$12.99

D0287193

Family Dinners

Middlesex County College
Library
Edison, NJ 08818

Family Dinners

A Memoir of Hard Times, Hope, and Laughter

A.X. McKneally

© 2017 A.X. McKneally
All rights reserved.
ISBN: 1974286711
ISBN 13: 9781974286713

This book describes the author's experiences and reflects the author's opinions.

Some names of individuals mentioned in the book have been changed to protect their privacy.

Cover picture – the family at the Hofbrauhaus in Munich, Germany.

For all my children

Table of Contents

Introduction

The moving van turns out of the driveway and heads down the street. I walk back inside my empty house; it has been a major character in the story of life with my husband Dan and the children.

Now I walk slowly from room to room, passing into the vacant dining room where echoes of dinner laughter rise around me. I hear voices of art friends who gathered here for lasagna after class and see my children who stayed up on school nights to sit with them. I hear again Dan's dinner table stories of his encounters with the top brass at work. We always ate in the dining room; the kitchen hadn't room for us all to sit.

I remember the night at dinner when I said, "I want to make this a rule. We have to get together to eat dinner every night, no matter what. Otherwise we are not a family." And they agreed.

Loose window panes rattle and the sound makes me jump. When the house was full of children, I never noticed. It *is* a big house, and its size emphasizes how lonely it is now.

I stop at the bay of windows in the dining room and look out across the broad lawn. I spot the apple tree Beth and her friends climbed in their nightgowns on a summer night. They began singing hymns, then lapsed into "Ninety-nine Bottles of Beer." I can almost hear again their beautiful harmonizing to "White Choral Bells."

In the early years, Dan and I would sit outside when he got home from work and watch our children chase each other across the grass, climb up into the trees, call to each other. I listened while he processed his workday. Later, as he recovered from his chemo treatments, he would sit out there.

This yard has so many memories—the kids making an ice rink there in the winter, swinging on the rope swing in the summer, walking up the driveway after school, washing the microbus if one of the boys had a date. Memories of each of them on the rider mower cutting grass, Matt high in the branches of the great maple tree with a snack, Greg shooting baskets, Justin splashing the hose at Mart and Beth as they ran squealing past.

I turn from the windows and enter the hall. I walk up the broad staircase to the landing and stop. This is where I stood the night I wanted to kill myself. I had gone from an abusive childhood to a marriage that became abusive–one I believed I had to endure. I remember the sense of despair—of wanting to die—and I feel a rush of gratitude that I survived and grew to know a happier life.

I go back downstairs and walk into the living room, vast and empty now. I scuffle through memories piled in the corners like autumn leaves—Matthew calling from the piano, "Mom, mom, listen to this!" He and Beth rolling on the floor, fighting over who had the right to play *Für Elise.* Their teacher had assigned it to Beth. I hear again Justin and Martin contesting points of chess, Greg and his friends playing cards and drinking beer while Dan keeps an eye on them, making sure their parents said it was okay.

I remember Matt walking about on his hands for gymnastics practice, and see again the long couch that often held a kid with a sports injury, recovering in the noisy midst of siblings and friends.

It has been my job to care for this house, keep the utilities going, the heat on, its bills paid, and the household secure for the night. When Dan and I divorced, I knew my children had a strong attachment to the house, and I was glad I could keep them in their familiar home. In exchange for my care, the house gave us shelter from the Midwestern winters and humid summers. Sometimes I was scared that I would lose the house because I couldn't pay the mortgage and other times I was angry at it, like when the wind blew through cracks around the windows, its roof leaked, or its basement flooded.

Together this house and I provided a home for us until the last child went to college. And now as I stand at the open front door and look out, memories of a far earlier time come back—of where it all began in a small town in New York's Hudson Valley.

Getaway Plan

"No daughter of mine is going to college!" my father said one night at dinner. He ate hunched forward, elbows on the table, in spite of my mother's "no elbows on the table" rule. Reaching for the butter, he went on, "College adds nothing to anyone's life."

Mother, who had gone to teacher's college, said nothing. We children listened in silence to his dinner table monologues. We had no idea where these came from. He just started talking, usually about something he and his mother discussed at lunch. He ate lunch at his mother's; had they talked about what I'd do after high school?

We were forbidden to speak during meals with Dad. If we dared to when we were younger, we would be beaten—usually with a leather strap Dad had made himself. Even our dog, Cinnamon, kept quiet under the table.

Dad had quit high school to work in his father's plumbing business here in upstate New York, and he prided himself on his common sense and political smarts. He was on our town's city council. He went on, "Do you think for one minute that college matters in a marriage?"

He glared at me, his eldest, making me think yes, they talked about me. My younger brother Paul dug his toe into my shin as if to say, "This is aimed at you."

With my eyes on my plate and using as few motions as possible, I helped myself to my mother's stew, more edible than usual. Dad blamed her bad cooking on her education. He often told us—at dinner—she should have stayed home and learned to cook.

While Dad chewed, I signaled to my brother Mark. We children used silent signals and eyebrow semaphore—like my staring at Mark until he looked up from his plate. Then I tilted my head and eyes at the bread, eyebrows raised. He touched the milk pitcher; I gave my head a tiny shake, "No."

He widened his eyes in his "What do you mean?" glare.

I tilted again. His hand moved to the breadbasket. I bowed my head, closed my eyes, "Yes."

"Of course not!" Dad, his mouth full, went on, "Is a man going to look at his wife across the dinner table surrounded by a battalion of children"—there were four of us—"and say, 'By the way, dear, did you ever go to college?'" Was he this sarcastic with his city council buddies? I wondered.

That night as we washed dishes, my mother scrubbed hard on the stew pot as she said, "Once you're through with high school, you *have* to get out of this town. There's nothing here. Nothing for anybody."

"What if . . . I got a scholarship to a college?" I said. This idea had come to me one afternoon when I talked with a neighbor's son who went to a state college. He had a scholarship, and he said, "I think someone like you would like college." I began thinking that since I had managed to get a scholarship to my high school, could I do it with college? I often plotted getting away from Dad but more like running away than going to college. We were terrified of his outbursts. Beatings usually followed. Even trying to talk to Dad, my brother cried and couldn't finish his sentences.

He and I used to say to each other when we were in first and second grade, "What would normal people do?" Now, I thought, maybe normal people might try to escape to college.

Mother brushed the hair out of her eyes with her forearm, hands dripping. "Yes, that might ... If you apply for a scholarship, *he* will be a problem. But if Dad lets *you* go, it would easier for me to get Mark to college."

With me, the eldest, paving the way, Mother could get her favorite, Mark who was 15, to a climate where his brain would be truly appreciated. His brilliance lay under a bushel in the dungeons of St. Patrick's High School, as his report cards proved; his grades were often lower than mine. The Christian Brothers there also taught him that "Girls can never be as smart as boys," and that "Boys always beat girls at math." He and Mother agreed on this; my being a girl meant that my brains *had* to be inferior to his, "especially in math!" they said.

The very next afternoon I studied the bulletin boards at my high school, Mount St. Mary. I saw notices for colleges I'd never heard of. These Dominican Sisters who taught here had put brochures at eye level from colleges run by Dominican nuns including one way out in the Midwest. I noticed they had tacked ads from colleges run by other nuns like the Franciscans at the bottom, where they slipped off and got stepped on. I looked for postings from non-Catholic schools; there were none.

I wrote down the dates to apply, application fees, and scholarship exams I must take: for the state, individual colleges, and Scholastic Aptitude. Each time the mail came I pounced, and I hoarded letters and forms from schools I had written to in a big envelope between my mattress and box spring. Dad never looked at the mail. A scholarship might get me to college, but winning one was not my greatest challenge.

Getting Dad's signature on the applications was. Back then in the '50s, the forms required the signature of the applicant's father. Not her mother. And Dad, looking ahead to my graduation from high school next year, had already started looking for my full-time job; in fact, he talked to our local bank manager about my working there. Soon. He dropped this news into another dinner monologue, adding, "The manager says tellers can make really good money." My stomach turned over. If I stayed in this house, he couldn't even let me look for my own job. I said nothing, of course.

I filled the applications out and hid them. When I mentioned Dad wanted me to work at the bank after graduation, my English teacher said, "That's ridiculous! I know your father. He'd love it if you went to college!"

My French teacher said, "There's another way around this, you know. I have always thought you would become one of *us*. If you enter the convent here, we would put you through college.

"And remember, Anne, we faculty never do housework. That's for the lay sisters." Housework! Everything here smelled so clean, I loved how clean it was. Not like our house. But to live here, all I had to do was sign up for life. And would life in the convent be an escape? Better than being a teller?

I talked with my brothers and little sister, Elaine, about getting Dad to sign the applications, and their fear of his rage made them beg me not to upset him. Yet now that I had a possible way out, I knew I had to have that signature. When I said, "Mother, what if I forge it?" and showed her my efforts, color drained from her face.

Lying awake one night, I thought of another approach. I had often noticed that my father seemed to change when he was with people outside our family. In public—at church and as a city councilman—we saw him politicking and being cordial. "Hiya!" Dad would say, all smiles when we ran across a friend from city council politics on our main street, "Howza boy?"

We *never* saw him like that at home. I knew how much other people's opinions mattered to him; we could never tell outsiders what went on inside when our front door closed. Most people thought we were "such a good Catholic family."

Some of his public friends were priests, teachers at a local seminary who trained missionaries for India and Africa. Dad did their construction work and often bought them cases of whiskey. My brainstorm was, what if *they* were around when I asked Dad for his signature?

Although my parents did no entertaining, once in a while Dad invited the priests to our house to "have a few drinks" in his study. From the basement where we ate and did homework, we heard them laughing. And with Father Buckley up there, after a while they sang "Stand Up and Sing for Your Father!" They never ate dinner with us, but a gathering like that could be my chance. I never knew when one would occur . . . unless I set it up. So I asked, "Mother, what if we invite some priests to dinner? If they're at the table, I could talk."

"Yes!" Mother said. "He'd want to look good in front of them."

Mother's cooking complicated my strategizing. Suppers she cooked often came to the table lacking necessary ingredients. If she made chili con carne, she'd forget to put in beans. Or she would put Apple Crisp in the oven without mixing it first, so one portion was mostly apples and another, just sugar and cinnamon. At my friends' homes, dinners seemed to get on the table much more easily.

I didn't realize then why my mother was like this, but I knew Dad had a point about her learning to cook. She was still "in charge," but ever since I was ten, I had taken over making more and more of our family meals. Still, I couldn't handle this special dinner alone.

Getting everything to the table at the same time was another hurdle. I was trying to learn how. I recall no meals with us all seated the whole time. Mother often jumped up to get horseradish or mustard or rolls she'd left in the oven. Or she'd start to make iced tea from scratch after we started to eat, and my father would roar, "Alice, please! Sit down!"

I talked with my siblings about what to serve, provided Dad agreed even to have this dinner. "Steak?" said Paul, who was eight.

"Those priests might not like the way it curls up, all gray and everything. And it's always so hard to cut," said Mark.

"What about pork chops with stuffing?"—my sister's suggestion.

"You know how Dad feels about undercooked pork—he says we'll get trichinosis and die," Mark said.

"That's right, he won't eat it, but he'll remind us what the symptoms are and how we're all eating our way to the grave," I said.

"Say, then Father Shanahan can give us the Last Blessing!" Paul, an altar boy, knew a lot about Church rituals.

I threw a pillow at his head. "What about turkey? It has a lot of side dishes."

Mark really liked that idea. "There's turnips and potatoes and dressing and cranberry sauce and salad and rolls. And gravy!"

"And with all those sides, even if the meat is tough, nobody will notice," Paul said.

I went downstairs and asked Mother if we could serve roast turkey, "Mom, it's one of your specialties." I knew I'd have to do most of it, but I needed her help with the shopping.

"Why, turkey! Of course!" she said, and started clipping recipes from *The Evening News.* She kept piles of these in the pantry. I sometimes sorted through and catalogued them for her. Some were crumbling, but she never allowed me to throw any out. Putting the supper dishes away later, I noticed she had scrawled in the margin of one recipe, "For Turkey dinner." It was for Broiled Grapefruit.

I concentrated on asking Dad if we could invite his priest friends to dinner. I rehearsed in the mirror, "Dad? What if . . . we had your friends over?" with my stomach churning, and to my brothers, and as I fell asleep at night. Then one evening at supper, my father appeared in less bad spirits than usual. He had just referred to his political enemies as a "pair of retired whores" and the whole town's electoral process as a "turkey." I saw my chance and cleared my throat.

"Speaking of . . . . " I was about to say "turkey," when my mother's eyes stabbed me into silence. I looked around the table. My siblings glared the same glare, the family glare. Did they think I was about to say, "Speaking of retired whores"?

My father looked at me, eyebrows raised.

I had spoken during mealtime.

Turkey. Think: turkey. "Dad? You know . . . ahm, Father Buckley and Father Shanahan?"

"Faintly, yes." he said, still in his sarcastic mode—a good sign. He started chewing again.

Now or never. "Dad, I was thinking we haven't seen either of them in a long time, and I always liked them." I saw my mother look down, then realized her eyes were closed. "Do you, could we have them over some night for dinner?"

My father looked up from his plate, then at me from under his black Irish eyebrows. "I don't know, Anne ...."

Not a real "No" yet! Steady on. "Dad, I think it would be nice for all of us if they could come."

He glanced past me out the window to the mountains in the distance. Then he looked back at his plate, and bent over it. "Well, I suppose . . . it would be all right."

He didn't look at me again.

Electricity circled the table. I didn't look at Mother, but I saw from the corner of my eye that she had let go of the breath she had been holding.

We selected the date; my mother called the guests who accepted delightedly, my father heard this news with a grimace, and I bought the makings of the feast with Mother. We ironed the tablecloth and napkins, cleaned the dining room, hid the family junk, tied Cinnamon up in the garage, and put the turkey in the oven.

It was a Sunday evening in late fall. The roasting turkey filled the house with a delightful, anticipatory aroma. Mark stood around commenting and asking, "Can I help?"

I cut the grapefruit and dug around each segment with a grapefruit knife I had bought that week. Paul washed the salad greens, I checked the place settings, and our banished dog sent out a howl from the garage. Mother, strands falling from her carefully pinned-up hair, put a pan of frozen rolls in the oven below the turkey.

Since we never had company, we had no routine to follow. Some families can have everyone in the kitchen at once, and they work together like a paramedic team. All ours managed to do was trip over each other. Dad stayed upstairs. Mother barked out commands—"Make sure the carving set is on the table!" "Find the napkins!" "Wash your hands!" along with wails of "I don't know!" and "Get out of the way!"

When the doorbell rang, we went to a state of alarm.

"They're here!" Paul shouted and stumbled over the dustpan. I ran to the door to let the priests in, and they headed upstairs first to Dad's study. I hovered in the stairwell until I heard signs of joviality, then hurried back to put candles on the table. The thump of heavy male feet on the stairs stopped me in mid-task. They were coming down *now.*

Waving the gravy ladle, Mother said, "Get those grapefruit under the broiler!" I spread brown sugar on them and obeyed.

Father Shanahan came to the kitchen and shook hands with Mother. Father Buckley went on directly to the dining room, and at a signal from Mother, Paul asked for his blessing — to buy us some time. We knelt, and were blessed.

After that, Mother said, "George, will you light the candles?" and my father gave her a look of horror.

"Candles? *Candles?* We need to see the food."

The priests chuckled.

"We can leave the lights on, too, if you like, dear," Mother said, playing along.

Paul rolled his eyes at me when she said "dear." The lights stayed on.

My father assigned places, leaning heavily on the table at his end, saying, "I have to make sure this won't collapse with all the food."

Mother and I opened the oven door and moved the brown, shiny turkey onto it. Together we hefted it onto the carving board. The sound of knife against whetstone announced Dad's readiness to perform. I set the gravy boat down, and Mother placed mashed potatoes nearby. As I placed rolls, butter, salad, turnips, dressing, cranberry sauce, our old table creaked a bit. Mark opened his eyes wide in fear, but it held.

I brought out the broiled grapefruit, serving carefully from the left.

"My, this looks good, Anne. What ... is it?" Father Shanahan said.

Mother and I locked glances. Didn't everyone serve cooked grapefruit?

"That's the, um, *Pamplemousse*," I said, hoping it sounded better in another language.

"Oh, I see! French, is it?" said Father Buckley, picking up his spoon.

Dad plunged the carving fork into the turkey and flourished the knife. "What can I give you, Father Shanahan?" he said.

"Some white meat, if you will, George, " Father Shanahan said, spreading the huge napkin across his lap.

Dad began slicing the breast from the wishbone. Then stopped.

We children looked at him, at each other, then down at the table-cloth. Red juices flowed from the wound Dad had made. Our turkey was quite raw.

Mother jumped up saying, "I think it just needs a few more minutes." She slid the turkey from under my father's carving knife and ran it back to the kitchen.

During this awkwardness, Father Shanahan asked what I was studying this year. Since our guests were priests, I thought I had better talk about their subject.

"Theology. We have to read St. Thomas Aquinas, then make books with the Virtues and Vices he writes about. We put one virtue or vice on each page and label it like it's a tree trunk. Then we cut leaves for lesser virtues or vices and paste them on the branches."

From the kitchen came the crashing of pans. I raised my voice. "We make green leaves for the virtues and black ones for the vices."

"Well, that sounds like fun. Can you name the major vices for me, Anne?"

"Pride, Lust, Envy, Avarice, Anger, Sloth and Gluttony."

"Good!" Father Buckley pointed his butter knife at me. "Back when I was in seminary, we figured out PALE GAS used the first letter of each vice, so we'd remember for exams."

Paul choked on his roll at the word "gas" and left the table briefly. Dad and Father Shanahan talked for a long time about adding on a dormitory at Father's school. Then my brother Mark began signaling me with his eyebrows, "Get to the point." The men continued to talk about "service lines" and the "sewer main" as I looked for an opening to ask my question.

Mother reappeared, hair awry, with the turkey. She said, "I think it's done. I turned the stove up to 550." Dad stood and began again to carve.

Dad lay slices of meat in a circle on the platter while we watched in silence. This time, it looked done. As he filled his plate, Father Buckley said, "It's certainly good of you, Alice, to make this nice dinner for us. We priests don't get the home-cooked meals you lay people enjoy. This is a real treat."

Mother smiled, forehead shining with perspiration. "We're glad to do it."

Was it time? Or should I ask during dessert?

"Would anyone like more rolls?" Paul passed them, helping himself to two. Mother got up to start the Baked Alaska, another experimental recipe. If that didn't succeed, my question about college could distract everyone.

I followed her into the kitchen. "Go back and sit down!" she hissed. "Make conversation! I'll handle this."

Baked Alaska had to be put together at the last minute. No telling how long it might take. I turned back.

Paul wanted to help, I knew, when he said to Father Shanahan, "I hope you don't think we eat like this all the time," then winced. Mark must have kicked him to signal, *Don't* call attention to Mother's cooking."

I needed to get the talk back to school. "So, Dad, what about my going to college," would be too abrupt, but I felt desperate to get started. Then Father Shanahan mentioned he had just returned from Rome.

"How are the schools over there?" I threw out wildly.

"The . . .schools? In *Rome?* I have no idea, Anne. Why?"

Everyone turned, looked at me.

"Oh, I just wondered."

"Speaking of schools, you should see the grammar schools in Africa! When I was stationed there . . . " and Father Buckley was off on a ramble about his missionary years. He then explained how to say, "Good evening, Father" in Swahili ("Sahli gashli, Oobaba"), and had Paul repeat it.

Father Shanahan had begun talking about mission work in Patna, India, when Mother reemerged with the dessert. She tilted her head toward the dessert plates, signaling me to set them out.

"Well!" Father Buckley became more and more mellow as Dad kept refilling his highball glass. "What have we here, Alice?" he said, smiling mistily around the table.

Mother set the singed mound at my place and handed me a carving knife. "Mother," I said, "Could I have a word?"

We went into the kitchen, and I asked her how to serve this dessert, since it was new to me.

"Just cut it!" she said through her teeth, brushing hair back from her face. She marched back into the dining room.

Our guests had never heard of Baked Alaska. Neither had we. Father Buckley said he was more familiar with roast water buffalo and baked python. Mother explained she had put ice cream on cake and wrapped it all in whipped egg whites, then broiled it.

"Why?" said Father Buckley. Father Shanahan gave him a warning look, and we began passing the plates of gooey meringue along until each was served. Everyone looked at the others to see how to tackle it.

And I could wait no longer. "Dad, I want to go to college. May I? I have to apply for scholarship exams now so I can pay for it myself. I mean if I qualify."

"What kind of scholarships are these, Anne?" Father Shanahan leaned forward, the light from the candles shining on his glasses.

My father lowered his head and shot me a look of fury and betrayal. I met his eyes, then looked away. He *knew*. I had set him up and our battle was joined, sword on sword.

I swallowed hard. "Father, there are scholarships for tuition, board and room. I want to try for one of those."

"Why, that would be wonderful. George, you must really be proud of your girl for wanting to try for something like that! Chip off the old block, isn't she?" he said smiling at Dad.

Dad said evenly, "I can always count on Anne to come through." The edge to his voice would cut through armor on a tank.

I held my breath. The others stopped eating. Father Shanahan looked at Mother for a long moment, then he said, "Anne, I'd be really interested in hearing how all this comes out. Will you let me know? When is the first test?"

Mother, limp, sat back in her chair.

Paul stood. "I hear Cinnamon. He hasn't seen me all day." He ducked out the door, leaving his dessert half-finished.

Father Shanahan looked at me, and then turned to Dad. "You know, George, I think that would be wonderful for this family." He put his napkin at his place. "I notice you have a piano in the other room. I'd like to play for you after dinner if I may. Who here likes to sing?"

Everyone else scraped back their chairs, retrieved napkins from the floor, said again what a good dinner it had been. Mark muttered, "Remarkably good! Even that dessert thing." They went in then by the piano, and I could hear Father Shanahan rolling some chords to get started. I still sat there, relieved, happy, and numb. I had won.

I looked up; Dad lingered at the door, staring at me, alone by the fireplace now. Oh no, what was I thinking? "Wait here a minute, please, Dad!" I said, as I dashed upstairs to grab those applications while I still had the priests there.

Dad slowly sat back down at the table, surrounded by the remains of our dessert. I handed him my pen as he scowled at the forms, saying, "Why so many?" And as he inscribed his name I thought, all I need to do now is . . . win some scholarships.

At graduation the next year, our school chaplain announced the scholarships my classmates had won. He read my name last, then said: "She has won a New York State scholarship," and went on to announce eight more, so that when he got to the end, the audience drowned his voice with their laughter, a reaction that startled me. I expected clapping, but not laughing.

I had been so afraid I wouldn't win any.

DROWNERS

The same winter that I applied for college scholarships, I took Red Cross lifesaving courses at the YW. I hoped to land a summer lifeguarding job. My younger sister came with me. It being a small town, Brownie, the teacher, didn't mind. At twelve, Elaine was way too young for lifesaving class, but she was big for her age, my height already. And frankly, she swam better than I did.

Together we simulated drowning rescues at the deep end of the pool at the YW, and the others in the class liked to watch us. She and I took turns being the drowner. She would throw her arms in the air, shouting and splashing. Then I'd move in close to practice breaking a drowner's hold.

As she grabbed me, I'd breathe deep then go below the surface pulling us both under. When I came up beneath her, I'd slide her into the rescue grip and scull her to the side of the pool. The others applauded. We had signals in case it got out of hand, but we understood each other so well that we didn't usually need them.

Then we'd walk home in the winter air with our heads not quite dry, and our frozen curls would tinkle in the wind. And when Mother met us at the door, she'd yell at us for not drying our hair; then we'd make cocoa together and go to bed. In those years we were each other's best friend, even with the four years' difference.

That summer, right after my graduation, I started my lifeguard job. I soon realized that our boss, Woodrow Prochnow (Woody), supervised like a drill sergeant. He made us clean the First Aid room, make up the cot, take apart the resuscitation apparatus and scour it, inspect the tires on the wheeled stretcher, go through the bandages kit, count the grappling hooks, and make sure no cracks had appeared in the bamboo pole—the long one to be used for pulling in drowners—since the last time we checked. When his back was turned, redheaded Farley, the heavy-set male locker attendant, would imitate Woody Woodpecker. Then snicker.

When the sun shone on the pool and the kids, it all seemed worthwhile. This was the 1950s and ours was the only public pool in town– open to everybody, no segregation.

Woody liked to appear with no warning on the pool deck to make sure we weren't lounging in the guard chair or on the benches along the fence. We could sit only during our turn in the guard chair. Otherwise we had to stay on our feet even with two or three people in the water. Those were the Rules. While he reminded us that we had the authority to kick out anybody who misbehaved (fighting, running on deck, refusing to get out of the pool on time, etc.), he also said we weren't there to "work on our tans and stroll the deck" in our bathing suits. "All right now!" he'd shout. "Stay alert!"

He'd work himself into a lather. "You people don't realize lives are at stake!" We told each other he was humor-impaired. As if to prove that point, he'd say, "You may be girls, but try to look like *professionals!*" We would snort with laughter and turn away. He'd look hurt.

This being the only city pool, we had a lot of daily kids. The rich kids went to the country club pool at the Powellton Club. We never saw any of them. Our "dailies," black and white, came in at the start of each summer with their heads shaved, and smelling of turpentine. Their mothers sent them whether sun shone or thunder roared.

When the pool was open, they followed us guards around as we changed posts. We spent fifteen minutes at each station, rotated to the next spot, and once an hour we got a turn in the guard chair at the deep end. The dailies liked to sit in its shade, or when Woody wasn't looking, climb up the side and talk. When I was in the chair, one of the seven

Reeds, Junebug, always climbed up to give me his little gold ring from a Crackerjack box, a snake with ruby eyes. He was five, and I wore the ring for him while he splashed in the shallow end. He'd come get it just before he left for home.

The pool was the dailies' bathtub, it used up their boisterous energy, and it was cheap. If the pool was closed due to weather, and staff hadn't left yet, we could look up the entrance steps and see chubby six-year-old Cielie in her sundress, alone, raggedy towel tucked under her arm waiting for the sun to come out. The Reeds — all seven of them — would be there smiling and waving, "Gonna open, Woody?"

"No, now go on, you kids. Beat it! And you people (turning to us), you don't have to talk to them," Woody would scold.

The kids stayed. Their mothers had Rules, too: "You come home before five, and you'll get the beating of your lives." So they stood and waited in the rain.

Rain for us meant polishing the beat-up locker tags. When it rained, we'd plan which movie to see, but first we had to report at the pool reception desk. Else we'd get no pay. Woody would take attendance with his clipboard, then hand out rags and smelly brass polish. "Get busy, everybody!"

"Oh, come on, Wood, these old tags spend their *lives* in the pool. All that chlorine, they're clean to begin with!" Farley argued, as usual, while Woody pulled tags from long hooks behind the registers. And we'd set to work grumbling, and try not too hard to improve their appearance.

Next Woody forced us through rainy weather emergency drills or "dry land drill," where guards *walked* through rescue practice, using locker attendants as drowning victims. Much laughter, especially when Woody was out of hearing and Fat Farley was the victim. Rumor had it his father's connections got him the job, so he knew he couldn't be fired. When he wasn't smoking, he usually slept at Checkpoint Toenail, where attendants had to check for athlete's foot before swimmers could hit the pool.

If Woody's mood was foul, he would get out the janitor's brooms so we could clean the locker rooms. We had to peek into every locker, remove candy wrappers, abandoned socks, and used condoms. If Woody weren't around, the females made the male locker attendants handle those, despite the men's shouts of "Where is the Justice in this?"

Finally everything was shipshape, tags back on the hooks in exact numerical order—and if any were missing, we had to scour the place looking for the lost tag—so Woody let a few of us leave at a time. Kind of like jury duty when there's no case to try. When just two of us remained, we could pull down the roll-top door, lock it, and head home in the rain. So much for our plans to walk to the double-feature at the second-run theatre, the Cameo.

Sometimes after hours when the water was calm, I watched Woody swim laps alone. He had been on the U.S. Olympic team, but the Korean War came along and a bullet in his forearm ruined his stroke. He looked pretty good to me gliding through the still water.

Day's end was often a peaceful, perfect time with the tree shadows laying long across the deck and the sun warm on us. Sometimes my sister and I swam, too. Brownie, our lifeguarding teacher, coached swimmers when she didn't teach lifesaving. She had really liked my sister's swimming and encouraged her to compete, so Elaine worked out at the pool while I was there.

And the dailies, all relaxed from hours in the water, liked to hang around after hours and watch, too. They couldn't come on deck because during suppertime, we were closed. While they waited for the pool to open for the evening, they dared each other to walk the stair rim at the entrance and cling to the fence, just to get yelled at and chased to safety.

My being a lifeguard meant that the female locker room attendants usually came to me with problems. One time, a "locker" came on deck to ask me to help with a young black girl who was showing a knife around the locker room. I went down. She was a sturdy, well-fed-looking ten-year-old; I saw her knife was a switchblade.

"Where did that come from?" I said, standing well back. The "locker" crouched behind me.

"My mom gave it to me. It's mine!" she yelled.

"You can't have it in the locker room," I said, trying to appear calm though I could feel my heart beating hard in my eardrums. "It's against the Rules. Here, give it to me."

"No. My momma told me to keep it with me all the time."

"Okay," I said. "You brought the knife here, so I have to kick you out of the pool for a week. You can take it home, but now you have to leave."

She began sobbing, big, loud sobs. Getting thrown out was a big deal back then.

I said, "Next week you can come back, but do *not* bring your knife. Get dressed now. And I'll walk you out."

I stood there while she yanked her clothes from the locker and pulled them on.

We walked to the entrance and she snuffled her way up the stairs and out.

The next afternoon, a bright sunny day, I was called down from the deck to the front register. A tall black woman in a white suit, heels, and sunglasses stood at the steps. She was much taller than I was. Suddenly, the cashiers melted away, and no one else was around, no locker attendants, no boss.

"You the lifeguard threw my little girl, my Vinia Lee, out of this pool?" Her voice was low, menacing. The sunglasses reflected the overhead light and I couldn't see her eyes.

I had come down in bare feet from the pool deck and I licked my dry lips and said, "Yes. I told her to leave. She had a knife. The other kids were scared. It's against the rules." My hands were shaking. She could see them.

"I don't think that's why. I think you threw her out because you is prejudiced against black peoples."

Oh, no! I had no back-up, no witness, but I said, "That's not true. We have rules and Vinia Lee has to obey them like anyone else." My voice shook, but I was not giving in. "She can't come back for a week."

After we talked a few more minutes, and I refused to give in, the woman left.

That night at dinner, my father turned to me. "Anne, what's this I hear about you throwing a little girl out of the pool yesterday? The cops called me about it."

I thought for sure my dad would at least be proud of me for making the kids obey the rules.

I told him about sending the little girl home and why.

"Anne, you don't understand. This little girl's mother, Barb, Is one of my best constituents. She's good at getting the votes out. I can't have you making problems with her."

Tears slid down my cheeks. I had been scared but proud of doing the right thing. Now I felt crushed. I said, "I can't let a kid bring a knife into the pool, Dad. She could have cut somebody."

"So what are you going to do about it?" he said.

"I'm not letting her back in for a week. I said, 'No.' I have to stand by that."

I was so disappointed. Why were the rules different for him, anyway? Why didn't he say, Good for you?

Instead, he said, "Well, all right, see that you do" in a grudging tone and went back to eating. I learned more the next day at the pool. Another lifeguard told me, "Barb works with Big Nan at Treetops."

"What's that? A bar?" I said, making sure I faced away from her so Woody wouldn't see us talking.

"Nah, a whorehouse. Down by the docks. My boyfriend says they tell people, 'We don't discriminate.'" She pulled her hat down to shade her eyes and went back to her post.

The local whorehouse? I knew about Big Nan. She was over six feet tall and drove a white Cadillac. Her license plate said, "NAN." I had seen it parked in front of the town's only police station, right between the two signs: "Absolutely No Parking." So if Vinia Lee lived there with her mom, no wonder this little girl needed a knife.

Our town was a few miles from an Air Force base and near West Point, and my dad pointed out it was important to make sure the women who worked there had police protection. Before he left the table,

Dad had said, "You need to understand some things, Anne. The cops keep an eye out for them for good reason. There's more to this than you know. Both Barb and Nan make sure destitute families have food and clothing. Another of my best constituents, Dr. B, takes care of the girls there."

Here was another side to my dad. I had been taught that prostitution was a *sin*. Dad must know that—this man who knelt each night at his bedside to say his prayers.

The next week, I saw Vinia Lee floating in the pool. Her time "out" was up, and she was back. At five o'clock, when I went up the stairs to leave, she was waiting at the top, nicely dressed and with a smile on her face. She fell into step beside me, and said, "I gonna walk you home!" And she did; she became one of my groupies, who liked to walk along with me at day's end. I felt good that I had said "No." I learned I could say it and make it stick.

A few weeks later, on a hot and sunny Sunday afternoon, about 700 people had clocked into the pool by mid-afternoon. Woody closed the gate; we were up to capacity. I was in the guard chair at the deep end, and Elaine sat along the scum gutter on the far side opposite me. It was really noisy—kids and adults shouting, splashing, jumping in between swimmers, landing on some with great screams and squeals, shrieking if they lay drying on deck and got splashed.

I scanned the deck for runners, the water for faces, the fence for climbers, and tried to keep my concentration. When I glanced at the entrance, I saw two men in Air Force uniforms heading down the steps. I noticed them because most adults were here with children.

A small, plump girl like a Campbell's Soup kid bobbed through the water in the deep end (ten feet), and I thought she was in trouble. I started to get out from the chair. But she smiled and waved at me. I checked behind me. Three boys climbing the fence from the sandy beach ball area saw me, thought better of it and dropped back down.

It was really hot.

Elaine caught my eye and pointed. At the bottom of the deep end right at the drain, someone stood, arms lifted above his head. Preparing to surface?

Only he stayed down. With the crowd in the water, I couldn't see his face. He sure was big. How long had he been —

Uh-oh.

I jumped up. Yanked off my hat and sunglasses. No dive: Hit the water running like in practice. Kept eyes on the drowner, my head up. Sculled to center pool.

Elaine met me. We surface-dived. The drowner's arms waved slowly above his head, long brown underwater stalks beneath us.

Below surface I opened my eyes. He seemed stuck. I dove to see, was his foot caught in the grate? No.

I surfaced, dove again. I pulled him. Elaine pulled.

Nothing worked. Up for air. Dove again. Grabbed his chest. Frog-kicked and yanked. Big guy. All muscle. No fat to float him up. We shoved, pulled. Somehow got him to start rising. At the top, gasping. Lungs burning. Our training came back: I went behind him, set him on my hip. He opened his eyes, twisted and lunged for me. Bloodshot eyes wide. Pulled me under.

Brownie's voice came back to me: "Break his hold!" I jackknifed to kick hard at his stomach. Got free and rose. Air. I scissor-kicked to jump up high enough to hold his head under. Wrestled him back into Tow position. Elaine towed too, side-stroking next to us. People started yelling. We dragged him through the water, tried to keep his face up. He sank, his eyes shut. Not helping. Not like practice.

Pool so wide. Deck, way far.

My legs were lead. His deadweight kept sinking. . .

I bumped my head. I was at the ladder. Panting. Grabbed his hands, put them on one rung. Held them there. His head slipped below the surface. His whole body slid under. I was punchy. Why didn't he climb out? Say "Thanks"?

He wasn't moving. Elaine and I pushed him back up, got his chest against the rungs. Above water, he weighed much more.

Then Woody was on the deck near my head yelling orders. All I noticed, he was in his Hard Shoes on deck. Against the Rules. I realized he was talking to me: "Okay, we got him, Anne. Let go. Anne!"

What were all these people on deck for? Someone in street clothes reached down and pulled on my drowner so Woody could grab hold. The drowner slid down again, a great, brown slippery fish we couldn't land. I said to him, "You OK?"

When he said, "Huh?" I knew he was alive. I got set to give artificial respiration when Woody said, "Get that oxygen mask!"

With all the men now around me, they got the drowner finally all the way up on deck. But he kept flopping all over, out of control. The guys wrestled him onto the low wheeled stretcher. He rolled off. They put him back. Finally Farley sat on him, and the others could roll the stretcher to the stairs as Woody continued to yell orders.

Somehow the police were here. And they were in hard shoes, too. And the pool was empty. Hundreds in bathing suits all around us on deck. Not talking.

And my mother! For crying out loud, what was *she* doing here? She never came to the pool.

Still groggy, I climbed back into the guard chair. Was my fifteen minutes up?

Swimmers splashed back in all around me, and as the quiet ended, I realized how silent it had been. My mother climbed the side of the guard chair with a towel and a cup. "Here, dear. Drink this. It's coffee with cream and sugar."

"I never drink coffee, Mother."

"*Do* it. You need the strength. You're all worn out. All white."

Mothers! I drank. I was shaking from the adrenaline. And from trying to heft that 200-pound drowner.

Noise in the pool rose back to its normal deafening level as I sipped my coffee, hot and sweet and good. It tasted even better because it was against Woody's Rules, but he was down in First Aid with the drowner. Junebug Reed, all smiles, handed me my sunglasses and hat. I put them on, shivering. I was still wearing his snake ring.

More yelling on the deck. It was Woody coming toward me, looking annoyed. "That drowner of yours! Just puked. All. Over. My. Oxygen Mask. I just cleaned that mask! Now I gotta clean it all up again and *sterilize* it."

He climbed up next to me, whispered, "That guy was so drunk. We just got him to come to now. He said the last he remembered, he was on the high tower, he jumped, and everything went black. Next thing he knew I've got the mask on him. Then he throws up. And we open his locker to get his clothes and find a uniform! He's from the air force base. We also found a gallon-size jug of red wine in there! Half empty. The rest of it went onto my equipment."

"Wood? Was it like this with the others?"

"What others?"

"You know. Your other drowners. The ones you talk about during drill."

He got red. "To tell you the truth, this is *my* first one too, Anne. I been in charge eleven years now, and we had some near misses but nothin' like today.

"And by the way, nice going."

"I'm glad you were there, Wood."

As he climbed down he said, "The cops called the MPs out at the base. They're on their way to pick him up."

He turned back, shading his eyes with his bad arm, and said, "Hey! What are you doing with that coffee? You know it's against the Rules. Give it here."

As Woody walked away, Junebug climbed up the side away from him and with his widest grin said, "Can I have your autograph?"

MY KIND OF PEOPLE

Home from my first year at college during Christmas break in the '50s, I faced my Aunt Margaret's scouring the Hudson Valley for a suitable spouse for me. Earlier that week, she had called to invite my parents and me for an evening get-together. "There's *someone* I want Anne to meet," she said, sketching her plan as my heart sank.

While I listened on the extension, she scolded Dad, "George, you don't realize what a challenge marketing our daughters is! Someday I'll have to help mine find the right husband, but for now, we *have* to make sure Anne meets the right kind of people. We can't let her get involved with another boy like that Rick."

Dad agreed emphatically. Rick, a handsome ex-Marine (dishonorably discharged), had taken himself out of the running anyway due to an incident that landed him in Elmira Maximum Security State Prison. Dad had gone berserk last month when he saw the story in our local paper. He called my dorm that same day in November to shout, "All right, Anne, when's the last time you were with that Rick fella?"

Studying for a World History exam, I was memorizing the British line of succession (William, William, Henry, Stephen...). I felt blindsided.

Dad kept on, "Right here on the front page! The lead story! *Your* friend Rick! His *picture!* In *handcuffs!*"

"Dad, I haven't . . ."

"You! Went! Out! With Him!"

"Daddy, listen. The last time I saw . . ."

"Armed robbery! Him! *And* his brother! Jail! Prison!" Shouting still, he hung up before I told my side. He was furious also because he liked to call the police chief to see if any guy I even talked to was "on the blotter." Back when he proudly told me this, I wanted to die.

Rick was my first real love, and my feelings for him made me dizzy every time I thought of him. Yet all we'd done last summer was swim together, hold hands and go for long walks to talk about moving together to Alaska where he could raise horses. It didn't occur to me to wonder why Rick needed to get so far away. He told me he'd left sixth grade once he turned sixteen, and before that he hot-wired cars when he played hooky with his older brother.

"My parents are divorced. They're alcoholics," he said. I felt so bad for him; I'd never met anyone whose parents had divorced. After grammar school (he was kept back several times), he went into the Marines on a fake birth certificate, he told me. A few times I got a letter from him neatly written all in lower case. In one, he said he was "back in the brig and don't know why."

A note along the margin from the brig officer made the reason clearer: he had slept on watch. I wrote back enclosing two sticks of gum, one for Rick and one for the censor. Rick seemed so gentle and ingenuous. I was 17, and that summer my family and other problems seemed far, far away as we walked together in the sunshine to the pool.

That fall, when I went away to college, Rick's picture came too. In his dress uniform, his hazel-eyes and dark-gold-blond good looks smiled right at me. At first, I'd hidden his picture in my top drawer. I took it out only when I was alone with his picture, but my room-mate had dug around and found it. After that he smiled out at all of us. I came back from class once to find five of my dorm-mates looking at *my* boyfriend.

But Dad had to face the locals in our little town; his reputation as City Councilman was at stake; whereas, my world now involved only an all-girl campus, semi-cloistered nuns, and midterms.

Anyone who escaped our mill-town for college usually stayed away even during breaks, then after graduation migrated to Manhattan or points west. Occasionally one or two returned, settling in to join the town's eccentrics, people who babbled about existentialism and Theatre of the Absurd. They were first in line for tickets when the Metropolitan Opera Touring Company brought *La Traviata* or *La Boheme* to the high school. And they set up little salon-type gatherings, drank sherry. and read plays to each other.

Meanwhile the plumbers, butchers, steam-fitters, and car salesmen who dominated the town's social life ridiculed people who had to go away to study political science and Jacobean melodrama. Our family dentist couldn't hold his head up in public once word got out that his son, the brilliant one now majoring in Spanish, had taken up flamenco dancing. The local paper ran his picture—in a ruffled costume and boots with heels! Not only that: next summer he'd "tour South America as an exhibition dancer"!

Other dads stood around drinking at Previdi's Tavern or the American Legion hall, guffawing about poor Dr. Kessler. None of that for *their* kids who wouldn't dare leave home for college, thank God.

My confidantes were my brothers and sister, all younger than I. So I went to them for help after my aunt's phone call. Mark, 16, sat arranging pieces of a model plane as I walked in and slumped on his bed.

"You'll never believe," I said.

"What?" he said without looking up.

"Aunt Margaret's at it again. Finding my future husband. I don't think I want to get married. But—I don't have a vote."

"You're exaggerating. As usual." Mark stood up, stretched, said, "This glue is making me dizzy." He opened a window, then sat next to me. "So what's your problem, again?"

"Aunt Margaret. She wants to set me up with some guy she knows from, I don't know, church or something. But it's not just a date. It's a gathering for us to meet. She's invited Uncle Mac. Worse, Dad and *Mother* will be there. And it's all happening at her friend Cornelia's house."

"So? What's wrong with that?"

"It's them. I don't *want* them choosing friends for me. Boy or otherwise. Look what happened the last blind date, with that chemist shrimp from the plant." I picked at the balding chenille on Mark's bedspread. "All he talked about was sex. I never heard so many unfunny jokes about it."

"Probably figured you wouldn't put out," my brother said.

"And it felt like he had six hands." I rolled over. "Please. Help me get out of this."

My little sister, 14, had come into the room by then, and when the two of them said, "Oh, no, you don't!" I realized they'd be no help. Who would? I thought suddenly of my Theology teacher, showering us with, "Girls, desperate diseases call for desperate remedies!"

"If you don't go along with Aunt Margaret, she'll be mad for weeks," Mark said. "And *we're* the ones who'll catch the flak."

"'Cause you'll be back at school, and we'll still be here," my sister said.

"Look," Mark said. "It's only one night. You'll live. Offer it up."

"Easy for you to say. And what am I going to talk about with them sitting there like buzzards at a wake?"

"For starters, what you can NOT talk about is how marriage is legalized prostitution," Mark said. "Aunt Margaret might laugh because it's Shaw. But . . . maybe not."

My dad's mother had wanted all her children to go to college. My dad refused, but his sisters had returned prepared to teach English and Math and Latin, then found their students dropping out at 16 to work in the "pockabook" factory, starting families, and spending their nights joyriding our Shawangunk Mountains down the condemned Old Storm King Highway. Without brakes.

In our town, opportunities to "meet one's own kind," as my aunt put it, were few on the ground. And I knew she cared about me and wanted to help. Her criteria for "our kind" included people with substantial family money. Her other criteria included being Catholic and Republican. (She had married a handsome and charming guy who supervised our paper's newsboys, usually from his regular spot at Previdi's.) That's why she had also fixed me up with Joey, the bank president's son. He took me to a dance at the country club, where he went directly to the bar without me to spend much of the night.

And when I told my father I felt scared when Joey drove over curbs on the way home, Dad called Margaret to lambaste her. His shouting could be heard in the next block, and another season of their Not Speaking ensued. Icy silence alternated with sulphurous battles, and in our small town every wake, wedding and Communion breakfast provided opportunities for friends, kin and neighbors to speculate which McKneallys were Not Speaking. They observed this as strictly as Lenten fasts; Irish loyalties kept phone lines crackling past midnight.

Enemies for life got passed unto third and fourth generations. When a cousin got drafted and was asked if he thought he could kill, he said, "Well, my relatives, certainly. But . . . I'm not so sure about total strangers."

Should the leading adversaries—for instance, Dad and his brother—appear at the same reception or politico's wake, use of third-person vindictive covered the niceties ("Moe, tell my brother I wouldn't be seen sitting at the same table with him!").

As eldest of the next generation, I became a combatant as soon as I could talk. The right answer to "Who's your favorite aunt?" gained me affectionate access to the laps of my father's sisters. Sitting there, I learned to read from Aunt Margaret when I was three. When she proudly took me to the library for a card, the Children's Librarian handed me my favorite book, *Madeline.* Since I never read to her as I sat in *her* lap, I stood silent, feeling my cheeks redden as Aunt Margaret prompted from the sidelines.

I just couldn't read for a stranger.

Back in my brother's bedroom, I said, "Besides, I have nothing to wear, nothing that's clean."

"No excuse," said my sister, leaving the room. She returned with a teal blue dress still tagged from the factory outlet where she bought it for $3.

"Not my color," I said.

"Try it on," my brother said. "If it fits, you're all set."

Unfortunately, it fit. I mewed, "This makes me look sallow!" but my siblings said, "More rouge! And no one will notice."

Attired in my finery, I arrived with Uncle Mac at the pre-Revolutionary home of Cornelia. Another English teacher, she had set her cap for my uncle years ago. And so while we were assembled allegedly for my sake, it was also her chance to entertain my eligible bachelor uncle. Though my father was considered handsome, Mac's Black Irish looks turned heads. (In the heart of our family we referred to Mac as "not the marrying kind," yet women followed him everywhere. Once when he attended the funeral of a national politician, the man's widow proposed to Mac as they drove together away from the graveyard.)

On our way in, Uncle Mac muttered, "You haven't met her yet. She has a nose you could cut cheese with."

As I stood in the doorway of Cornelia's living room, I saw everyone else already seated: her tiny mother, Caroline, wrapped in a beautiful white lace shawl; Aunt Margaret; Dad; Mother; a woman I'd never seen before and a nice-looking blond man in his late 20s (the Someone?). Standing there, I acknowledged introductions as I had been taught in Deportment class by the nuns. I felt a beam of light surround me as everyone stared and nodded. (Was it the $3 dress?) The woman turned out to be Someone's mother, and he was José Vargas, scion of the local coat factory family. So, he met Aunt Margaret's first criterion—lots of money. About my height, slender, he had a handshake that felt like warm, raw liver. We stood looking at each other.

He said quietly, "I hear you're away at school."

"Yes."

"What are you studying?" he said.

No one else moved or spoke; they just watched us. Then Uncle Mac cleared his throat and said, "Ah! Cornelia! How's about some drinks?"

Everyone seemed to let go the breath they held. Starting like a guilty thing, she scurried to the dry sink and brought Mac a water glass filled with whiskey. The same for my dad.

I tried to speak quietly, scarcely moving my lips, "I plan to major in English. Rhetoric, actually."

"That's . . . interesting," he said. The other sound was ice tinkling in the grown-ups' glasses.

"Where … where did you go?" I hoped he'd gone to college.

"Colgate. I majored in Business."

Business? Wasn't that for dumb kids? Wait till I tell my brother!

"Nice," I lied. "I suppose you really use some of that over at the, ahm, factory?"

As he murmured something like "Yes," I could hear the other guests gulping at their whiskey. Caroline's chair creaked.

Gales of silence.

Caroline broke the quiet, "Cornelia! Has Anne seen the house?"

Uncle Mac raised an eyebrow at me and said, "You really must see this."

Cornelia rose and led me to the hall. She didn't invite José and when I looked back, he had gone to sit with Caroline.

"We have 35 rooms here," Cornelia said, "most of them closed off. When you walk through, you'll see why. Wiring and plumbing can't fit into these walls." She patted one next to the stairs. "They're so thick. We do have electricity in the rooms where Mother and I live. The rest…."

She sent me off to explore with a flashlight. Odd to send me off alone; what if I got lost? I wondered why José didn't jump to accompany me. But just as well; he might be a grabber. Though after that hand-shake, probably not.

As I walked along, I realized that the rooms connected to each other with no corridors. The ceilings came to just above my head. Though I knew from visiting Washington's Headquarters that people two centuries ago were quite a bit shorter than we, I all but scraped my crown.

I kept going, hoping this would be historic and romantic, then feeling bewildered as I went from one room—no fireplace, no furniture, and no lights—to the next, each opening into another white nowhere.

Eventually I came back to the hall where I had started, feeling a desperate need for a deep breath. I took several, there in the hall. Why was I here? José had scarcely acknowledged me.

I re-entered the living room with its candles and warmth. Everyone stopped talking as I returned the flashlight. I began to imagine their ears growing out on stalks.

"Well. Anne dear, what did you think of our house?" Caroline said.

"Really . . . most interesting. These walls must hold a lot of history. Thank you," I said into the quiet and the bank of eyes.

I wanted to hide. I turned to sit on a hassock near my uncle's feet and whispered, "What should I drink? I . . . just had my first cocktail this past Thanksgiving."

Taking a thoughtful sip, Mac said, "Cornelia doesn't serve soft drinks. You might try some scotch." And so I did. It tasted like fur and made me feel like a grown-up. I should have asked for water. She had offered scotch, bourbon, and gin—with a small piece of ice or none. No snacks, cheese, pretzels, nothing to absorb alcohol.

My uncle was by far the most interesting person in the room, and I wished he would tell stories about his boyhood like when he was punished by being locked in the parlor to memorize Butler's *Lives of the Saints* or how his father would fly into a rage and beat his children with whatever came to hand. (Often his tie.) But my uncle was not in a mood to entertain; he was in a mood to drink. Steadily, and heavily throughout the evening.

I felt something touch my hair. I turned to see José's mother had moved to the chair behind me. Her hand had lightly stroked my head.

"Dear, do you like to . . . shop?" she said.

"Shop?"

"You know, go down to New York, see the fashion shows." She seemed dreamy. Her eyes shone. "See the latest dresses and coats and suits."

I looked down at my factory outlet lap and said nothing.

"I'll be going down next Wednesday. Would you like to come along?" she asked prettily.

I felt uneasy. Why did she call him José when he was born here in the Valley and his late dad was "Joe"? She was a local steamfitter's daughter, not Hispanic. And why invite me to New York with her? Did she want me to see what being really upper-class wealthy was like?

I wished there were someone I could talk to about this. I really wished my sister and brother had come with me. And José still sat on the far side of the room talking pleasantly to Caroline. Going to join them didn't seem appropriate or welcome.

And then I began to feel sick. At first it was just that the scotch had stopped tasting like fur, more like oatmeal and ground glass. Then my mouth started watering, and I knew: Soon I would throw up. Really soon. But where in this house that predated plumbing could I find a bathroom?

My aunt who spent the evening leveling a fierce look at my every move came swiftly to my side, whispering, "What's wrong?"

"I need to be sick," I said, miserable.

Her face clouded but she quickly led me upstairs. In the bathroom (running water, thank God) she said as if to herself, "These things happen even in the best of families."

I clung to the rim of the toilet bowl with both hands; sick as I was, I knew she meant that I was no longer a member in good standing of any family—best, worst, Most Shameful Family. Cast into outer darkness, no relatives. Not even these.

José and his mother, Cornelia and her mother, my father and mother, my uncle, no doubt sat drinking in silence below us. Listening. I wanted to run down and tell them I'd never had scotch before. That I didn't drink. That to celebrate my turning 18, the one time I'd had a cocktail was this past Thanksgiving with my father.

But I was sicker than I'd ever been. I couldn't lift my head, couldn't even talk. I don't remember what happened after that or how we got into the car. I recall waking once to see tears glittering on my aunt's cheeks as we passed streetlights on the way home.

The next afternoon when I sat with Paul drinking my way through two quarts of orange juice, unable to eat, José telephoned. Astounded, I had thought I'd never hear from him. But he asked how I was and then, "Would you like to go ice boating? This afternoon? With some friends of mine?"

I wondered if his mother were listening in.

We did date a few times. He took to calling me at school once a week with not much to say. Eventually he mentioned that his mother would like to see him marry soon. (My brother referred to him as "EZ Pickens.") But with not even a spark of what I felt for Rick between us, it seemed cruel to continue. Though my aunt said, "It's as easy to fall in love with a rich man as a poor one," I told him "There was someone else."

His mother started a new search.

And that spring Aunt Margaret called me at college. "There's a really nice boy who's in his second year at Annapolis, Phil Brillstein. His mother teaches with me, and she wondered if you'd like to go to a formal weekend in June at the Academy. She'd come with us."

"Us?"

"And there's a ball–you'll need your formal–the boys wear their dress uniforms on Saturday night. And there's sailing on Chesapeake Bay! You'll love it."

Wait. I knew this guy; his dad made a killing in wholesale produce. Another one of "our kind"? Phil had been ahead of me in grammar school, fat, freckled "Brillo."

Back then I was too young to appreciate the efforts my aunt went to so that I might have a life of comfort. I thought of telling her I wanted to enter the convent here, but that wouldn't solve my problem. So, yes, I did go to that weekend, and his mother came with us, along with *my mother.* The two moms had fun, but there wasn't any spark between him and me.

He didn't follow up after that. I realized that mothers of certain boys, who had gone away to college, were anxious to have their sons settle down here. These moms usually had beautiful homes that looked out on the river and mountains, and were worth keeping in the family. Too many of those who left for college never returned.

And so, several mothers in town arranged dates for their sons—they picked out the girl and made it happen. Reaching out to me was only one instance; I learned this later when I talked to girls drawn into dating these soon-to-be eligible bachelors.

Did I want to marry soon after college? Would that mean living near my parents? Was a wealthy marriage worth giving up my own dreams? I was set on getting a job in advertising in Manhattan. My future seemed wide open and back then it was easy to find a job. I expected to meet lots of guys at work, and that's exactly what happened.

But not a husband. Not yet.

GETTING TO KNOW DAN

I first met Dan when my brother Mark arranged a date with him for a football game weekend at their college. Dan and Mark were members of the Purple Key, a society similar to a fraternity. Catholic colleges including their Holy Cross College did not have fraternities, only key societies. Members were responsible for morale, "spirit," and were relied on in crises. They were not volunteers, but were chosen by the society, a great honor.

I loved my brother Mark; he was a year younger than I, and we had been great friends and allies against our parents. I remember the two of us sitting on my bed when we were six and seven discussing, "What do you think *normal* people do?"

This was a serious worry and we talked it over many times. We knew our family was not like others; we just didn't know what the differences were. "Normal" was a fantasy we had heart-to-heart talks about. This subject was prompted by not only beatings but also spoiled milk and food. Then too, we had parents who threw things at each other and us. These events bonded us.

Any guy Mark chose for me to date was sure to be a wonderful person, I thought, a reflection of his own wonderfulness. Mark met my train and introduced me to Dan, a tall, affable, heavy-set redhead who greeted me from inside a cloud of cigarette smoke. During the game I sat next to Dan. His friends would stop by, say, "Hi, Mark," to me, sit for a few minutes on the step next to me, then get up and walk away. They continued to call me by my brother's name. I assumed they wanted to check me over.

After the game and bantering with his friends, Dan wanted us to go to the Bancroft Hotel, one of his favorite haunts, for supper. He ordered two pizzas, and asked for one to be flipped upside down on top of the other. He began to eat them like a sandwich. He flirted with our waitress, and when I looked at her face, I could see she was in love with him. I felt shocked and realized I was a rival.

Sunday morning we all went to Mass together in the chapel. Dan fell asleep in our pew. My brother excused him to me in a whisper, "Dan was out late last night." I knew this probably meant out drinking.

That Monday, when I got back to school, at breakfast my friends were waiting to hear about my date with Mark's friend. They all had the same reaction to the pizza story: "You aren't going to go out with *him* again, are you?"

"No," I said. "No, of course not."

Two of them rolled their eyes, and said, "You'd better not!"

But I did. He was quite persistent and I was flattered and then delighted. I had never met anyone who was so self-confident. My brother and I were the opposite, and Dan's sureness at every turn was like a flame that drew us moths to him.

It was now senior year for both of us, and he invited me to be his date for the Emerald Ball held near St. Patrick's Day. This gala was attended almost entirely by those of Gaelic descent; true to our heritage, the ball involved the traditional imbibing of vast quantities of spirits.

I was not much of a drinker. My dad was so strict that my chances to catch up on drinking were few. He always insisted that I be home from a date by 10:30 p.m. "and no cars." If my date brought a car, Dad called us a cab. Sometimes he made Mark take a date and come along with me so I had a sort of male *duenna*. I had little experience with drinking until I was legally eligible at eighteen.

The Emerald Ball, which continues to this day, was started in 1839 by the Emerald Association, a charity that raised funds to care for orphans in Brooklyn and Long Island. It was strictly black tie, women in elegant long gowns, no expense spared. Judging from the clothes, these attendees ranged from comfortably wealthy to the kind of rich known as "filthy."

Dan had taken another girl from my college to last year's Ball, and he suggested I ask her what it was like. She kindly agreed to talk about it, but said, "I can't see why he would want me to tell you about it. He seemed to spend most of his time in the bathroom. I hardly saw him at all. I had fun with his friends, though."

This didn't make sense—why did he think talking to this girl would encourage me to go with him to the Ball? But later I realized he must have had a lot to drink that night and didn't remember enough about it. This was a time—the Fifties—when collegians tried to mirror the eating and drinking exploits of Gargantua and Pantagruel. For instance, my brother told me that Dan's sandwich pizza became a legend at his college.

To attend the Ball, I stayed at a friend's flat on Manhattan's Sutton Place, an amazingly elite neighborhood where everyone was at least a multimillionaire. Dan called for me in his tuxedo. My dark blue formal sparkled. I was terribly excited. The hotel was aglow with light everywhere, along with Ancient Order of Hibernians banners, and flags in orange and green with the traditional golden harps. Everyone around me was drinking. I saw one beautiful redhead in green satin from my college. I went to speak to her; she tilted her head back and seemed very drunk.

Mostly I felt bewildered; I had never been in such a huge and elegant place. Dan kept me close to his side, and gathered his college friends about us. They toasted and bantered amid hearty laughter, often convulsed with guffaws. Tonight was my chance to see what Dan was like in person.

Much of time we were together, he kept himself surrounded by his courtiers. He had an entourage both here and at college, ever the center. Our spending time one-on-one was almost impossible. But when we took a breather from the dancing, we sat on the sidelines, and started talking. "Does my eye bother you?" he said.

I looked at his face, close to mine now. "Why?"

"I wanted you to know that two years ago, I had cancer. At first, I had flashes of light that sent me to an eye doctor. My parents took me to New York and California to see what the flashes were all about. The doctors decided it meant cancer."

"Why? How?" I was startled. Why was this coming up?

"My older sister had just had cancer, so they were really scared when the doctors told them it was likely cancer that was causing my eye to have lightning flashes. My sister was in college. She died and we had the wake at our house. Hundreds of people came through.

"The doctors in Chicago said there was no other choice. They had to remove the eyeball or the cancer would spread to my brain. So they removed the eye, and I got a plastic eye." He bent down then, and gently lifted the plastic eye out and held it out in his palm.

I felt shivers down my back, but I looked at it. It was the same coloration as his other eye. "They did a good job, to match it," I said, trying hard to say something positive. I was shocked but didn't want to tell him. Cancer in those days was not common and here his family had it twice.

"The priests at my college were great, very understanding. I wanted to get my degree; I had been majoring in math, and I switched to English lit." He sipped at his drink.

"Doesn't that mean a lot of reading? Can you do that?"

"Oh, the other eye is fine, and so, yes, I can. I'm writing my senior thesis on F. Scott FitzGerald. I really like his books. And he's Irish!"

"I don't know his books."

"Then you must read *This Side of Paradise*. I'll lend you a copy. It's really good, one of my all-time favorites."

The orchestra had switched back to slow-dancing music and he rose, took my hand and we went out on the dance floor. I had a lot to think about.

Other than this conversation, he and I spent little real time together. He gave me his copy of that book and he wrote to me several times, mostly after he had been out in the evening drinking with his buddies.

When I wrote back, he told me he read my letters aloud to his friends. I cringed at the idea.

Soon it was graduation time for both of us. My mother made me come home the weekend of my own graduation for my sister's graduation from her high school. Because I left campus on graduation weekend, I got demerits for leaving. Not that it mattered since I would graduate that weekend. However, graduation activities for the entire weekend were scheduled by our faculty—High Mass each day, final luncheons with our professors. My parents did come to see my graduation.

The following weekend, I went to Dan's graduation and senior prom. His parents had driven in from Chicago to Worcester, Massachusetts, for the weekend. Dan brought me to meet his mother at her hotel room.

The first thing she said to me was, "My, you're tall. I thought Dan liked only little girls."

"Yes, I am," I said, "tall." And I thought what an odd comment. Guess I'm not going to make the cut. Dan slipped away and she and I chatted a bit. Soon she said, "You do know, don't you, dear, that Dan wants to be a priest?"

"No," I said. "He hadn't mentioned it."

"Well, dear, it's only fair to you that you know that."

At first, I ignored her words, but it began to irk me. And then, I felt betrayed. But both Dan and I were products of the Catholic school system and the pressure on young kids to become priests and nuns was heavy. Was it motivated by a genuine wish to recruit more soldiers to spread the word of the "one, true, holy, and apostolic church" or by "Misery loves company"?

There was also a betting pool at my college that year as to which seniors might "enter" (as in, enter the convent). Rumor had it that ten percent of the class every year became nuns. I was horrified to learn I was considered a likely candidate. The universal sacrifices called for by vows of Poverty, Chastity, and Obedience might enthrall idealistic youngsters.

But as time went on, I foresaw that loneliness and deprivation were served up instead. Hard crusts for the hungry to gnaw.

Further, Dan had talked about our marrying, never even once spoke of entering the priesthood. I had found that many guys liked to bring up marriage as a topic of conversation. In those days, girls loved hearing it, and usually thought it meant the guy was giving some thought to commitment. It didn't seem to occur to any of us that this gambit was a ploy to get us more willing to make out.

After all, it was senior year, and at that point, many girls were engaged or about to be. It was in the air. In dorms as graduation neared, girls sat on each other's beds speculating about who was about to be engaged, and wondering what their own chances for marriage might be. Marriage and children—these were most girls' expectations at that time.

I was dazed. It was still Prom night, and I had to change into my prom dress and dance in the arms of this man who was headed, not for me, but for the priesthood. As we sat out a cha-cha, I asked him about the "vocation" I heard about from his mother. "Dan, your mother said…you're thinking about being a priest?"

"Yeah. Well, she shouldn't have told you."

"Is it true?"

"I was *going* to tell you."

"When? All this time, and you invite me to your senior prom, and you never said anything?"

"I'm really upset about it myself. I'm not sure—is it the priesthood? Should I be a priest? Is this what God wants me to do? Or do I marry? I'm making a retreat to think about it."

The music started up again, and couples wrapped themselves around each other in the dim light and swayed to "Memories Are Made of This." Then, "My Prayer" and "Love Me Tender."

I was broken-hearted.

The next day I dragged myself over to the train and headed up the Hudson River to my home. I couldn't talk. I had been sure Dan and I were meant for each other. I had prayed for years that God would send me a good husband; since Dan was a Catholic and my brother's friend I was sure that God had answered my prayers. Dan was the One.

I had a summer job waiting for me, head lifeguard at the Delano-Hitch Recreation Pool (the Rec) from one p.m. to nine p.m. daily. I also took classes in shorthand and typing in the mornings, eight to twelve. I left myself no time to brood, but I turned quiet. I did ask my dad one night to talk with me. I told him about Dan, that I had been in love with him, and I said, "Now he is on his way to a retreat. He said it would help him find out if he should be a priest."

"A man like that can never love you as you deserve," Dad said, as he changed out of his steel-toed work shoes. He was settling down to watch television, back then mostly wrestling and baseball games. And the once-a-week highlight, Milton Berle.

I felt startled by Dad's words. It hadn't occurred to me that there might be a flaw in Dan; I thought his rejection had to be my fault. I wasn't good enough. And how could I compete with God? Another woman, maybe. Not God.

I didn't think about how Dan's mother fit into the picture, but from our talk, it was clear that on having a son become a priest, she was hell-bent. Or heaven-bent. A lot of Catholic mothers thought a child who entered religious life in those days meant that their moms had done an exceptionally fine job as a parent.

My grieving had me down and monosyllabic. One day when I didn't have work, Mark and I went swimming with one of his friends. Since we had no car, Mark and I were adept at getting friends to give us rides to swimming holes. Unfortunately for the friends, we usually brought our siblings. These "rides" came mostly from my boyfriends, who thought at first they were taking me alone for some possible romantic moments. Guys were mostly good-natured about the carful.

This time Jerry took Mark aside to ask, "What's the matter with Anne?"

"She's had some very bad news," my brother told him.

I didn't realize that I was also exhausted from the six-day week on the job and school four hours a day. But mostly I was mourning. College was over and I was about to begin my life, get a job, but now *not* marry . . . I had thought marriage to Dan was my future.

Though I had to take myself in a new direction, I was doing poorly at it. Eating was no help. I began to lose weight. There was no joy anywhere. At the pool the sun shone on me, but it was not my warm, friendly sun. This sun was harsh, glaring. I wore sunglasses, even inside, still shocked. I was beyond tears.

I continued to plod through my days

Then one lunch-time, the phone rang as I passed it in the hall. It was Dan, all affability and good spirits, in his most Friendly Bear mode. "Well, hello there! How are *you?*" he began.

My mouth dried. What was he calling for? I had closed the door on him–and my feelings. I thought it was all over. Final. The end. Over and done with. I stood there in the hall with the phone to my ear. "Hello. I'm surprised to . . . hear your voice," I said. I didn't know what to say.

"You don't sound very happy to hear from me," he went on, like this was just an ordinary, everyday call.

"Why. . . why have you called?" I finally got the words out. It hurt. I lost my bearings standing there. I sat down hard on the hall stairs, twisting the phone cord with my other hand.

"Well, I wanted to tell you that I finished my retreat and that I don't think I'll be a priest after all. The priest that I talked to said, 'Get back in touch with Anne. She's too good to let go of.' And so I want to come out there. And see you."

"Here?" I couldn't think. What was happening?

I was due back at the pool in twenty minutes. "Can . . . can I call you later?"

"What's wrong with now?"

"I have to leave for work. It's a long walk."

"Well, I wanted to tell you the good news, and set up a time for me to come see you."

My brother. I had to talk to him. He was out, driving a Seven-Up truck for the summer.

"I thought I'd fly out the week after next."

"Where are you now?"

"I'm back in Chicago."

"I need to think...."

"I thought you'd be happy."

"I have to go. I'll talk to you...tonight."

I hung up the phone. My mother was in the kitchen, humming to herself. I never knew when she might blow up as she so often did. To avoid trouble, I said only, "That was Dan. He said he isn't...going to be a priest. Got to go. I'm late."

I grabbed my hat, whistle, sunglasses and ran out. My feelings were all over the place, and they were not good. I was confused and I should be happy, I told myself, this is what I wanted.

Or was it?

At the pool I ran up the stairs from the locker room to my post at the far end. just as the hordes were let loose from the basement locker rooms. Like suddenly freed prisoners, they raced up the stairs yelling and hit the still water, scattering it into rough waves. They shouted, exuberant with joy and the freedom that vast expanses of water offered.

Boys charged up the three-meter tower and began cannonballing into the deep end. Their goal: soak my co-worker in the lifeguard chair with their watermelons.

She caught my eye, lifted her eyebrows, and shook her head.

I blew my whistle, shouted "NO Running! Or you're OUT."

Soon chaos settled into the usual hullaballoo.

I set my hat farther down on my forehead and walked from the Kiddie Pool to the stairs and back, sentry duty. We four guards weren't allowed to sit but rotated around the perimeter every fifteen minutes. It was tiring to be alert every moment, watching for distress in the deep end, fistfights, boys picking girls up only to throw them screaming into the water.

"Bella Donna, Bella Donna!" A small blond boy in too-big navy trunks tugged my hand. Most kids in the area spoke Italian only. He was trying to hide behind me from another kid he pointed at. He looked too young to be here alone; I figured his mom dropped him off. These were the days of no day care, and this daily pool was ideal for over-stressed moms. I sometimes heard them yelling as they walked away, "And don't you dare come home till after this place closes!"

I was in no mood to babysit. Still, little Beppe was part of my job. He looked up, worship in his eyes. At least someone appreciated me. I knelt and put my arm around him. *Come va?* (What's up?)

The kid pestering him was in the water holding on to the scum gutter, just his dark eyes and the top of his damp head visible over the edge of the deck.

"Aaah!" A scream halfway down the deck. A girl had settled herself on her towel to sunbathe. A boy roaming the deck had filled a bathing cap with water and splashed her out of her sundoze–his way of saying, "I like you!"

He was one of a bunch of boys from Washington Heights, the "dailies"– past the age for babysitters, too young to drive, but old enough for mischief. They called themselves "the Huskies." They were our groupies.

Right now, I needed to think about Dan's coming visit. That night I talked with Mark about where we could put Dan for that weekend. He could not stay with us in our small house. Dad would never allow it; we knew better than to ask. We arranged for a room at the Hotel Newburgh, the best our town had to offer. (Dan refused to stay at the YMCA.)

On the appointed day Dan agreed to come directly to the Rec, since I had to work. To avoid any unpleasantness with our dad, we didn't want Dan showing up at the house. We of course had not told Dad Dan was coming. For some unfathomable reason, perhaps he suspected something, Dad came home and offered a ride to my sister and me. To work. At the pool.

What was this? He *never* gave rides. Had Mother let it slip that Dan was on his way? My sister, Mark, and I piled into his convertible, and he pulled up to the pool entrance.

There at the top of the Rec steps was this enormous red-headed man in a business suit with a huge suitcase.

Oh no! My heart stopped. Early! Damn it.

Standing at the gate, Dan looked as out of place as a bush growing from the ceiling. He stood chatting in his Midwestern friendly way with kids waiting for the pool to open so they could run down the inside steps to the cashiers.

"Who do you suppose that man is?" my father said, pointing with one index finger extended and both hands on the steering wheel. "Does he know you?" Dan had looked over and spotted me. (Take me now, Death.)

I crouched behind the dashboard. I had to get out of Dad's car, but I wanted to put off my boyfriend's welcome–that my father would surely see. "Thanks for the ride, Dad." I tried not to rush to greet Dan until Dad got out of sight. My sister and brother scrambled from the car.

It couldn't be helped: Here came Dan, bounding down the entrance steps to grab me in a bear hug. Curious six-and-seven-year-olds collected around us. "Is he your boyfriend, Anne? Is he?"

I struggled out of Dan's grip to check on the departing convertible. Yes, it seemed to be gone. What had it witnessed?

All we had to deal with now was dinner.

Tonight. With Dad.

But first, Mark and Dan had to go to the Boys' Locker Room so they could change into swimsuits. Dan tucked his big suitcase behind the cashiers' counter.

That afternoon at the pool I walked my guard beat while Dan swam and then lay down on the benches that rimmed the pool's perimeter. He soon fell asleep, and some of my followers, black and white, crept over to stare at this tall, red-headed white man in red plaid bathing trunks. He lay large along the benches. I heard whispering, "Anne's boyfriend" as they gathered near him. Some squatted down to look straight at him.

One of my groupies, Junebug, went to sit silently on the bench next to Dan's substantial feet. After studying Dan for a few minutes, he reached over and softly touched Dan's pale toes and their tufts of red hair.

"Jesus Christ! What the hell?" Dan woke with a start and leaped from the bench. "*What* was that?"

Junebug and the other kids scattered. I was near enough to see all this.

Dan came from then-segregated Chicago. He had never been by black people; they lived mostly on the South Side then, and to have even a small black person touch his toes was beyond his experience. Since my town didn't segregate—we had just the one swimming pool—I didn't understand how upset he was.

Dan couldn't seem to stop talking about it. He walked along with me as I patrolled my beat, but he did all the talking. "Whew! That was really something! I can't believe it happened. I've never had someone scare me like that!"

I still had to keep lifeguarding, so I murmured a few soothing, "Yes, must have been hard...." I had to concentrate on my job. No talking, or Woody would be at my side

Dan went to lie on the grassy berm outside the pool for the rest of the afternoon until at five, we guards chased kids and adults from the pool. Shortly after, the water settled into a tranquil calm until seven, when the hubbub would return. This peaceful time was when I loved it best, and our supervisor, Woody, must have felt the same. It was often his time to take a long swim by himself.

I usually liked watching his expert crawl, but tonight I had just time for dinner. Dan was joining us; Mother was serving a rare treat, steak.

And then we had to return for my stint from seven to nine, the evening session.

Dan, my sister, my brothers, and I walked through the streets in the still-warm late sun. Dan continued with his, "I can't believe that happened. That little kid touching my toes!"

"It was no big deal, Dan," my brother said. "They all had been in the pool. They were clean."

"That's not the point!" Dan went on. "They shouldn't have touched me."

"We'll be back here tomorrow, so you should get over it," Mark said.

Now we were walking down Broadway, facing the river and Mount Beacon...

"And another thing, the mountains! They look like we could reach over and touch them,"

"Know why it's called Mount Beacon, Dan, do you, huh?" Paul didn't want to be left out.

"No, I don't," Dan said. "Why, Paul?"

"Because in the Revolutionary War, our side lit signal fires at the top to warn our soldiers when the British were coming up the Hudson." Paul at twelve wanted so much to be part of his older siblings' lives. He had been lonely when Mark and I were away at school. And right now, he was part of the "in" group.

Some of my younger groupies fell in behind us, nudging each other and giggling.

At home, we five stood in the hall to wait for Dad to come in the front door from work. Dad always used the front door–the rest of the family always came in the back. We stood there as aromas of seasoned beef cooking rose from the kitchen. And then, here Dad was, coming up the steps.

I went forward, opened the door and said, "Dad, I'd like you to meet my friend Dan."

Dad's face was thunderous. Dan smiled and had his hand out in his friendly Midwestern way.

My father batted it aside. He looked furious, and scowled at me. "Where's your mother? Was this her idea?" he barked. "What's going on? Why wasn't I told any of this?'"

He then turned, ran out the front door and down the steps.

I felt like he slapped me. What a way to treat a guest, I thought. No one spoke. I thought Dan might have said something, but he kept his mouth shut. We went downstairs to the dining room. Mother naturally had listened below stairs so we didn't repeat what Dad said.

Dan did say as we sat down to dinner, "Shall we wait for Mr. McKneally to join us?" No doubt thinking that is what normal people would do. But not our family.

Paul, Mark, Elaine, and I met each other's gazes with that penetrating Family Look That Needs No Words. We knew Dad wouldn't be back, probably not for the rest of the weekend. But no point in telling a stranger—Dan–about it. There was no explanation possible.

In a rare moment of tact, Mother said, "He may be delayed. Why don't we all just go ahead?"

She served the steak, spinach, and baked potatoes. Dan was his jovial self. "Say, what is this meat?" he asked. "It is delicious!"

"Why, Dan, that's steak," Mother said. "I thought you'd recognize it, being from Chicago!"

"It sure is good. Say, do you mind if I make a sandwich? My mom tells me it's uncouth, so I'm asking."

Dan, I had noticed, made sandwiches out of almost anything– ketchup, mustard, baked beans, what-have-you. He helped himself to the bread and made a steak sandwich. The steak had been broiled as usual, and it was a well-done piece of meat about a quarter of an inch thick, grey, and curling at the edges. All my relatives served beef well-done. When I had steak at Dan's house a few months later, I had one–well over an inch thick and medium rare.

Dan continued in a pleasant mood, thanked my mother graciously, and then he, Paul, and Mark left to walk with his suitcase the half-mile or so to the Hotel Newburgh. None of us had cars, and we walked everywhere. This must have seemed quaint to Dan who had the use of his family's car. He said nothing.

After they left, no one talked about, "What do you think Dad will do when he gets back?" But I dreaded having him return, whenever that would be. Years in the future, Dan would regale friends and relatives with the story of how Anne's father greeted him when he first came to our house. "Let me tell you what it was like to meet Anne's father! He wouldn't even speak to me! He left the house and didn't come back! What a welcome!"

I don't remember much about that weekend; I had to work both days, and Dan had to fly back Sunday night. He came with me to the pool, and we went for some long walks without my siblings. This would be just around our neighborhood or to Downing Park, a block away.

"Sure is beautiful scenery here," he said. "Reminds me of Colorado."

"Yes, well, can we talk about your retreat? You said you decided not to be priest?"

We were at the pond called the "Polly" (short for Pollywog) where we always skated in the winters. Dan skimmed a few stones across the surface. I did, too.

"Oh, that. Yes. Well, I thought God was calling me, but turned out He wasn't."

"How did your parents take it?" I thought he dismissed it pretty lightly, but didn't really know what to say.

"Well, Mom was disappointed, of course. She would have liked to have a son who was a priest. Say, I'd like to see you again. Soon. Would you come out to Chicago for a weekend?"

We settled that I would fly out to Chicago for Labor Day weekend. Before that, I would line up a job in Manhattan at summer's end and get an apartment with three college friends.

I had continued to believe that God wanted me to marry Dan, but what now? My feelings were still numb, stifled; I didn't know what I thought or felt. I knew I should feel happy. Mostly I was exhausted and tumbled into bed each night to sleep long and hard until it was time for my 8:00 a.m. class in shorthand.

Getting in Deeper—to Know Dan

Before I met Dan, my mother met him. It happened at a Parents' Weekend at Holy Cross College, where my brother Mark was a junior. Dan was the chairman of the weekend and he made a great impression on her with his friendliness, efficiency, and courteous attention to his mother.

My brother had already set Dan and me up for a football weekend blind date a few weeks away, so my mother wrote to me that "If you don't like Dan you are crazy." Since she often told me I was crazy, I paid no attention.

However, I was now a senior in college, and my mother's family often asked me, "When are you getting married?" before I even had a prospect. I dreaded having my mother's sisters stop by for a visit. Their way of making conversation usually started by their saying, "So, Anne, how's your sex life?"

In those days, I never knew how to answer. I didn't want to marry since I was still in school, and I felt put on the spot. Besides, neither of them had married. Why did they ask? All I could do was squirm. If I answered, "Fine," I figured they would press me for details. I didn't know what a "sex life" was, and I felt too intimidated to say "what is that?" And I always felt I was rude not to answer.

Later on, I might have answered, "How's yours?"

Part of Dan's allure for my mother may have been that he lived about a thousand miles from our home. That meant that I would be gone, out of our town and out of her hair. For years, she would say to me, "You have to get out of Newburgh. There is nothing for you here." I wondered if she were talking about herself. Before she married, she had taught in Manhattan and lived in Greenwich Village for seven years. Our little mill town was limited in comparison, and she had married a Newburgh man so she had to move back here and leave her New York life.

And so, my mother from the start really wanted me to marry Dan.

At the time, I was still living a life that was almost convent-like. Our all-girls' college was more sheltered than we knew. I didn't know what I didn't know. We were all pretty much cloistered. I often thought it would be an easy step to pass through the convent doors and "enter"—the life would not differ much from what we knew as students.

No males were allowed in the dorms unless they were our brothers and fathers helping us pack up to go home. Usually a Sister would lurk nearby to keep an eye on things.

Handling social situations where we needed to understand appropriate behavior and conversation was unknown territory. Some of us had brothers, but they weren't really knowledgeable about how we girls should act with the opposite sex. Somehow we had to fumble through the college mixers on Friday nights, try to appear self-confident, figure out how to encourage a guy we were interested in and discourage the ones we didn't care for. I ran the mixers committee senior year, and had to OK legions of males from nearby colleges who flocked to our campus. Security stood by in the background.

At lunchtime and after classes, boys swarmed on campus and sat about on the steps to the library or the dining hall. They didn't set foot inside the buildings. If a gentleman caller came by a dorm building, he had to approach the desk in the front hall and indicate whom he was there to see. He was allowed to sit in the vast reception room to wait until his requested lady friend joined him while Sister sat within earshot.

For example, one afternoon I had just come in from a dress rehearsal, when the Sister at the desk rang the bell over the loudspeaker that I had a visitor. I was not expecting anyone, and I was already made up for my role as "Lord Byron's Lover."

At the time of the play, my character was in her eighties. I had powdered my hair with talcum, applied grease paint foundation, and drawn wrinkles on my forehead and cheeks. My roommate took a look at me, and said, "You're not going down like *that,* are you?"

"It took me ages to get made up like this. I can't change now and put it all back on before the curtain goes up tonight. I'll have to see who it is," I said. I also planned to go to the dining hall like this, but the whole school knew about the play. Others might be in their makeup as well. I honestly didn't care–the play was what mattered.

So down I went. I had no idea who it might be, but there in the living room was George D, a guy who sometimes drove me from school to my home in Newburgh. He drove a terrifying 95 miles an hour on the Thruway. But it saved train fare. He wasn't anyone special to me, just an occasional ride home. I wondered why he happened to stop by.

As he walked toward me with bulging eyes, his look of horror was as gratifying as a standing ovation. I must have done a great job on the wrinkles. He babbled, "Are…are you all right?" and choked.

"I'm in a play tonight," I said. "I didn't know you were coming." In my heart I thought, "Serves you right for not calling to tell me you'd be over."

But back then, it was unthinkable that I didn't "pretty up" for him, and my dorm mates scolded me later. I never heard from him again.

However, my immediate concern was with one guy, Dan. It was time to get on with my life, and my summer lifeguard job would end. I had thought long and hard about whether I should continue to see him. I had been so sure before he announced he wanted to be a priest. While I mulled this thought, he and I talked about my flying to Chicago to visit him over the Labor Day weekend.

I had never been inside a plane. My brother drove me to LaGuardia airport and when I saw the plane on the runway, I felt panic wash through me like a true country bumpkin as I said to my brother, "Oh, no! That plane is so big! I don't think I can do this."

"OK," Mark said, "We can go back home."

Very funny.

I got on the plane and sat between two servicemen who were about my age. We had fun flirting. They teased me when we passed over Detroit and I thought we had missed Chicago. They were going on to Minneapolis where they were stationed, and they wanted me to stay on the plane and come with them.

Dan met my plane. He said his parents had dinner ready, but he wanted to show me something first—a White Castle restaurant. Where I came from, we had nothing like it. Dan insisted on our ordering burgers, "Sliders," each two inches by two inches. He was going on about how wonderful they were, and I was concerned that his parents were expecting us.

I apologize to Slider Lovers everywhere. To this day, I fail to feel their enchantment. I couldn't believe Dan had stopped to have these–with dinner waiting at his home.

"Well, what do you think?" He asked several times.

I much preferred the substantial burgers at the Dairy Queen back home, or at Bill and Gene's Greasy Spoon. I tried to be polite. "They . . . are interesting."

"Is that all you can say?"

"Can we go now? I am really tired. And I want to unpack," I said.

When we entered the house, his parents were quite angry. Dan's dad scolded, "We have been waiting all this time. And I'm trying to grill steaks for you. Where did you two go? Dan, I told you not to be late."

His mother looked really annoyed, and called me "dear" with an edge to her voice. But his father did the talking and it wasn't comfortable,

As the weekend progressed, I heard a lot of scolding from his dad. But then, my father hadn't even spoken to Dan, but snubbed him.

I weighed the pluses and minuses of continuing to date him. The minuses included his living in Chicago, my plan to share an apartment in Manhattan with three college friends, and working in advertising and loving that part of my life, so not wanting to give it up.

The pluses were that my brother liked him a lot, that I had liked him a great deal before he mentioned his call to the priesthood, and that I was sure that God had intended us to be together. My faith in the power of prayer was strong back then. Having prayed for a good husband when it was time to marry, I assumed that was Dan.

After graduation, Dan had started working at a Chicago bank, and when he visited that first time, he asked my mother and siblings to each open a savings account. His bank had a campaign to increase its savings accounts, so he brought signature cards with him, and asked even my Uncle John to open an account, just for $5. They all humored him for my sake, without pointing out that their money would be in Chicago. I was embarrassed, and hadn't known he was doing it until it happened in front of me. Having their money out in a Chicago bank didn't make sense to me, but they did it.

After that summer, I got a job in Manhattan and shared a tiny apartment with my college friends. I had wanted to work in advertising and I did. If I ever married I would have liked to marry and stay in New York. As Dan and I dated on occasional weekends that fall, we talked about our futures. When Dan asked me to marry him on New Year's Eve, the main obstacle I saw looming ahead was getting my father's consent.

One request from my mother had been that I was not to tell my father that Dan had had cancer. She was sure he wouldn't allow me to marry him because of it.

And so, one winter Saturday I went upstairs to where Dad was watching TV. If I thought getting his OK to go to college was a hurdle, this was worse. My mouth went dry.

I felt like a toreador entering the bullring for the first time. I had no one at my back. I stood in the doorway, took a deep breath, and said, "Dad, I want to get married. Dan has asked me,"

His immediate response was full-on fury. I braced myself as my bull charged, shouting, "Absolutely not! Over my dead body! You'll do nothing of the kind!"

His volcanic eruption all but flattened me. He was shouting so loud and hard that he rose briefly from his seat.

I knew I had to persist—to the death. I did not lose my temper. I was terrified, alone in the room with a mad bull. In that small house, I knew my mother in the kitchen was listening. No help for me there. This, like the scholarships struggle, was my own problem.

"You. Have to. Stay. Here," he roared.

"Why?" I said.

"Your mother needs you," he said.

"What does she need me for?"

He didn't seem to have an answer. I found myself crying, mostly from rage. I hated getting shouted at by him, and I knew my engaged friends had their parents' delighted blessing. I had been a good child, seldom in trouble.

That was no help to me now. Into my mind flashed one night at dinner when Dad said to me, "Joanie over at the Health Department told me she saw you walking down Broadway today with some boy–Bob Farrington. I called the police chief and asked him to look the guy up on the blotter. Seems Bob pulled a knife on someone. I don't want you spending any time with him. Hear?"

Bob was a nice-looking guy I met at the pool. He worked as a lifeguard in Florida during the winter. But I had only walked home from work with him.

Dad's spies were everywhere. I *had* to get away from this town.

I continued to press. "Dad, I really want to marry him."

I would not give in. With a lot more shouting on both sides, suddenly I saw him crumple. In a weak, sad voice, he said, "All right. Anne. You can marry him. It . . . it will be a nice wedding." His voice was full of tears.

I could hardly believe this turnabout. Yet here it was. I won against him. Again. I hardly noticed that the bull's ears and tail were in my hands. A triumph, but it didn't feel like one.

With my cheeks wet with tears, I went down the two flights of stairs. Mother had been listening in the stairwell. I told her, "He said . . . it would be all right."

I was too wiped out to talk about it. I went to my bedroom and lay down.

Ahead of me were more fights—fights over who could be on the guest list—many local politicos—what dates were open, where the reception would be held, how we could accommodate my godfather's schedule since he was slated to become National Commander of the American Legion, and so on. I was eldest grandchild of an extended family, so I had to spread the news through the family tree. But all these were anticlimactic; my biggest battle was behind me.

I did not foresee that I would never be forgiven—the Irish hold grudges over decades, generations, and for years beyond. Dad barely spoke to me after our fight. On my wedding day, he took me aside and said quietly, "You can never come home. Do you hear me? Never." He never really forgave me.

Most of the wedding preparation was mine; I knew other girls' mothers plunged into the planning, but mine let me handle talking to restaurant owners, choosing the menu, getting prices, going to New York's garment district to find a dress.

I was keenly aware that I knew almost nothing about sex, and I decided I needed expert advice. I went to our family doctor, a good friend of my father. I gulped and choked my way through "Doctor, I will be married in a few weeks, and I wondered if you could tell me something about . . . what to expect on my wedding night."

Doctor Fred reached behind himself, and extracted a book from his medical literature. He handed me a fat volume: *Sexual Hygiene and Pathology.*

Saying, "Here. Just read the beginning. You don't have to read the Pathology part," he ended my visit. I took his book home and, of course, looked into the long Pathology section, which generously quoted Krafft-Ebing's texts. Awful, awful, awful—details of depravities and savagely cruel behavior set out on every page.

Not the answer I had hoped for. I was afraid to go to sleep the first night I peeked into his book. I took it back to his office; he wasn't in. I said nothing to my parents.

Looking back, what was in that doctor's mind? I knew he was re-nowned as another of our town's alcoholics. I had no idea whom to go to for help. Certainly not the nuns who educated me. And I surely couldn't ask my parents. Books, in the past my source of help, offered no light at our library.

Dan insisted that we live in the Chicago area after the wedding where I knew no one, except of course, him. A few months before the wedding, Dan asked me to quit my New York job. As he put it, I had "too much fun in (my) apartment and job." It would be boring to be married, he anticipated, so he wanted me to live at home with my parents and Paul. That way I could get used to being a housewife, he said.

It all seems preposterous now, and in today's world, it would be. Back then, my friends who married just stayed home until the babies came along. Remember, these were the days of no birth control, and for Catholics, having a child right away was the norm.

When I went to talk over the wedding plans with the priest, I asked if one of my friends could sing at the wedding. Father said, "No. We have to have Marian. She's our organist and soloist. We can't offend her."

Her voice offended me; she sounded like a bullfrog. I begged, but Father stood firm. We had to have the designated soloist. I picked out some music and asked her in advance to play it. She said, "No. This is not in my *repertwahr.*"

When I pressed her to learn it, she again said, "I can't, because it's not in my *repertwahr.*"

We also had a battle over Mendelsohn's "Wedding March."

"Everyone loves it," she said.

"But I don't. Please play this instead," and I handed her music from my choir mistress at college. But that, too, was scratched. The organ music she chose as my new husband and I went down the aisle was dread-ful, and my horrified face didn't look like a new bride's, my sister said. I suspect the organist punished me for not embracing her Mendelsohn rendition.

For our honeymoon, I had picked out a local resort in the Catskills, Lake Minnewaska. The setting was beautiful, and Dan wrote to them to order a king-sized bed. They accepted his down payment, but didn't tell him they had only small double beds with no box springs. The mattresses were old and thin. Dan weighed over two hundred ten pounds, and when we lay on the bed, it caved in the middle. I clung to the edge of the mattress, but I still fell into the middle where Dan had slid. We lifted the mattress onto the floor so we could sleep without falling into each other.

We were the youngest people there by two generations. All the other guests were about the age of my grandmother, and when Dan and I entered the dining room, all the white heads rose and we had everyone's attention. Later as we went toward the stairs, one tiny little old lady popped out of a corridor to giggle and say, "Are you two having fun?"

The first three days at the lake ("Laughing Waters"–the translation of Minnewaska), a dense fog filled the bowl of our mountains, so dense that the management would not allow anyone to step off the porch. I have never seen such a fog before or since. Dan and I were getting cabin fever. It was like a whiteout and there was no visibility. We were in the mountains, so a romantic walk could be suicide.

When the fog lifted, I dove for my suitcase. I could swim this morning! But alas, I could not find my bathing suit. My sister had borrowed it, I learned later. I put on my shorts and a top, and Dan and I went swimming in the beautiful Laughing Waters.

As I swam luxuriously in the clear, spritzy water, I thought of how years ago, my sister and I used to row to center of a lake, put out the anchor and get in the water. We removed our bathing suits and swam near the rowboat. Occasionally a boat load of boys would see us swimming near our rowboat and shout over, "Hey, Girls! Can we join you?" We were submerged to our necks, and this lake was murky. We laughed and chased them away. Luckily, they left. We giggled a lot knowing we had to slip back into our suits before we could climb into our boat–Dad's boat.

I wished I could have done that skinny-dipping at Minnewaska, but with so many little old ladies around and the Laughing Waters so clear, I would have died of embarrassment. Dan and I could see to the bottom of this deep lake.

The rest of our honeymoon days passed slowly. Once we figured out that we might sleep better with the mattress on the floor, we moved it down there nightly, and every morning the maids placed it back where it belonged.

As the days went by, I was getting to know Dan as never before. We had all our meals together, and we enjoyed the fresh trout from the lake below us and local farm tomatoes, carrots, and salads.

Also, Dan relayed this very Irish message to me: "Mom told me that after she met you, she said that Anne seemed like someone who could handle a great deal of suffering." He thought it was a great compliment, as did his mother.

I didn't feel at all complimented. While I knew from my own experience that the Irish Catholic culture prized suffering and often heard people telling each other to "Offer it up" when they had troubles or pain, I began to realize that Dan's mother had made a career of it.

I knew he and I had never spent much time alone, and now we were together around the clock. He seemed different from the Dan who surrounded himself with his entourage—quieter, more thoughtful

One aspect of this honeymoon resort I had not known was that it was "dry." No alcohol was served or permitted anywhere in this state park. Dan had brought some bourbon with him, but for him to have no cocktails or beer at dinner was a hardship. The first time we went down to dinner Dan's "Unbelievable!" could be heard from one end of the building to the other as he roared his displeasure.

The other diners' chatter suddenly stopped at that.

The next day, he headed into town and found a package store. He had grown up with all kinds of liquor available. No family gathering or dinner was without. Minnewaska was an alien universe.

Soon our honeymoon ended, and we went to my now former home to gather clothes and a few books: Shakespeare, *Bartlett's Quotations*, poetry. I wanted to bring more, but Dan thought there wasn't enough room, and besides, he said, "My parents have plenty of books. You can read those."

My mother drew me aside to say, "I can't stand the way he talks to you, and neither can your sister." She had overheard him scolding me about not packing fast enough, or as he put it, "I want to see sweat on your face, Annie, while you get packing! We don't have all day."

"Mother, this is how he is. This is how he treated his roommate. I just have to accept it." I didn't like it, but he laughed when I asked him to stop. He was in the habit of finding fault, I realized, like his dad. I told myself, "This is what I wanted–this marriage. I've made my bed. Now I must lie in it."

My mother made it a point to take Dan aside to tell him, "You need to know that Anne sometimes has mental problems. She often cries. Some day she might have a nervous breakdown. I just wanted to warn you." He told me this later. For years this failing of mine came up when he and I argued. He usually clinched his argument that I was wrong about whatever because of my "mental illness."

My mother-in-law occasionally would say to me, "You know you've always had mental problems," when we disagreed. This accusation came up partly because my younger brother, Paul, had been in a clinic throughout high school, and they assumed it ran in my family.

It was hardest to say "Goodbye" to Paul. He hugged me close, and we didn't speak. I cried.

And after the goodbyes, it was time. With my belongings safely in the car, we started on our way to the Midwest. Dan wanted to take a side trip to Minnewaska; when we got there, he asked the proprietor if he could rent a hotel room for a few hours.

I didn't see this coming. I thought we were going there for lunch. The man's face when Dan asked was a picture of outrage. I was mortified. If the floor would open and I could sink into it, I would have been grateful.

I took Dan aside to say, "What is the matter with you? This isn't a hot sheets motel."

"I didn't think it was. I just thought it would be nice to spend some time like on our honeymoon."

"*He* knows what you thought. I'm ashamed—embarrassed."

"Don't be ridiculous!" he said. "Anyone else would understand." He laughed it off.

"Let's get out of here," I said.

We left the Catskills and drove through the Poconos and on through Pennsylvania. Dan was right about the scenery; it was spectacular—I was used to mountains in my Hudson Valley, but this drive was one beautiful expanse after another.

When I remembered my dad telling me I couldn't ever come back, my heart sank. I tried to think about other things—the scenery, a new life, a chance to start over.

I had no idea then that the East Coast world I knew would give way to an entirely different atmosphere in Chicago. Dan's mother had said to me at our wedding feast at a riverfront inn, the most elegant in the valley, "This place is rich in scenery, but Chicago is rich in people." She and I stood looking out over the Hudson River toward the Shawangunk Mountains.

It flashed into my head that this was her way of commenting about our wedding reception, where Dan's family was isolated at one large table. Only my mother's brother John went over and talked with them. As the bride I circulated, of course, but no others of my blood kin went near them, like they were "other." They were Midwesterners.

They did seem to be having a fine time among themselves. All the other guests were Dad's political cronies, Dan's and my college friends, or priests from the several novitiates and parishes. For anyone to introduce themselves and chat with strangers at a party like this would be to invite ridicule; that was part of *our* culture. It simply wasn't done, but the Midwesterners didn't know that. I was told later that my family was "unfriendly." Where I grew up, even next-door neighbors didn't greet each other as they passed.

I was still to learn how different it was in the hinterlands.

Before I left my home town, Dan's mother advised me to return several costly items, such as a silver gravy boat, to my hometown jeweler. His mother had said, "Everyone does this. If you can't use it, you ask for the money."

When I took the silver item back, I had no idea that in our town, this simply was not done. As I stood at his counter, I could see the jeweler's face turn a deep red. He shouted, "What is wrong with this gravy boat? Why are you returning it? It's one of our top line gift items!"

The jeweler called my father at his office as I left–cash in hand. I heard later my father hit the ceiling and called my mother to berate her. Now that he was our mayor, this reflected badly on his image.

It may have been a Midwest custom, but in Newburgh, my inelegant attempt to placate my new mother-in-law became an item of gossip for weeks.

Dan was fond of his Midwest and wanted me to love it, too. He was proud of the spectacle of Gary, Indiana—its towering smokestacks with gas flaming from their tops, the vastness of Lake Michigan, Chicago's skyline.

My heart hadn't quit my Hudson River Valley just yet. It needed more than a road trip to migrate. The days that followed were the usual moving in and settling our apartment, opening a great number of wedding gifts, mostly ornamental items—huge ashtrays, place settings, flatware, linens, cocktail shakers, wineglasses–things donors assumed we needed for entertaining. Because Dan was expected to enter the executive ranks, these would be required—twelve place settings of everything.

I stowed them in our cabinets with dread. Yes, as engagement gifts I had received two copies of Emily Post's *Etiquette* and one of Amy Vanderbilt, heavy tomes, so no excuse for not knowing the proper etiquette. My parents never "entertained" and would have no occasion to host people on the executive level.

My college prep high school gave us girls mandatory lessons in social conventions—curtseying to bishops and cardinals, addressing royalty, making gracious conversation, correct tea-pouring etiquette. Some class-mates were daughters of ambassadors and other diplomats who required such training. Ours was the equivalent of a finishing school.

Once I settled in to my new home, most of all, I was lonely. I had no one to talk to during the day and my new husband was at night school in the evenings. I missed my family and my New York friends. I thought a job would solve that. The family I married into expected me to have a baby as soon as I could. This was their culture. Everyone I met in my new life was a member of a large family. I met no one who had only one or two children.

At first there were parties to welcome us as a new couple to Dan's extended family. At a swimming pool party a few weeks after I arrived in Chicago, a man shouted from across the pool to Dan, "Is she pregnant yet?"

I was mortified. I hadn't even met this loudmouth, but he was part of the family weave. My husband's mother seemed to think it was needful to instill what she considered appropriate behavior in me. She had me meet and visit with her friends, all in their 50s and 60s. We had lunches: "Now tell me, your father is the mayor back home. What is that like?" these women said politely.

I knew I needed to keep it bland, but part of me wanted to tell them my father wore a handgun late at night in his shoulder holster. (The cops insisted.) Also I didn't mention Dad's other family. But as I picked my way among the briars of these visits, I avoided mention of my young-er brother—just out of a mental clinic; my mother's sister—harmlessly insane and currently spending time in Matteawan State Hospital; my beloved uncle–Commander of the American Legion; my grand-uncle--a sheriff and a member of the Ku Klux Klan. He could keep an eye on their activities, and the Klan was intensely active in our area.

These women had maids, lived comfortable lives, and had never worked a day job. My husband's mother told me that "All politicians are from the gutter" so although I was proud of my kin, these nice ladies no doubt saw me as a woman from hill country; after all, I did grow up in part of the Appalachians, our Hudson Highlands.

Dan had a sister in Wisconsin who invited us up for a weekend. Martha and her husband had six children then, and I had been struggling to memorize the names in all the families I had landed among. His sister lived near the American Club, so Dan and I went with them for dinner on a Saturday night.

Everyone at our table drank water glasses of whiskey, some with no ice. Soon they were singing *"Dein Ist Mein Ganzes Herz," "Du, Du Liegst Mir im Herzen,"* and neighboring tables joined in.

In the midst of all the *gemuchtlichheit*, I began to feel really ill. Was it the food? I couldn't tell, but was embarrassed that I was sick. Was it the whiskey? I didn't have much, and I hadn't felt like eating. On the way home from the Club, I had to ask them to stop the car so I could be sick outside.

In the morning, Martha talked to Dan and me about having "brats" for supper that night. I asked what brats were. She just looked at me. "They're . . . brats!" It sounded like brots. This was Wisconsin, so everyone understood about bratwurst, a local specialty like White Castle sliders. "You'll love them!"

Brats turned out to be sausages to be eaten on rolls, like Kaiser rolls. "Milwaukee and Madison have Bratwurst Festivals twice a year," Dan's sister told me. I still felt ill, and talking about sausages wasn't helping. I wanted to be a good guest with this part of my new family. I did my best, but all I could do was mope and provide wan smiles. What was the matter with me?

When Dan and I returned to our apartment I called his other sister who guessed at once, "You may be pregnant. Do you have a doctor?"

Of course not. I just moved here.

She kindly arranged an appointment with her family doctor and I reluctantly went to his office. His reception area teemed with children milling about among four mothers, two of whom were clearly pregnant. I saw babes in arms, in rebozo slings, in jumpy chairs, lap babies, creepers, toddlers and several school-age kids who looked ill.

Whoa! I had never liked children. Here I was, in the heart of a swarm of them. My doctor back home seldom had more than another patient or two in his waiting room, and those were usually adults.

As I started to the door, the receptionist called, "Are you Anne?"

Nailed!

Somehow it was my turn, and I went in dragging my feet. There wasn't much for me to say. I gave as little information as possible, did not tell him I didn't like children and was not happy to be having one. However, he may have assumed I was more than uneasy, because after we talked a bit, he handed me a book, *Childbirth Without Fear.* He wasn't much of a talker I noticed. He did say, "If you read this, and you have questions, come back and we'll talk."

I vaguely recalled that this doctor was a great proponent of home births. I had met Dan's sister when I visited over a year ago. I was impressed with how well and happy she looked the day after her son was born, compared to how I remembered my anesthetized mother after Paul. But I didn't want to think about having a baby at home. Or, truly, I didn't want to think about having a baby. I didn't want to tell anyone yet.

In those early months of marriage, Dan's parents kindly invited us for dinner many times. To me, it was a mixed blessing. I was grateful for the delicious steaks that we could not afford. But I was also uncomfortable with the dialogue that accompanied the good food.

"The Fed's raising the mortgage rate a quarter of a point," Dad would start in, as he swept his napkin across his lap.

"What's that got to do with the price of tea in China?" His wife liked to dip her oar into the conversational flow.

Dad turned to her with an annoyed expression.

I, of course, knew nothing about banking, and Dad was president of his bank. Dan must have heard a lot of this kind of talk when he lived with his parents, but like me, he had majored in Liberal Arts, meaning literature and not finance. Now he worked at one of the biggest banks in the country.

This was back when students were encouraged to follow Liberal Arts, because we were told, they would teach us to think and therefore master any task in the business world. With the tools we picked up from Socrates, Rimbaud, Dante, Schiller and their ilk, we could handle any mental challenge that came our way, we were told. At my college, we were assured that a B.A. was *the* ticket to any career. The CIA and FBI were particularly keen to hire graduates of Catholic colleges—us. We were assumed to be loyal, trustworthy, and faithful to our convictions. And yes, they did come on campus to recruit.

Nobody told us that entry-level jobs usually involved grunt work ("Here, kid, sharpen this bunch of pencils." / "Run this down to the mailroom, sweetheart." / "When I come in each morning, I want my coffee on my desk, hot, black, two packs of sugar.") The fun of talking with lively classmates was replaced by elevator conversations about sports, radio soap operas like "Ma Perkins" and "John's Other Wife," or any television programs our workmates might have seen.

And so the price of a good meal at my in-laws was to be lectured to about the banking industry rather than the political scene of my growing-up years. Also, Dan was in for a barrage of comments: "What's the matter with your hair, Dan? No time to get it cut?"

"Why do you wear your pants so low? Don't you have a belt?"

"Dan, you didn't wear that suit to work today, did you? It's so wrinkled."

I wanted to take a class in drawing at Northwestern U. I hadn't mentioned it, but Dan had told them, so the topic changed to, "Dear, why do you think you need to take a class? None of the other girls in the family take them." My mother-in-law had a special emphatic tone when she called me "dear" and I came to hate the word.

And although they were in comfortable circumstances, Dan's mother made some economies that baffled me. She had a group of friends, all wealthy women like herself, who got together to make little girls' dresses to give to "the poor" through the Child Welfare Society. I was invited to participate, but declined after I saw their products.

They cut out the dresses using patterns and stitched them together; then the maid washed and ironed the little dresses. The row of pretty cotton dresses on hangers was impressive. When I was at her house, she showed me the products of all their hours working together. I reached for one and rubbed the fabric between my fingers.

"Do families you donate these dresses to have ways to wash and iron them after the girls wear them and they get soiled?" I said to Dan's mother.

"Well, no, dear, I don't suppose they do."

"Could you buy material that's permanent press or wash-and-wear?"

"Oh, no, those cost too much! I buy only fabric that's on sale. We need to watch our pennies," she said.

To me, dresses distributed to women who would have to wash and iron them after they were worn was no charity, when permanent press was now available.

"Wouldn't it be kinder to give them clothes that didn't need care? You have a maid, but they won't," I said realizing too late that I had put my foot in it. Dan's mother was proud of her charity work. She gave me a memorable glare and turned away.

I went downstairs.

Another night at dinner, Dan's mother somehow got to talking about how some priest friends thought she was a saint. She said to me as we cleared the table, "What do you think, dear? Do you think I'm a saint?"

"I . . . I haven't known you for long," I said as I tried to come up with some inoffensive prevarication. What was she thinking? I'm not the Pope or anyone like him. "I think you are saintly. You go to daily Mass and Communion...."

"Saintly isn't the same thing! Father Mannix thinks I'm a saint. I asked him if he thought I was a saint, and he said, 'Yes, certainly you are a saint.' And you know, dear, he *is* the president of a university." She batted her eyes at me in a manner that once might have been fetching.

"Well, I'm not in any position . . ." I said. "I've never known any saints."

"Mother!" her husband interrupted. "Stop the talk now. We want to play some bridge."

Fall had come and I enjoyed the changing colors. I said one night at dinner that I missed the mountains and the river I grew up with. My father-in-law said, "Dan, take Anne down to the lake so she can see how beautiful it is. It's every bit as beautiful."

And so we borrowed his car that weekend and walked along the Lake Michigan shore. In my heart, I thought, "How flat this all is!"

"Isn't this wonderful?" Dan said, waving his arm to gather in the view.

"Yes, yes, it is," I said. But my mountains had given me a sheltered feeling that Flatlands never could. I tried to think more positively—that this broad expanse to the horizon opened out my spirit, where mountains had enclosed it. Yet my familiar childhood view was gone. As a child I woke up one morning to a dense fog. In a panic I called to my mother, "The mountains are gone! Who took them?"

She said, "It's just the fog. When it clears, they will be back. Now eat your breakfast and get ready for school."

Still here I was now, homesick for mountains. Better not mention it to any Midwesterners; they seemed somewhat closed-minded in their view that everything in the Chicago area was superior to anywhere.

For instance, one night at dinner, a brother-in-law asked, "What in the world do you miss about New York?" He had grown up there and like me, was a transplant.

"Well, the scenery, the river, the museums, Times Square . . ." I began.

"Everything you could possibly want is right here in Chicago," my mother-in-law said.

And that was that.

Soon Christmas in my new life would be here. I wondered would it be anything like Christmases I had known back home—getting excited at finding the right gifts for my brothers and sister, climbing down our steep hills to hometown stores close to the waterfront—Kresge's 5 & 10, Kresge's 5 & Dollar, Schoonmaker's, Berger's Bookstore up on Broadway, picking up orders at the Montgomery Ward outlet. We always shopped at the last minute—Christmas Eve, assuring ourselves that the "Christmas spirit" would strike us then. As kids, when we went down the hill to shop together, we would ask each other seriously, "Do you feel the Christmas spirit yet?"

Now as a newlywed, I was in for a surprise.

CHRISTMAS-IN-LAW

Having married into a huge Irish Catholic family near Chicago, my new in-laws expected Dan and me to spend our first Christmas with them. I looked forward to it, and Dan's father said he did not want me buying gifts. "I'd much rather have something home-made, a pie or a poem," he said. "Just something simple. Dan's sister always makes me a Christmas poem."

A *poem*? Like Yeats or Eliot? Or doggerel? But this was my family now, and I wanted to fit in. I decided on home-made bread.

As Dan and I turned up the street to his parents' house, a life-sized Santa on their front porch beckoned us. Spotlights shone on bushy garlands that swagged the doorway, lined the stair rails, and twinkled with hundreds of tiny Italian lights. Four-foot scarlet candles guarded the entrance; on the foil-wrapped door sat an enormous gilded wreath. My new husband knew just where to reach in for the knocker, and did.

At once the door swung open, letting out a fragrant cloud of roasting turkey, balsam, mince pie and whiskey. Highball in one hand, my father-in-law kissed me warmly, shook hands with his son, said, "Merry Christmas! Come on in. Dan, you been too busy to get a haircut? Here, here, give me your coats. Put your gifts by the tree. Mother! Where's she gotten to? Mother, they're here!" Piling our coats on his free arm, he said, "What'll you have?"

"Bourbon's fine, Dad, and I can get it," my husband said. I thought, cocktail time at 3:30! They start early here, and said, "Ginger ale, please."

"What do you mean, ginger ale?" Dad asked laughing. "It's Christmas, isn't it?" His highball arm waved toward the living room where an un-countable number of children milled about their parents. Women in jeweled Christmas sweaters—teal blue, rose, and cobalt—and men in sports coats stood chatting amiably, old-fashioned glasses already in hand. Above their heads an enormous blue-flocked fir tree glowed with tiny lights, sugared candy canes, and sparkling pastel fruit. Beneath it sat brightly colored stacks of wrapped gifts. Little girls in red or green velvet with bows in their hair and small boys in white shirts and ties chased each other to the dining room and back.

Dad bundled the coats up the garlanded stairs as he muttered, "Ginger ale! I ask you!" I glanced down at my feet to see a Santa face smiling up at me from a fluffy mat.

Dan's mother fluttered towards us with her wife-of-a-bank-president's smile. "Dear! At last! Dan, that hair of yours! We've been waiting and waiting!" Her long velvet skirt matched her glass of Dubonnet perfect-ly. "Come along and see my poinsettias!" Red and white, these stood massed in corners of the long hallway beneath streamers of Christmas cards, all picturing Madonnas. Garlands of white-flocked balsam draped the bannister and chandelier, and from one wall, the Resurrected Christ gazed at us from the arms of a large ceramic cross.

As I took this in, she touched my shoulder and said, "Now, dear, I know this is your first Christmas away from your folks. I do hope you'll be happy here with us. And that you'll think of Dad and me as parents. You know, I think it's about time you called me, 'Mother.'"

Inside I flared. My own mother was Mother, and bad as she was, my only one, Murmuring, "You're very kind. Thank you, M-mother," I looked away, thinking ". . . in-law" and choked. She went on, "Now, today you'll meet my three brothers and their families. Some are not here yet. And Dad's cousins are on their way. And John and *his* children, of course. Martha and Rick came early, along with Harry, Kate and Dr. Dave."

So many names! She went on about someone "down with the flu." My head buzzed. Did I have to remember them all? Dan, fidgeting during this chatter, brushed past us through the swinging door ahead, throwing over his shoulder, "Come on, little girl, let's go out here." Trying to match her smile, I nodded at Mother-in-law and followed him into the high-ceilinged kitchen. A tall, brown-skinned woman in a white uniform fed giblets into a grinder. A dark-colored highball stood at her elbow. "How you, Dan? And Anne!" She gave me a generous smile revealing all her teeth, and kept cranking. Dan went directly to the pantry to fix drinks. I felt awkward and said to her, "Could I maybe do something to help?"

Raising a lid from a pot, she poked at an immense clump of potatoes with a giant fork. Looking through the steam at me, she said, "You? What in the world could *you* do?" The idea of my being useful brought on a fit of laughter then wheezy coughing. A long swallow from her drink soothed the cough.

"You seen the dining room?" She gave me another warm smile. "Bet you isn't never seen nothing like how *this* family fixes up for Christmas! You just go on in and take a look! Bob Junior's got it fixed up *real* nice. You know he's a designer, even has his own design company."

I pushed through another swinging door, this one with a framed copy of "A Kitchen Prayer" on it. Inside the dining room, only candles lighted the massive room. They gleamed from the polished wood and reflected on the glassed-in Infant of Prague statue. A sequinned white feather tree with tiny sugarplums and glittering gumdrops stood on the sideboard, and another crèche surrounded by fresh holly crowned the center of the twelve-foot table. I felt peace in here, and breathed it in. The romping children seemed far off.

I thought back to my home far away and our Christmases. My father always bought a live tree, and I decorated it with those big, colored Noma bulbs, glass ornaments, and tinsel. Though my dad said he'd help, he'd work late and come in the back door just as I turned on the tree lights.

My mother's sisters were kind about giving us sorely needed clothes rather than toys, and in the true spirit of Christmas, we children mightily resented getting them. My brother Mark saved tips from his shifts as an altar boy, and I'd done chores for my aunt, so we two had money to spend. We bought gifts for each other and our parents that we pondered at length at the 5 & 10 or Kresge's. These had to be just right.

And I especially liked walking in the snow late on Christmas afternoon past Perrott's Funeral Home, a huge old mansion looking out on the Hudson River, to see candles in every window of their three floors. Out of respect for their clientele, mostly Greek, all the bulbs were purple. And at the end of the day, I'd have a satisfied feeling that *this* is Christmas.

Now at my in-laws' house, I went on to the next room—the Front Room, Midwesterners call it ("Fronch Room"). More like a library. Two walls were lined with books, and a third was windows. Every flat surface held a miniature crèche set in straw, or a small tinseled tree, or a mirror with tiny figures skating. There was even a white Bisque bust of the Pope. On the far wall high above my head hung a three-foot straw crucifix with a straw Body of Christ. I could imagine my brother Paul saying, "Amazing! Every room has a crucifix!"

Below the crucifix on a spinet, sheet music lay open: "The Rosary." I glanced at the lyrics: "The hours I spent with thee, dear heart / Are as a string of pearls to me…/ I kiss each bead and / Strive at last to learn / To kiss the Cross, Sweetheart! / To kiss the Cross!" The cover called it a Love Song. Other music was Schubert's *Ave Maria* and Christmas carols, the ones my brothers and I sang at our piano last Christmas. Paul had taken it so hard when I left to come out here.

Tears started to my eyes, and I set my ginger ale on the windowsill. Taking a deep breath, I turned to the bookcases. I saw *The Imitation of Christ* and *The ABCs of Scholastic Philosophy.* I pulled out *The Catholic Guide to Sex and Marriage.*

"Oh, there you are! I haven't seen you since the wedding!" I startled, then turned to face a tall, slender redhead, Dan's older brother, Bob junior. Today he had on some dark-green knit, very close-fitting trousers. He flashed his smile, then said over the rim of his martini, "Well, what do you think of them?"

"The books?"

"The *decorations!* The tree, the whole works! I came in yesterday from New York to do the tree. How do you like it?" He waved his martini hand to embrace our view of the presents, the garlands, the tree.

"Beautiful. Really. Magnificent."

He beamed. "My theme this year is the 'Sugar Plum Fairy.' And I've been told my designs are the Cadillac of the industry." He closed his eyes, raising his eyebrows. He opened them to look sharply at me, and said, "Why are you in here by yourself? Does having all these in-laws around make you feel like an outlaw?"

I gasped, thinking he knew my thoughts, then said, "A bit, yes. Even the way everyone talks is . . . different."

"I know. You worked in New York, and I live there now. New York is the International Metropolis and Chicago is Big Town USA. But …"

Just then his mother came in to call us to dinner. A welter of perhaps twenty-seven adults lined up at the buffet with plates. "Women and children first!" Dad called out. Several women helped children near them to food amid cries of "But I don't *want* salad," and "I *hate* stuffing!"

Mother-in-law supervised each grandchild's portions, telling them "to at least try" everything, and saying as she placed generous portions on each plate, "Now, I know how much you children like these candied yams with marshmallows! And this year we have *two* kinds."

"Oh, *not* turnips! I just ate some *last* year," I heard a tearful small boy say as he took his plate to the Children's Table, a lower table neatly covered with white bedsheets. The one time they all stayed seated. I counted fourteen children. The oldest seemed about eight.

Other adults helped themselves to salad from a gigantic Waterford bowl. In turn I heaped my plate from the mountain of sliced turkey, snowbank of mashed potatoes, the hot gravy, rolls, and cranberry sauce.

"Honestly!" Bob junior seated himself at the Children's Table. As I stood at the Big Table looking for my name, he said loudly, "Mother's been doing this to me for years, Anne. She won't let me sit with the grownups because I'm not married yet. And I'll be thirty-four this month." Dan must have sat there last year. (Years later my unmarried cousin Bryan stationed at Great Lakes Naval Training Center visited us one Christmas, and he also had to sit at the Children's Table—using paper napkins while the grownups had linen.)

Bob turned toward the Big Table. "Mother! Mother, this is ridiculous." But his mother was asking Dad to "say Grace. *Now,* dear." The two tables hushed into a wordless, noisy silence. The cook, called in from the kitchen, stood by the swinging door with her head bowed.

Dad's blessing ranged over the "goodness and generosity of God for providing this feast before us," and then to "gratitude of us whose health is equal to letting us enjoy it." Here his wife broke in cheerfully, "Amen to that, say I!"

With "Quiet, Mother, don't interrupt," Dad continued, remembering "the poor souls in Purgatory unable to share this good turkey dinner, along with our dear, dead departed daughter," and the possibility that the one calling down this blessing, himself, "may not live to see another Christmas."

My head bowed over my steaming plate, I glanced under my brows at him. He had closed his eyes and tears slid down his cheeks.

"Sst, Dad!" his wife hissed. "Don't bring up *morbid* subjects. We're supposed to be enjoying ourselves. It's *Christmas.* Remember?"

I wondered if we were supposed to say Amen, wait for more, or just dig in. Looking around I noticed one of the smaller boys sitting by Bob junior had quietly begun to eat mashed potatoes with his hands. My husband across the table winked at me and said, laughing, "Dad, you've been saying you might not be here for next Christmas for the last fifteen years."

"And don't start in on that 'Some Day You'll Look Down on Me in My Coffin' routine, either!" Bob junior said.

His mother, smiling at everyone, held her wine glass high and called gaily, "I think we should have a toast." I reached down and touched my gravy with a tentative finger; it had begun to gel.

". . .and further, the joy and happiness possible only through marriage to a wonderful man like Dad. . . "

Bob junior rolled his eyes and said, "That is aimed directly at me!"

"Well, dear, why *don't* you get married?" she said. What happened to her toast? Was this their Christmas tradition, too?

"Here we have all these happy marriages right in the family. Even your little brother is married." (I remembered she asked me to fix Bob up with my sister, who had said, "Never!") The other adults suddenly busied themselves with passing rolls, butter, salt, wine carafes, and murmuring, "Isn't this delicious!"

"Yes, marvelous!"

Bob junior rose abruptly and banged into the kitchen, leaving the door swinging hard behind him. Everyone else continued eating. I could hear Bob scold the cook for letting the marshmallow topping on the yams get so brown. Dad said in a loud whisper, "Now, Mother, don't start in on *that* again. You know Bob isn't the marrying kind."

I felt my hair rising to stand on end and held my breath. Then Mother said, loudly, "What? Bob is, too, the marrying kind."

Her daughter Maureen said hoarsely, "For heaven's sake! Mother. Dad. He'll *hear* you."

Dad said, "What in the world difference does it make if he heard?" Giving himself another refill, he said, "Bob knows we all love him, don't you, Bob?" as Bob re-entered the room.

His sister Maureen tried to change the subject saying, "You know, *Dan* has really always been the favorite. But now I don't mind, really, not anywhere near as much as I used to," and poured herself more wine.

Her mother said, "Dear, Dan *was* the baby."

"And awfully cute!" his sister said and began to pass dessert plates with wedges of warm mince pie.

Soon after dessert, a lot of scraping and moving announced the end of dinner. The children made for the front hall to run up and down the great staircase, squealing with joy. The boy cousins tried to see who could jump farthest from the landing. From the living room where they sorted through piles of gifts, their parents called offhandedly, "Careful!" and "Don't hurt yourselves!" as great thumps and delighted laughing announced successful landings. Mother-in-law came through the swing-ing door to stand directly in the target area where red-faced boys panted, their shirt tails out and ties askew.

"Come on now, children, it's time for presents!" She and Dad herded them to the great tree where various parents handed out beribboned, wrapped parcels. Their voices bubbled around the children as they called "Here's one for you, Bobby," and "This has your name on it, Pete!" "Look, *another* for Wendy!" "Mark, here you go!"

Maureen and I sitting together by the tree stopped talking. She had just said, "Mark is three now. He likes to get up in the middle of the night and ride his tricycle down the block. We know because it squeaks! But we don't want to oil it, because at least we know where he is!'"

Mother-in-law came over to where I sat, saying, "Did you find your pile of gifts yet? No? Come with me, dear!" and led me to a stack of gifts with my name on them. I opened one to find a small, decorative yellow box. One foot had broken off. Next came a white satin belt trimmed with false pearls, rhinestones and gold thread. My sisters-in-law tried theirs on across the room and found the belts didn't quite reach around their waists. "Bob junior likes to give things his models wear to us. Otherwise they go to waste," said Maureen as she discarded her belt.

Another gift, an ounce of Chanel #5, when unsealed had only dark sediment in the flacon. Mystified, I held it to the light, then looked around for Mother-in-law. When I asked her about it, she laughed. I asked if I could return it, and she laughed again. She had bought it on her last trip to Paris, and it dried out. Returning it was not possible. I felt bad; the welter of wrappings and chatter drowned out my thoughts.

The children surrounded me, ripping and tearing through the wrap-pings, tossing bits and pieces into the air with glee. Dan's mother called, "Please! Children! Save those wrappings! I can use them again!"

As his sisters laughed, Bob junior said, "Mother! You've still got used Christmas gift paper saved from the last ten years!"

"Come on, half the fun is tearing off the wrappings. Let them be," my father-in-law said. He tilted his head back, sipped at his empty highball glass, smiled sheepishly. "Guess I need a refill, " he said and headed for the kitchen.

The children settled in to compare gifts, open books, puzzle ("What's *this* thing?" from one small boy) and mourn ("Oh, no, not *clothes!*" from another.) My father-in-law adjusted his camera and massed the whole gathering for a group picture by the tree, placing unavoidable in-laws at the edges.

As the crowd broke up, Mother-in-law said, "All right, children! Take your toys down in the basement! The adults want to play Charades."

She turned to me above the hubbub. "You do know how to play Charades, don't you?"

"Well, yes...." I did know how. I saw myself back drinking hot cider with my brothers and sister as we acted out *The Joy of Cooking* and *Webster's Dictionary,* and we had roared, laughing.

"Oh, surely, you know how. We just act out the name of a song, or a movie. A book title."

A book title, from *their* library? What if they assigned me *The Catholic Guide to Sex and Marriage?*

"Come along, everyone," Mother-in-law raised her voice. "Dan, you set up the chairs. We have to choose teams." Dad busied himself getting fresh drinks to all charaders. Veteran players quickly chose teams and huddled to brainstorm. One aunt sat back, silent and glassy-eyed. My suggestions, *Encyclopedia Britannica* and "Ave Maria," were dismissed with "Please, dear! Some won't get those! This game is supposed to be for everybody."

Dad, up first, studied his slip of paper at length, then shuffled back and forth, shading his eyes with one hand, holding on to his drink with the other. Answers shot up like corn popping. "Long Way to Tipperary!" "Going My Way!" "On the Road!" "Kandy-Kolored Tangerine-Flake ..." (*"Don't* say things like that, dear.")

"Old Man and the Sea!"

"Yes!"

"That's it??"

"Yes, yes! Good job, Dad. Who's up next?"

I heard the knocker at the front door and, at once a small boy ran to open it and said, "Good afternoon, Father!"

On the doorstep stood Father Foley, the parish priest, black hat in hand. Dad hurried up to him, "Come in, come right on in, Father. We're all just after having dinner, but there's plenty left. How 'bout a glass of something to warm you first?"

"I wouldn't say no to that," Father said. "Scotch will do nicely, thanks, Bob."

"Coming right up," Dad said, taking Father's coat and hat. Father turned to stand in the wide doorway to the living room where our two groups faced each other. Dad bustled in with Father's drink and a fresh one for himself as others went to greet the priest and rounded up their children to speak to him. The boys shook his hand, and the little girls crowded giggling around him.

"All right now, kids, that's enough!" Dad called. "Let Father come in and sit down. Don't be all pushing and shoving . . . Father, we're playing Charades. Like to join in? If not, we can wait and play later."

"I'd like to sit here for just a minute, Bob, and catch my breath." Several children had settled in by his feet. "And then . . . maybe I'll play a few carols for a bit, and the children can sing."

"Sure, sure, Father. That's fine," Dad said, waving away Dan who had started to protest, "But our side hasn't been up yet . . . "

Father played "Silent Night" skillfully, sipping his drink as he segued one-handed into "O, Come All Ye Faithful," and the adults clustered around to sing. Father sang, too, and Maureen reached to draw me closer into their circle. The children stayed politely but briefly, then went back to their game of Chase in the hall and on the stairs. Under the music I heard shrieking and squeals from the bedrooms upstairs as their parents sang on, harmonizing now to "Away in a Manger." That carol brought back my brother Paul, now 14, and our last Christmas together.

As my tears came again, I stepped out to the darkened hall. I had loved him so—as though he were my own child. And soon I'd have a baby to take his place. He was alone now with my parents. And my mother mentioned in her last phone call that lately he came home after school and drank whiskey. By himself.

"I think it's good for him—it relieves the tension," she said. "His I.Q. scores have gone down again. I think he just isn't as smart as the rest of you."

I had argued with her, "Oh, yes, he is!"

And now the old carol made last Christmas rush back. He never drank back then, not when I was around.

Through my tears I saw my father-in-law step away from the carolers to slip a twenty in the pocket of Father's black jacket on a hassock in the corner. And then my husband came quietly up behind me to say, "Well, here you are!" and hug me. "I've been all over the house looking for you."

I reached to put my arms around his shoulders as he said affectionately, "Are those tears? Oh, honey, all this was a lot for you, wasn't it?"

He tilted my face up and gently brushed at my tears with his handkerchief. "The gifts, the crowd, I'm sorry! You aren't used to it. And we always do this." He wrapped his arms around me and hugged me hard, standing there rocking.

"It's not this Christmas, it's . . . Paul," I said. "I'm just thinking how much I miss him." Dan gently blotted my tears as I sobbed, "I tried to be there for him . . . when I was home and now . . ."

"But, honey, home for you is here now," he said as he held me, gently patting my back as I had patted Paul's when he was little. "You can't raise Paul, any more. Not now," he said. "You'll have your own baby—ours—next May."

And then around us, the families started gathering coats, boots, scarves and sorting out children, "Where's Mark? Anybody seen Mark? MARK! Get down here! Right this minute, young man," a fusillade of Goodbyes, ". . . call you early next week," hugging, kissing... and they were gone.

As we went down the snowy walk to the car, I slipped my hand inside one of my husband's, and he tucked them both in his big coat pocket. What a Christmas! I thought back to Christmas dinner with my old family, Paul, our dog—and even those purple candles at the funeral home, far away now.

I turned back to wave at Santa on the porch and look again at my in-laws' house outlined in twinkling lights.

Our new family—Dan's and mine—could eventually fall into what I saw that day in his family and known in my own.

His mother had said she saw me as an answer to her prayers for him.

ENTER THE CHILDREN

I prepared for my first child's birth in 1958 with great dread. First of all, I had never liked children. Baby-sitting and being eldest of four kids had cured me of any wish to have my own. Further, I had almost no one to talk to other than my in-laws; my real friends were all back in New York. I had made one friend, Maddie, out here and we met occasionally for a quick supper at Wieboldt's Department Store. She was a Hungarian refugee from the 1956 purges, a bright girl who was grateful to be safely here in the States.

Although I never talked about being lonely, I was very much so; she seemed to figure that out. She told the family who sheltered her, "It's amazing that a young married woman would be so lonely!"

I had met her through my husband Dan's cousin and that comment was repeated to my mother-in-law, who saw it as a slur on her family. She shared it with her son Dan. As a consequence, Dan asked me not to spend time with this friend, who had been a ray of companionship for me. As he put it, "I can't be home any more than I am, but I want you to stop seeing her. And don't say I told you. I don't want the blame to go on me. Just tell her you can't do it anymore."

This really hurt and I cried. I felt trapped by what I needed to do to keep this marriage going. I had begun to realize that above all, Dan did not want to look bad. As he put it to reinforce his point, "Your parents don't have a good marriage, and my parents know a lot about successful marriage. So, if you want this marriage to succeed, you have to do this– stop seeing her."

This was preposterous. The family I married into seemed to have a need to control my activities, so different from my earlier life working in New York.

Dan was correct in that I had no idea what made for a happy marriage. I just knew I wanted to have one for my own. The night before my wedding, my father had said, "I have never known any happy marriages."

Shortly after Christmas my mother decided to visit me. She and I and Dan went out for dinner one Saturday to the Italian Village restaurant in Chicago's Loop. It was one of my favorite places. I remembered showing her the little village scene that I liked so much. She was polite about it. "That's nice, dear." She didn't talk much with Dan around. Dan talked enough for all three of us.

I also remember coming back to our apartment and being sick. My mother already in bed heard me and began putting her stockings on. She thought I might be miscarrying, and came out to see if she could help me. It may have been the spicy meal or my anxiety at having my mother visiting. But I recovered, and we all settled down.

Mother, a grammar school teacher, had come for a long weekend. She told me that she and my brother Mark, then in medical school, thought they each should come and see me before the baby came because, and here her voice trailed off as she told me they thought "something could go wrong. You might die, or your baby won't be normal." Their low expectations of me were not new, but always surprised me.

It hurt—I believed that she and my brother were people who loved me, and knew me, and they thought I was not normal. This made me feel shaky, but I didn't think I was not normal. I never thought, yes, they're right. I was disappointed that my beloved sister agreed with them. Yet no one tried to put me in a hospital, as they did our brother Paul years ago.

After mother's visit, Mark came for a different long weekend. He must have had his obstetrics rotation around that time, because he told me the dismal possibilities–I might miscarry, the baby might be abnormal. He and Mother didn't want to see that, he said. He also said they thought I couldn't handle an abnormal baby. Clearly they had spent a lot of time talking over the negatives that faced me.

My situation didn't feel that way to me at all, and it struck me as odd that my doctor hadn't said anything about any abnormality. Because I was on my own a lot, I'd been reading many books such as R.D. Laing's *The Divided Self.* I began to see a pattern of family dysfunction. As I read, I saw the climate I grew up in as creating schizophrenic behavior through physical and verbal abuse over a long period. It was certainly true for my younger brother, Paul. I thought the family life we had known was just that kind of atmosphere. I determined to avoid that with any child I might have.

When Mark came with me for my routine checkup, my doctor and he had a chat about Mark's future calling. Dr. N talked to Mark about how "medicine was mostly routine things like lancing boils." I watched my brother listen politely; I knew that face of his.

Mark did not want to hear about what a GP like my doctor did; he told me so as we drove home. Being a general practitioner held no appeal. What he really liked was surgery—organ transplants, lung resections, and so on. He excelled at those in later years. (As his studies continued, he practiced transplanting organs in families of dogs in his labs. One dog family was named after Dan and me, and later he used our children's names as each came along. He named his other dog families after our friends who were Catholics and had large families.)

After Mark went back to med school, the expected baby made signs he would soon make his entrance. I went to the doctor's office, and he told me that labor had begun but likely wouldn't get into higher gear for quite some time. I called my in-laws and my husband. Although I had alerted Dan, he didn't come home. Dan's father came over and waited with me. Dan and I had originally planned to have the baby at home, since our doctor specialized in home deliveries. But another mother was about to deliver, so this time, I had to go to the hospital.

I still wasn't worried. Dan's father was concerned because "Dan should be home for this," he said. Dad was quite annoyed at Dan for not getting home; in fact, he was fuming. But he was often annoyed at him.

He took me to the hospital and waited with me. Dan still didn't come. The doctor popped in from time to time. Dan came by at about 9:00 p.m. His father lambasted him, "What is the matter with you, Dan? You should have been here as soon as you knew she was in labor."

I didn't really understand what was going on. I felt calm; things were progressing normally, if slowly. It was not at all like in the movies and TV comedies, where the expectant father dithers around like Rob Petrie in the "Dick vanDyck Show," completely losing his common sense and his mind.

Months before, I had started attending meetings of La Leche League–a group of mothers who encouraged each other in breastfeeding their babies. A seasoned, experienced mom led discussions. They emphasized nutrition, exercise, and good mothering. They had books to lend like John Bowlby's work on Attachment, Winnicott on the "Good-Enough Mother," Adelle Davis on nutrition, Gesell Institute's studies on normal child development and so on.

I had time to study these books because I was alone quite a bit, so I spent my days reading up about having a baby and what that was like. My doctor had lent us his copy of "Emergency Childbirth"—which he had written for police and fire departments–in case we had a sudden birth.

I thought what I saw with my own mother and Paul was bad patterning, so I determined to have a baby who turned out well and happy. Luckily for me, my mother wasn't around to give advice and point out everything I was doing wrong.

Many days I went to Dan's sister Maureen's house a few blocks away; she had three small children and I watched as she interacted amiably with them. Also, she had had her most recent baby at home, and had thrived. She seemed to be a kind and loving mom, and was kind to me as well. I hoped to learn as much as I could about raising a healthy child.

Having my own baby could be a chance to prove to myself that a child would not have to spend his adolescence in a mental health clinic.

That night in the hospital passed with not much progress. When labor started in earnest the next morning, I was taken to Delivery as Dan waited in the Fathers' Room. When serious contractions came, they were fierce, but when they stopped, I felt sleepy. A nurse stayed by me, hand on my left shoulder. I heard her say quietly, "Now when this next contraction hurts, yell and swear at your husband." Groggy as I was, I didn't see how that would help the pain; I didn't follow this advice.

After pushing so hard, I remember saying out loud, "I can't do this anymore."

She said, "You don't have to." So kind of her …. I could relax and I fell into a doze, telling myself I didn't have to push.

And then an intense contraction gripped me, and I *had* to push.

"Crowning!" someone called.

I heard sniffing, loud sniffing. I called out, "Who *is* that?" I thought someone had come into the labor room, interrupting us while I needed to concentrate. But it was my baby entering the room. He was breathing on his own, head and shoulders out. And then all the rest came out with one more push. That final push meant I was done. Done!

"Aren't you going to slap his back like in the movies?" I mumbled. Wasn't this ritual routine?

"Not necessary. He's breathing already." The doctor got busy again, now weighing our newborn, handing him off to the nurses who wrapped my still sniffing baby—it sounded like he was trying out what his nose was for. He was next laid on my chest, his huge eyes rolling around as he took in the bright lights of Delivery. He had been in the dark for so long–it must have bewildered him as he got surrounded by smells, brightness, voices, loud-speakers calling doctors' names ….

What a great feeling—to have it over, and so successfully. Back in my hospital room, and feeling greatly contented, I could talk with my husband. The doctor joined us and had me get up and "walk to the nursery to see the baby." As I walked with my doctor on one side and Dan on the other, I heard a nurse walking behind us refer to my doctor as "That butcher! She should be in bed," because he made me walk right after delivery.

It was his routine to check this way on whether there was hemorrhaging, though he did not tell me this until later. I stood at the window of the nursery and looked in at all the tiny cots. I couldn't tell which baby was mine, and picked out a cute boy with lots of dark hair. Looking closer, I saw the name on his cot: Durante.

When the nurse brought my good-sized, healthy, bald baby to me in my room, and I held him in my arms, I was thrilled. As my first child was placed in my arms, the intensity of feeling that washed through startled me. Mother love ambushed me: the smell of his baby head, his tiny hands with their perfect nails, his big, searching eyes figuring out his noisy new world. I fell in love–with my baby.

This was back when the babies were not kept in the mom's room. That night I woke over and over, excited, saying to myself "I did it. I did it!" After my family's predictions, I had been afraid that something might go wrong. When I called my sister, she told me she had spent all the time I was in labor in chapel praying for me.

This birth went well, and I gladly told my blood kin so. Each of them, brother, mother, sister, sounded subdued at my news. I was elated, and high on good spirits. Dan sat with me as I made my calls with my baby in my lap—joyful moments.

I didn't call my dad because usually when I called home, if my mother said to me, "Would you like to talk to Dad?" he came to the phone only after a long pause. I imagined my mother had to argue him into talking to me. I still hadn't been forgiven for marrying; all I got from him on the phone since the wedding were monosyllables, then he would cut off with, "Gotta go."

What might my life have been had I stayed behind? A job at our local bank? More dates with guys who went away to college but lacked the guts to seek broader horizons? I shrank inside just imagining it—working on my dad's mayoral campaigns, volunteering at the Ladies' Auxiliary for the American Legion? Being Dad's daughter, would I share in the animosity some people felt for him?

Better to make my own enemies in a new life, I told myself as I held my son close. At last I had a blood kin relative out here. From this start to my little family, I went on to have four more children; all brought joy into my life. As I held my firstborn to my heart, I had no idea he would be the start of a houseful of lively, sometimes rambunctious, children.

When my firstborn, Greg, was a sophomore in high school, he was over six feet tall already, with dark brown hair and eyes. His siblings looked up to him. I woke one night to hear him shooting baskets out by the garage. It was two a.m. I asked myself then if things would be different if my husband were here to deal with this. But he usually traveled, and it was always I who had to cope. I sat up in bed with a feeling of wonder that being the only parent made no difference for me—I still had to cope alone just as I always had.

Matthew, the second son, struggled to keep pace with his big brother. He was tall like Greg; he wore glasses and was seriously involved with gymnastics in high school. It became the love of his life. Blond, blue-eyed, he excelled at practicing his moves, especially on the trampoline. With other gymnasts, he got into Young Life, a religious group, and took to reading and quoting aloud from the Bible at the dinner table. The other kids would just tell him to "shut up."

Beth was the middle child and only girl. She, too, was fair like Matthew—blonde, hazel-eyed and quite pretty. She was a whiz at math so that her teachers would have her coach the other kids in class. She really wanted a sister and we prayed for one, but once she turned nine, she realized she would be too old to be close to another girl. Her brothers gave her grief about wearing anything pink, so she stopped wearing it. Her brothers were her early playmates.

Justin, the fourth child, wasn't as tall as his big brothers when he started high school and it concerned him. (He did catch up.) He was socially involved, on the student council, and also a gymnast. In second grade he had wanted a baby panther for a pet and hoped to keep one in our attic.

Martin was the youngest and loudest. Just to get airtime, he had developed his vocal cords to get heard at the dinner table. Like Greg and Justin, he had dark brown eyes and hair, but his was curly. In kindergarten he wore a baseball cap all the time to keep the curliness out of sight. "People will think I'm a girl if they see curls," he said.

For the next few years my focus was on these children and our family.

Paris Off the Map

I had settled into my identity as Mom and Wife of Rising Executive. My unwritten job description—typical for women like me in those years—included helping write talks for my husband, sorting through his work problems, and choosing his subordinates by having dinner with the candidates. As another corporate wife pointed out, "This boss gets two employees for the one salary." My routine was that I left the house mostly to buy groceries, take our five children to dentists and doctors, and give rides when needed.

When my husband accepted invitations to speak at conferences in Paris and Vienna, he wanted me to join him. It was May of 1971 and our five children were between four and twelve years old. Since we had a neighbor who had taken to chasing children with her pitchfork, I didn't want to leave ours behind, so we decided to bring them along. It would cost a lot, so we took out a second mortgage.

We asked the children to pack their own suitcases—with our overseeing the process. When I inspected four-year-old Martin's, I found his pajamas and a large teddy bear. His dad and I walked him through what else might be needed.

The others, with our prodding, did somewhat better. We also had each of them memorize "please, thank you, hello and goodbye," in French and German. I added *"merde"* and *"scheisse"* to make the lesson familiar. They had a great time, running around the house shouting these at each other (also *"scheisskopf"*) and calling, "I'm practicing!" as they ran past me.

Their teachers agreed to let them out of class during the school year only if they kept journals on the trip, so we bought one each. Martin at four was to dictate his to me.

We flew first to Paris. My husband had arranged for us to stay with his college friend and banker colleague, Tom. He had been with the Paris branch of Dan's bank for several years, and he and his American wife, Janet, had four children. Tom told Dan "the hotels would be full that week, and it would be no trouble" for us to stay with him. He and Dan had known each other since their Catholic college days, when they were big Irish campus leaders, but I didn't really know Janet.

On the way to Tom's flat, we had to take two cabs—the cabdrivers refused to allow more than four to a cab. My driver had the address I had written down, and he stopped in the middle of the street, slapped his hand on the paper, and shouted, "Merde! Merde! Merde!" when he couldn't locate the address on his map. My son Matthew (ten) turned to me, eyes wide. These were the first words he heard from a Parisian.

Emerging from our two taxis, we herded our children and our luggage through the front door to meet our hostess. She came towards us in a cloud of costly fragrance, and scooped Martin into her arms, hugging him affectionately. While I felt lightheaded with the time difference, it was bright mid-morning here. Janet called her children to the parlor to meet ours. Her housekeeper, or *bonne,* Hélène wore white go-go boots and brought us coffee in white bowls. She greeted us in French and apologized that she "spoke French only."

Dan looked at me to interpret, then said affably to everyone, "You know, I took French for seven years! And I still can't understand it, but Annie here can."

I winced—never liked the diminutive of my name but he refused to stop using it—as he shook his head, chuckling. We adults sat in a sunny room filled with antiques that our host collected when he worked with the State Department. This flat could pass for an antiques store. Windows ran from floor to ceiling, and I looked about me with sinking heart to note the white carpeting in this room.

Glass-fronted cabinets stood about on highly polished parquet floors elsewhere, and fragile porcelain figurines sat on each shelf. An enormous wooden rosary from Nicaragua—each bead a hand-carved rose—spanned the wall across from me. "Kids, be careful!" I thought, cringing inside as I fixed my Corporate Wife's smile in place and sipped the excellent coffee from my bowl.

Though we had come to Europe with the children because Dan had talks scheduled, there was another agenda: Senior management was considering us for a European post like Tom's. At this time, wives were considered part of the package, especially for jobs like Tom's. I had known, to my dread, that I and the children would also be on display, although I also thought an overseas assignment might be a nice change from dealing with the demands of charity work and from Dan's people.

Meanwhile, the children of our host showed ours around the flat, as all nine chattered happily in English. Our son Matthew stared up at the enormous rosary, then joined the others.

"And where's our friend Tom?" my husband said, stirring his coffee with a forefinger, "At work? He said he'd meet our plane."

Janet cleared her throat and blushed. Friend Husband had been called out of town on bank business. To Tangiers, she told us. "Suddenly. I'm sure you understand; it is . . . a crisis. With the franc and Euro currencies."

Dan and I looked at each other. "If I had known," Dan said, standing back up. "Look here, Janet, we can go to a hotel." He put his coffee bowl down. "Having us stay without him here is a terrible imposition!"

Janet refilled his bowl of coffee as she said, "But there are no hotel rooms available because of conferences! Tom insisted—before he left—that you stay here, sleep in our room."

Dan and I stared at each other; he barely knew Janet and I had met her only at bank functions. And now she would have to bear the brunt of our visit alone—all seven of us. I sank into my chair mortified.

Janet sat forward and went on, "He thought it would be fun for the children, yours and ours, to share sleeping bags in the study." Then she sighed. "I do wish Tom were here. It would do him *good* to see you."

Now, as Dan continued to look dismayed, our hostess rose and called her children in to meet us more formally. Exquisitely well-mannered, each shook hands with Dan and me. The three boys and one girl were similar in age to ours—from four to twelve. In chorus, they asked their mother, "May we go to the *Bois de Boulogne?* Please, Ma-*ma*, please?"

Although back in Chicago it was still nighttime, the children didn't want to lose a moment, so we all set off for the park. The nine children raced ahead of us through the streets, oblivious to stares from passersby. When we got to the *Bois,* I saw no playground. I had hoped for swings and seesaws to use up the children's energy; but there were none. "The parks here are restricted. Children are permitted to play in specified areas only," Janet said as we strolled the *Bois.*

On this lovely May morning, people walked dogs and pushed perambulators among the sparse shrubbery. We stayed a short while, then all our children ran back through the streets, laughing and calling to each other. The Parisians they passed turned to stare at them, then glare at us.

"Paris is no city for children," Janet said as we adults ambled along behind them. "There's no place for children to play. It's not like Chicago where you have forest preserves and parks. Children here go to school during the week and to the country on weekends. All families do."

Far ahead, the children stood panting and breathless as they waited for us at the entrance to the flat. We all went inside for chicken broth and baguettes. My children looked around the table politely after the baguettes and broth. Their faces all held the same question, "Where's the rest of our lunch?" Justin, six, stood and came to me, to put his arm affectionately around my shoulder and whisper winsomely, "Mom. Is there anything else? Can *you* ask? I want to be polite."

At that moment, Janet thanked Hélène for getting us the "delicious lunch," and I realized this was all of it. I gave my children warning looks, and they left the table with their new friends after excusing themselves, to wander about inside the apartment since the flat had no yard, balcony, or other outdoor space.

That night Dan and I lay in our host's bed talking about food, remembering hearty Midwestern breakfasts with steak and eggs. "How about a hero sandwich right now? Or a pepperoni pizza, thick crust?" Dan said.

I rolled over, plumped my pillow (Tom's?), and said, "That makes me feel worse. Let's get some sleep. Hope I don't dream about food."

Just then, Matthew and Mart slipped into our room. "Mom, is there any way we could get more to eat?" Matthew said.

Mart's eyes were tragic. "I think I'm beginning to starve!" I could hear our hostess somewhere in the back. Dan told the boys to hop under our covers, then he and I in our robes gingerly approached Janet.

When she heard we all felt famished, she put her head down and said, "I feel terrible! Let me see what we have." Her *bonne* had gone home, but by midnight we had gathered our children for soup, bread, and laughter. Janet stayed up with us, and again she said, "How I *wish* Tom could be here, to touch base." Dan, across the table, gave me one of those spousal we-have-to-talk looks.

I glanced at Janet and saw a tear slide down her cheek as she looked at our children munching on the crisp baguettes. Although we wives had to maintain a façade that everything was under control, I chanced breaking the Corporate Wives' Code by touching her hand gently and said, "What is it, Janet?"

She shook her head with her eyes cast down, wrapped her robe more tightly around her slim frame and said, "I'm just . . . quite tired. I had better turn in. You stay here as long as you like."

She rose quickly from the table, and as I watched her leave, my heart sank. What had we gotten ourselves into?

The next morning, the nine children woke each other early—they had all slept in the study together—and ran through the streets to the baker's to buy croissants while they were hot. And those were the best croissants! Unfortunately, the local custom was to have only one with morning coffee. I had specifically asked the *bonne,* and she told me that "it was unthinkable to have more than one."

When I was alone in the kitchen, I peeked into our host's college-dorm-size refrigerator and saw half an onion and a lemon. Butter. Empty space. Breakfast was always a single croissant and coffee. Lunch was soup and a bit of bread. Dinner was a stew or *cassoulet*—in the evening we adults sat down to a feast with excellent wine. All the women I saw in Paris were glamorously slim. They dressed beautifully.

How would my round self fit in, if *we* were assigned here? And I saw that the secret to their slender figures was that they starved themselves. Also, they smoked.

Another issue during our stay had to do with the water. First of all, there were no wonderful American tubs and showers here. This made Janet's hostessing even more difficult because there was one dark water closet at the back of their immense apartment and one full bathroom for the twelve of us. The first morning, our hostess called us all into the bathroom to explain, "This is how we take showers." I gathered that the French think our American habit of frequent bathing is unhealthy.

She showed us how the hand-held shower gadget could trickle tepid water onto her forearm and then into the tub. She then turned and said, "And this is the *bidet*. Do you understand how to use it?" She explained slowly, then said emphatically, "It is not ever to be used as a toilet."

Dan turned to the children, and said firmly, "Do you all understand? Never!"

The children all nodded their heads, yes. Clearly, they understood.

Also, we had warned our children not to drink water from the tap, and Janet reminded them again. However, her own children—accustomed to the Paris water—had told ours, "*We* always drink it." And ours followed their new friends' advice.

So our family soon divided into two groups: one was made up of Dan—who had insisted tap water would not affect him—and Justin and Mart. They could not see Paris because drinking tap water made them too ill to leave. The other group—who drank only Evian water—went exploring with me that afternoon: Greg, at twelve the eldest, Matthew, and Beth, eight. The four of us ate (heavily) in a cafe, toured the *Palais de*

Justice, and listened to musicians play guitars in the *Métro* underground passages. The first group stayed home and threw up.

When we four left the others to convalesce, we went first to a sidewalk cafe. When we spotted its sign, "English Spoken Here," I especially was delighted. We sat down quickly. The English speaker was not on the premises at the moment, I was told.

And somehow despite our ordering carefully, we ended up with two of everything. It may have been the waiter's idea. He was rather cruel about my accent. While we waited for our food, I puzzled over the numbered slips of paper profusely scattered on our table. Matthew held some up asking, "Mom, what are these for, anyway?"

When the waiter brought our food, he set the bread and *citron* on top of the slips, and added another handful. We fell to on hot dogs (French sausages actually) and pizzas made from French bread—like no pizza I had ever had, but tasty.

And so for the first time since we landed, we were hungry no longer. We sat back feeling satisfied. As we basked in the feeling of "enough," the waiter came to clear our places and gather up all the little slips of paper. When he returned, he presented the bill.

It was far higher than I had reckoned as we ordered—about three times that amount. In the end, he and I had quite a fight. The other patrons looked on, curious, and continued eating or slipping small bits of food to their dogs under the tables.

Soon there was much shouting (me) and arm-waving (our waiter). I told him in French that he assumed "because I was an American," he could cheat me! My children, off to the side, watched in amazement; this never happened at McDonald's or Bishop's Chili. Soon the manager came by to add his gesticulations to those of the waiter.

The manager calmly assured me this bill had nothing to do with my claim that our waiter viewed me as a "*stupide Americaine.*" The waiter continued to splutter behind him, tears of rage in his eyes. In the end, I persisted and the manager finally agreed to my calculation of the total in spite of my *abominable* accent. As he did so, his eyes sparkled, and he had a faint smile on his face. My win was a small step for an American, a giant step for tourist-kind.

We next descended to the *Métro* to study the wall map and plot our way to *La Madeleine* chapel—in high school my French teacher, Sister Marie Thérèse, had said that if I went nowhere else, I must see that. My children enjoyed watching the routes light up, pressing all the buttons to see what colors would show as several people muttered behind us.

At the *Madeleine*, one first needed to buy tickets. But after I left the ticket window with francs in hand, I realized I had been substantially short-changed.

"Why are you counting your money again?" Beth said. We had also asked our children to learn the money values for this trip. I asked her to calculate with me what change we should have received, and she did. Then together we returned to the ticket grill, and I shoved the change and our tickets back under it, explaining why.

The ticket woman was furious. Shouting words I never heard in French class, she threw our tickets back over the grill, this time with the correct change. Beth rolled her eyes at *"Merde!"* The other patrons waiting in line seemed quite amused.

And the *Madeleine* truly was the jewel that Sister Thérèse had promised me. What a joy to fulfill my long-ago dream. As I circled the chapel, sunlight fell through the stained-glass windows, bathing us in color. It was more wonderful than I'd imagined, so I said a prayer of gratitude to *La Madeleine* for Sister.

We went on to the *Palais de Justice,* where an older woman in tweeds stopped me to ask, "Excusay mwah. Oo ess the, ah, um, Loover?" My children looked at her, then drew close to me. I explained to her in English that I, too, was a tourist and shared our map.

As the woman walked away, Matthew leaned in close to say, "Mom, I need to tell you something. You know that big rosary hanging on the wall? Well, last night after we were in bed, I went out and took it down to look at it."

Oh, no, I thought, dreading the next sentence. Which, of course, was, "Mom, I didn't mean to, but I dropped it on that wood floor. And one of the beads, those rose things? Well, it cracked. A piece came off. So when we go back, could you try to glue it on? I have it in my pocket." If only I could get beamed up back to Chicago right now, and not tell our hostess! And Matt looked so upset that I told him I would do my best.

Later, as we headed for the Louvre, I said to Greg, "We've been walking a long time. I know you're tired. Should we go back to the flat?"

I sure wanted to. And my son surprised me by saying, "Mom, this is the chance of a lifetime! Even if we're dead tired, let's do it! Let's at least see the Mona Lisa." And so we entered the great museum; tourist season had not begun, so we easily approached Winged Victory and the Mona Lisa. My children's comments about the size of the Mona Lisa were audible only to me.

"Why is it so tiny?"

"Is this the real one–so little?"

Unfortunately, that evening in addition to dealing with her broken rosary, and she was not so angry as I might have been, Janet had to call us all into the bathroom for a meeting: Someone had misused the *bidet*. The incontrovertible evidence was down there in front of us. As all of us crowded into the bathroom, she became furious.

"You all were here when I told you what the *bidet* is to be used for. You said you understood. It was NOT to be used as a toilet. And one of you did just that!" Her voice was shaking with anger." She swallowed, then went on more quietly. "We have only this bathroom for everyone to use! Don't you *ever* do this again!"

I felt awful thinking that she had all of us as houseguests, and no help from her husband. No one ever admitted to the crime, although I did hear our three youngest talking among themselves, "Boy, everything here in Paris really is different, isn't it?"

"Yes, like the bathroom!"

"And those two little toilets right next to each other. What'd you suppose, are you supposed to sit together and talk? It's weird over here."

The next day at the flat I sat in the kitchen and talked with the *bonne*. Mam'selle Hélène was a warmhearted, likable young woman who told me she would always want to speak only French and to live in Paris. And she said, "Every weekend *Madame Janet* goes to the country with the children. They stay at a millhouse on a farm with her American friends who are also over here on assignment. But these Americans speak only English among themselves!"

Hélène said she usually talked with Janet in French as they worked around the house together. Janet was "developing a really good accent. But those weekends with the Americans destroy everything," Hélène said, throwing up her hands, "particularly accents. Those Americans simply will not practice their French!"

That night Dan and I had a dinner engagement with his Paris associate, banker M. Charles. Since this was a business trip, we were to have dined with Tom and Janet as well. However, with Tom away Janet begged off. Our children now seemed past further need for warnings about drinking tap water, and Janet and Hélène assured me they could handle the situation in our absence.

When M. Charles and his wife came to fetch us, they first visited with Janet and us in the antiques-filled parlor. Sipping a fine Beaujolais, we five conversed in French. Dan mostly smiled and kept the wineglasses filled. He said again, "I had seven years of studying French, and I can't remember any of it!"

The others just looked at him, then went on with their chatting. All the children—seven boys and two girls—were brought in to meet the company.

"I really am unable to tell the difference between the children, one family from another. They all look alike," Mme. Charles said as she shook hands with each of them.

"We have no children," M. Charles said pleasantly.

"Then perhaps you would care to buy two or three of these?" I asked, thinking to lighten the atmosphere.

My husband glared at me over the rim of his wineglass. His eyes said, "No joking with my business associates." I sipped my wine in silence—my humor had often been a problem for him. Clearly the time had come to leave for our dinner at the *taverne*.

We departed in the Charles's tiny Peugeot and rode at our peril along the River Seine. M. Charles's personality had changed from banker to madman as he drove over curbs and through traffic lights. Our car lurched and lunged along the narrow streets. With one hand on the wheel, he turned around to me in the back to ask, "Are you as terrified, Anne, as you appear to be?" Dan told me later I had turned white.

"You know the mortality rate here in Paris on weekends—it was Friday night—from auto accidents is really very high," Mme. Charles said casually.

The *taverne* was small and crowded and far from Montmartre—M. Charles considered that a great compliment to us as visitors. Beneath heavy, dark beams in the ceiling, the owner walked through the crowd to our table. With the parchment menu against his chest, he thoughtfully discussed our food choices.

We began with a superb onion soup and wine. A guitar player with a shaved head sang songs of the *Carcassonne* and played flamenco music as his girlfriend passed a hat. Somehow I got to talking about my work giving talks on marriage, childbirth, and sexuality in Chicago high schools. I spoke slowly and quite loudly because Mme. Charles had said, "Your accent is so bad that I have to work hard to understand you."

I then noticed that everyone sitting near us fell silent and leaned forward to listen as M. Charles asked me what kind of questions students asked, and I gave examples. Perhaps the *vin Médoc* loosened my tongue just enough. Students' questions were written up for us in advance. One girl asked, "Is it enough for a happy marriage that he doesn't beat you?"

And a sophomore boy wrote, "How do you get her to have intercourse? I mean, you don't just plug it in?"

I found this one a challenge to put into French. At first, I felt flattered that so many nearby ears attended to what I said. It was just as well that Dan did not know what I was relating. At the time, I hadn't thought my choice of subject was unwise for a candidate for an international post.

At 2:30 a.m. Dan and I returned to our hostess's flat. We entered to find Janet sleeping in her clothes on the couch where she had waited for us. "The children were really ill while you were gone," she said apologetically when she woke.

She must have had quite a time of it, because from the corner of my eye, I could see huge damp spots on the white carpet. "Hélène gave the sick children baths," she said, "And your oldest son told Hélène—using my oldest son as his interpreter—that he would take care of his siblings until his parents returned."

His night-owl parents felt terribly guilty that so much had gone wrong in our absence.

Dan and I all along had talked among ourselves about not hearing from Tom, in spite of his inviting us to stay here. The next day, Janet told us that Tom had wanted us all to see his and Janet's country place, the millhouse Hélène had mentioned. That morning, we drove a long time through beautiful Normandy farmland. And just before we left, six-year-old Justin had been ill again, so I had a steel bowl in my lap, in case he needed to throw up. All twelve of us were in Janet's American station wagon—more than equal to the lunacy of the Parisian drivers in their tiny cars.

At a stoplight, a man in a red car pointedly counted the children in the car and stared at me. I held up nine fingers, and he nodded. Dan, the only man, sat in the front seat with our hostess. To amuse myself, I pointed to him, and the man nodded again and stared at length at my husband, who looked like the father of them all.

The light changed, and we drove on through picture postcard villages. The homesteaders of this countryside had settled around their churches. I saw no sidewalks; houses abutted the road abruptly and kept their shutters closed, turning their backs on us tourists. Nowhere did I see trash or litter.

And then we arrived at the two-hundred-year-old millhouse rented by our host and Janet with their American friends. The mill faced a wide stream by a wooden bridge; weeping willows sat on either side of it. And near the bridge, a swing hung from a branch in an apple tree. Janet had told us on the way that one American, Merrie, now lived here full time since her husband had been reassigned to the U.S. As the car stopped, Merrie came to my side of the car while I was still in it.

Justin had vomited twice en route, and I still had the bowl with its contents in my lap. Merrie reached in the open window and extended a limp hand to me. I shook it, having carefully slipped the bowl to the floor of the car. I could see she, too, was starved to perfection and beautifully groomed. Her designer blouse was open to below her cleavage. Did she hope to attract another husband? Mine? I saw Dan gave her bosom a long look until I caught his eye.

We emptied the car (and the bowl) and headed for the kitchen with a huge casserole of *boeuf bourguignonne* that Hélène had made. All other preparation had been done by the help here—washed salad greens lay by the sink on paper towels alongside crisp bread in bakery bags. The refrigerator here was also diminutive; it was hard to believe this same country gave the world stories of Gargantua and his prodigious appetite.

I went with the other adults to the meadow where we sat sipping Beaujolais. It was not yet noon, but all the adults had wine. Later, I looked for my children and spotted them by the swing. As I came toward them, Beth screamed out in pain. She had touched a nettle. Janet quickly found a burdock leaf, saying, "Here, little one, rub it on the painful spot." It worked miraculously, and the other children then experimented—accompanied by much squealing—with causing and soothing each other's nettle stings with burdock.

A few drops of rain then chased us indoors, where some American neighbors appeared at the door. Among them was Trixie in a white cowboy hat, a woman with teeth like piano keys. Her bosom was exposed to exactly the same button as Merrie's. A local custom? Tight green Levis faithfully followed every curve of her pelvic area. She brought us more children, a girl and several boys, who at once ran upstairs to mingle with ours and Janet's.

My husband was the one male among these revealed bosoms. I saw him gazing intently at her cleavage, then he looked at me to say quietly, "Did she say her name was *Titsie?* Oh, no, Trixie, *Trixie.*" He shook his head, smiling.

Three of the boys had gone down the lane, then returned to alert us to a parade in the village. We went out to see it with them. It was May 8, the Liberation of Paris, and in the distance I saw elderly Frenchmen in dark suits, medals on their breasts, marching towards a monument in a small graveyard. The village mayor, wisps of his hair blowing in the breeze, gave a speech.

The children came along and listened in silence. Nearby, a woman opened her shutters and leaned out to attend. A solitary Peugeot raced down the one street, drowning the mayor's words in noise and exhaust fumes. Another man stepped forward and spoke. Trixie with the teeth inhaled her cigarette and said loudly in English, "I'd give anything for a camera!"

I sat on a boulder and watched, glancing back at Dan now and then. The town choir of six sang *"La Marseillaise"* with quavering voices, and their *directrice* waved her hands above their heads. They went bravely through all three stanzas, and they seemed to miss many words. Sister Thérèse would never let us get away with that.

After that, silence. The sky grew dark with clouds. The villagers reassembled quietly, all our children got into the thick of the group, then with drums and flutes everyone marched back from the graveyard to the inn where they broke ranks.

Collecting the children, we returned to the millhouse and the fireside where Merrie opened champagne. The thirteen children stayed outside to play Frisbee and tussle. From time to time, they came in to ask for food. When I asked the other women if they liked to cook, they said, sounding horrified, "I never cook!" "Never bake!"

I watched them casually offer pieces of cheese or fruit to their slender children. I felt an urge to whip up a batch of butter-laden, satisfying chocolate chip cookies.

Merrie came over to sit next to me companionably; she held a water glass of scotch. Facing me, she said, "I've been too long in Paris. No other place is worth living in." She sipped steadily at her scotch. "And all our friends are gone from where we used to live in the States. Or they're reassigned. Or, frankly, they've forgotten about us in the ten years we've lived here."

I started to murmur something comforting, hoping she would not share further revelations, but she went on, "You know, the bank has assigned my husband back to the States. He left last month, but I just can't . . . can't go back. I can't face returning."

I felt mild alarm, but to be polite, I asked why. She looked at her glass, took a healthy sip, and said, "How painful it would be—not just losing the allowances that make life so pleasant here, but I would have to face *real* hardships—like no servants! And then there's . . . much less money. So. I've made up my mind. To stay here.

"If I have to, I'll get a divorce." She held her glass, almost empty, to the light and looked through it. "I think Tom and Janet probably will, too."

I startled, feeling stabbed in the stomach. Then nauseous. Like us, Tom was still a Catholic, so it would be a serious sin as well. And for the bank, his divorce would be a disaster. The chairman liked Tom and Janet "as a couple," for this Paris assignment, he had told me.

Merrie looked off at the fire and rambled on, "You do know Tom lives with his secretary these days, don't you? On the other side of Paris. They haven't told the children yet."

My mouth was too dry to answer her. So that's why we had heard nothing from Tom. I stood abruptly. I had to find Dan. But he was nowhere in sight. And where was Trixie?

Merrie was unstoppable. "You know, being an expatriate means that I represent the U.S. I have to look nice and live well." She checked her manicure, then said, "You know there are nightingales here, near the millhouse? And we have robins in the apple tree." As she prattled on, I had the feeling time had stopped and run backwards to the artificiality of Versailles.

I finally spotted Dan on the far side of the fireplace, asleep. And alone. Merrie, still talking mostly to herself, said, "There's a cuckoo in the woods here. I think it's so important for the children to know what a real cuckoo sounds like, don't you?"

I backed away, desperately needing to talk with Dan and be with our children. I touched his shoulder and he woke, looked at my face, and put his arms around me. The children near us elbowed each other and snickered. "I have to tell you about Tom," I whispered. But Janet called us to the buffet table to help the children and ourselves to dinner. People swirled around us, and I barely got the news out to Dan's startled, "What? Tom? Are you sure?" before we were urged by the chorus of voices to "stop talking; come to the buffet."

I felt too stunned to eat, although the others dined from paper plates on the beef stew Hélène had sent with us. How hard it must have been for Janet to keep up the façade of the good corporate wife throughout our visit. I agonized for her. How would I cope with the same situation?

We made our farewells to Merrie and Trixie, and the twelve of us drove back to Paris. Once there, we circled *L'Arc de Triomphe* when we saw the city was also celebrating the Liberation. A huge flag hung from the underside of the *Arc*, and *M. le President Pompidou* was speaking. Janet wanted to continue driving, along with all of Paris who seemed to be driving around the *Arc*, watching the tri-colored spotlights and *La Garde Republicaine*, listening to the talk and the band music.

To subdue the children so that we could observe the ceremony, I told a horror story, an old favorite about people turning to mold. Then as we continued circling, my son Greg told Poe's "The Telltale Heart." He left out no detail and was an enormous hit with his peers and siblings.

That night we were finally alone. Dan sat on the bed with his head in his hands, saying, "This is terrible! How could this have happened? And Tom didn't tell me or call me? Why?"

"I feel worse because I got it from Merrie, and not Janet," I said. "She's such a private person! She'd have told us if she wanted us to know. I feel so bad for her—and with having us all here!"

"When the bank set this up, *Tom* came up with the idea for us to come here," Dan shook his head. "I can't think what to do . . . maybe the kindest thing is let her have time to herself this weekend. Let's leave early tomorrow. We can walk around Paris and wait in the train station. Give her some peace and quiet after our invasion."

I was grateful for his thoughtfulness. And the next morning, he went out to rearrange our reservations. On his way back, he bought every croissant he could carry, along with a huge tart with orange slices on top. We ate them all with enthusiasm. Janet didn't press us to stay; she looked drained.

As we made our farewells, I again with sinking heart tried to draw her aside, but she kept herself surrounded by children and would have no part of confiding. She called two cabs for us, we all thanked her profusely, but I felt bad leaving her alone, continuing to keep up her good corporate wife appearance.

Down in the street four of the children climbed into one cab. The driver shook his head at me, *"Non!"* as I, the fifth passenger, dared to get in with them.

He held up four fingers. *"Quatre!"* He started pulling away with my leg inside, and said again, *"Quatre!"* Greg looked at me, got out, I got in, and we moved off. Greg took the next cab with Dan and Matt.

Once at the station, we faced a long wait until our train to Calais came. Dan appointed Justin the quartermaster in charge of luggage. I watched Justin as he woefully pushed a handcart piled high with suitcases. At six, he couldn't quite see over the top. When I asked if he could manage, he said, "I'll just watch for Dad's head. I can see that 'cause he's so tall."

Then I went to find out where to board. I searched the station for someone who would pay attention to my French, having been told yet again that my *execrable* accent made me impossible to understand.

A man with a small boy came toward me asking in French, "*Pardon?* Are you missing any of your children?"

Pointing to the little group arguing among themselves, I assured him all ours were accounted for. I thanked him and we said good-bye pleasantly. Then beyond him in the distance I saw a huge pile of suitcases moving away from us to the far side of the station. Justin!

I ran toward the pile. The man, still nearby, came back and stood there smiling broadly. He spoke to his child, muttering something about Americans.

Justin told us later, "I was following a tall, red-headed man. I thought it was you, Dad. When I got to the other side of the station, I saw that it wasn't you.

"But there were these machines, and I still had some coins, those *centimes,* and you told us to use them up before we leave. Then this man and his little boy came over. He asked me if I was lost. I told him, No. I wasn't lost. I didn't feel lost. He told me I had to follow him until he found my parents."

At last we entered our train, and we seemed to cause a stir. Some passengers asked if we were Americans, "because of the clothes." We went to the dining car, hungry once more. Reading the menu, I mistook *veau* for veal. The order I put in was for calves' liver with french fries all around.

Dan detested liver. Four of the children refused to eat it, Dan roared "over my dead body will I eat liver," and I ended up with six plates of liver in front of me. The other diners gave us disapproving looks, whispered among themselves, and rolled their eyes.

When the train reached our destination and I stood looking out on the English Channel, a man with long sideburns and a blue jacket came to me to ask, "'Ere, missus, how'd you like a hand wiv all this baggage?"

My eyes filled with tears. I wouldn't need to talk with him in French! No more comments about my accent! I wanted to hug him and thank him for being British. Taking charge of our mound of suitcases, he got us on board the ferry for Dover and the UK. I sank into a seat and wallowed in sounds I didn't have to puzzle over. English in burrs and brogues and drawls, split infinitives, dangling modifiers, clichés spilled around and comforted me like I had come home.

Moving On

Our problem with the next-door neighbor was waiting for us when we came home from Paris. Long ago it had started with small things – "It's your fault," she told me many times, "that I have dandelions!"

Then she began throwing trash and used toilet paper over the fence onto our yard. Next came chasing our small children with a pitchfork.

"Don't pay her any attention," Dan said. "You're letting her get to you."

When she swerved her car almost into the path where my daughter was walking home from school, Dan went to the police with Beth, nine years old. She had to tell her side of the story.

They dismissed his concern, telling him, "You have made this woman into a monster." They refused to give our troubling neighbor even a warning.

But our family doctor understood her behavior immediately. He said, "Paranoids are unpredictable, and that's what she is. You have to get out of there as fast as possible."

I was the one she was angry at; when I first talked with her, she had been quite friendly. I had two small boys and she had raised two. I noticed a distinct change in her attitude towards me once I put on maternity clothes with my third child. She was sweeping her front walk and came over to me as I went up my front steps, to say, "My doctor told me I couldn't have any more children. It would kill me. And I've always been Catholic, I sang in the choir."

My arms were full of groceries and my little boys were running up the steps. I murmured some soothing sounds, like "Mmmm, mmm," but she was still ranting.

"If I obeyed my doctor and practiced birth control, I would be ex-communicated! So I left the Church!" she went on.

Clearly, she resented having to give up her religion to save her life. She had processed this a few times with me but as time went on, she became more and more difficult to talk with. And I had more and more children. Several neighbors said she told them, "I hate children."

Yet when we first moved in next door with our two little boys, she identified with me, and sometimes came over with her home-made soup. Dan tried it and told me to ask her not to bring any more. I didn't obey him. I thought she was kind, trying to be a good neighbor. When I was outside with my little boys, she would stop to visit over the fence, or offer me some peonies.

I did make things worse between us in 1968 when the riots broke out on Chicago's near West Side. Robert Kennedy had been shot and all hell broke loose. I had a black friend who lived in the 2000s on West Jackson with her five small children. She and I had met at my doctor's office and became friendly. When I heard her neighborhood had shut off the water and electricity, I called and invited her family to stay with us–at least overnight.

Since our neighborhood was composed of white people, Dan and I thought our neighbors should be forewarned that a black couple with five children were on their way here. Most neighbors were understanding, but when Dan talked to this neighbor, she said, "I'm so glad you told me, Dan. My son has his rifle from Korea, and he'll load it and set it by the front door."

The black family parked across the street from our house. They were dressed in their Sunday clothes, and Marnie had her youngest baby in her arms. We had a nice polite conversation with iced tea and lemonade;

I had borrowed sheets and pillows from Mother-in-Law, who said "This whole thing is foolish," but she did cooperate and lent me what we needed.

Since they had eaten their supper at home, we had my fresh fruit salad and lemon cake-top pudding with our iced tea. The little kids ran in and out the back door, and all of them behaved well playing tag happily. Marnie told me she kept a big spoon handy if they misbehaved, but it must have stayed in the car.

Her husband was a quiet man. As he and Dan talked, he said, "I am looking to move on from my present job. I've been married before and paying the alimony is really hurting."

"I hear you," Dan said. "I don't offhand know of any openings."

"Marnie and I want to move to Michigan. I hear there are opportunities there."

The two men went out on our front steps and looked toward the Loop. In the sky, they could see the bright fires of their neighborhood. I had been in their home and saw that their living quarters were strictly "bare bones." Their couch was the front seat of a car covered with a blanket. And their children were neatly dressed. Their kids and ours played nicely together. With nine of them, I could imagine the noise level if they squabbled, but they didn't.

I had a feeling that if we did use my in-law's linens, she would throw them away after our guests left. When the little girls went to the basement with our boys, they looked at all the paperbacks on our shelves down there. Two girls picked out books—"Winnie the Pooh," "Harriet the Spy," "A Snowy Day"–and asked if they could borrow them.

I had been in their house, and had seen no books. I said Yes.

At the end of the evening, the dad called his neighbors on West Jackson, and when he learned the water had come back on and the lights worked again, he told his little family. The girls said, "Please, Daddy. We want to go home. To our own beds."

I thought how gracious they were to accept our invitation, and come here dressed in their Sunday clothes. I was glad they came and it worked out. Afterward, I realized it took a lot of courage to come out to our neighborhood.

No shots were fired by the man next door. I did turn as I waved good-bye to see him peeking out as the family got in their car.

I worried about them and prayed mightily for their safety driving back. I felt a little bad that we had scrambled to help and they didn't stay. But they were safe, and that was the main thing. They called me when they got home to say all was well..

While it was more and more clear that we had to move away from Mrs. R, Dan and I had several arguments about it. Dan didn't want to. Any time he and our neighbor were both outside bringing in groceries or collecting mail, he stood on our porch steps while she stood on hers, yelling, "Why don't you people move?"

"No, *you* move!" he yelled back. This went back and forth getting louder, but not resolving anything. Their yelling made me feel sick, but it never bothered Dan.

Finally Dan agreed and began lining up possible house buying choices. He made sure our real estate agent, an old friend from the parish, understood what he wanted, telling him, "I want a *big* house. We're going to have ten children and we'll need a lot of room."

Dan's dad also thought it was time for us to move on. He pointed out that Dan was becoming more successful at his job, and a big house was more in line with his executive role. He was helpful in getting us to list our house for sale.

At first there were no bites on our house, and Mother-in-Law wanted me to bury a statue of St. Joseph in the front yard. This must have been a Midwestern custom; I objected and said, "That is superstitious nonsense. I won't do it."

We argued. Then one day when Dan and I took the children to the Museum of Science and Industry, we came home to find that Mother-in-Law had stopped by and buried St. Joseph in the yard. He was wrapped in plastic, I found out later.

When we went house-hunting, we took the children with us. I thought our kids should be in on the decision. "They will have to live there, too," I said.

Dan agreed, "100%!"

A friend told me, "Houses talk to you. Just listen. When you get in one you like, you'll know."

And so we looked first at a large house in Chicago's Austin district, spread about with trees and a large grassy plot. It was just off Austin Avenue but still in Chicago. The price made it a steal, and strangely our agent said, "It's never a good idea to have the biggest house on the block. It attracts thieves."

Why tell us this, if he wanted to sell it and collect his commission? I didn't much like it, but it sure was big. The kids didn't say anything, just stood looking. This was the first of many. Another house in north Oak Park had a swimming pool in the front yard, and hardly any land around the house.

The kids' eyes lit up at the sight of the pool. "Let's get this one, please, Dad?" But Dan's father nixed the idea. "Swimming pools are an 'attractive nuisance,'" he said. "You'll have to watch it day and night to keep strangers out. If you leave on vacation, you can't be sure visitors won't swim in it, have accidents, even drown. And legally, any of these would be your responsibility."

I listened. Dan's father had been a real estate lawyer before he was a bank president, and his experience was valuable to me. Although I had thought, "This house will be great. I love to swim," I re-thought it after he spoke. And it would be one more chore to maintain, check the Ph levels, clean out leaves and branches and bugs, stray children, dogs....

On Thatcher Avenue in River Forest, one enormous stucco house was priced to sell. We went in together to check out the seven bedrooms, all large. The house backed into a substantial wooded area, a forest preserve. The river was several yards away from the back door, and the woods made the house even darker. I had heard vagrants sometimes camped in these woods, but kept that thought to myself.

The owner's daughter showed us around the house. She was barefoot, about age 20 and had a glass of red wine in her hand as she walked us through. She showed all of us the elevator, used mostly by her father who had a disability (undisclosed), but was not there at the time. I saw lots of heavy exercise equipment in the master bedroom–a stationary bicycle, weights and strength training setups.

Our kids mostly followed us around—the size of this house was intimidating, so they weren't their usual noisy selves. I looked down long, dark corridors; many trees and bushes had grown up to cover the windows. It was like where Sleeping Beauty rested. Behind me I heard Justin whisper, "This place is creepy."

The black woodwork everywhere and the bigness and darkness gave me the creeps, too, but I frowned at Justin to make him be quiet in front of the woman ahead of us. I had already checked out the great front porch sweeping across the front of the house. Large black roaches swarmed in one corner by the barbeque kettle.

"You guys, I think this house is haunted," said Beth, almost ten, and the other kids agreed, sticking close behind me.

When we got to the third floor with its ballroom, Dan said to me, "This place is way too big. It will give the kids nightmares."

He was right. "And that ballroom!" he went on. "We can't use that." The ballroom was vast, deep, and dark. I couldn't see into the far corners. Good place for ghosts.

"We could set up a bowling alley," I said. "Ideal for above the bedrooms at night."

He turned and glared at me.

"Just . . . kidding," I said. Several houses in the area had ballrooms, a bygone luxury. What a lot of work it must have been to put on a ball—and to get people to climb all those stairs in their finery.

"With all this space, the taxes must be astronomical," Dan said mostly to himself.

Beth said on the way home, "That was so dark and gloomy! And it had that big ballroom on the top floor."

"What would we use that for?" Matt said.

"We'll give balls!" my husband said.

"Oh, *Dad!*"

We looked at five more houses, all enormous. I didn't feel "at home" in any. Dan, exasperated, said, "I showed you all these houses and you don't like any of them! What is the matter with you?"

"I have to feel good about where we move to," I said.

And then early one summer evening, we went to another house in River Forest. Dan and I took a quick look. As I stepped into the entrance hall, I had a feeling–a "this is it" feeling, right there inside the front door. Most people say the kitchen is what sells a house to the woman who will cook there, but I hadn't seen the kitchen yet. I just *knew*. Light poured down the front hall stairs from cathedral windows on the landing above us. All the rooms had lots of windows, and most faced south onto the wide yard. I felt safe there in a way I had not in the other houses we looked at. And I knew with all the space that our children's running and shouting wouldn't disturb neighbors. The feeling that there were lots of places to go inside the house and all the sunlight made it feel right to me.

We went back the next day with the kids. They tumbled out of the car and started running across the grass, playing "Chase." This game involved mostly running and trying to catch each other with much shouting and squealing. But they were far enough away from any neighbors so as not to disturb them. That alone was a fine selling point.

With them running off their energy, Dan and I went inside; the agent had told us to make sure we went "before dinner." I later learned that this phrase is real estate code for "Get there before the owners have too much to drink."

That part didn't work out; what with rounding up our kids and eating, we didn't get there until *after* dinner. The owner and his wife were sitting in their dining room, well into their highballs. He was a salesman for a major carpet company and was in the jovial phase of highballs. They had raised five kids there, four girls and a boy.

I asked the Mrs. If she did a lot of cooking—I was leading up to seeing what shape the appliances were in. Although I had turned on all the faucets, I did not turn on the stove top or oven. And unfortunately, I should have.

"Oh, *I* don't cook!" she said, laughing. "We usually go out to eat or order pizza."

I later thought of these owners as grasping connivers who dumped on us dangerously defective wiring and furniture they couldn't get through the doors after they had remodeled—a mattress, a sofa. They must have thought we were unsuspecting bumpkins. They even tried to sell us these things that wouldn't fit through the doors. When we refused, they left them behind anyway.

At least they did not have bedbugs.

As Mr. poured himself another highball, he said, "How 'bout a drink?"

We both said, "No."

The kids were still running happily back and forth within eyesight as we looked from the dining room windows that gave onto the vast yard. Mr. seemed anxious to show us some features of the house. I wondered why the agent wasn't doing this, but I went along. Mr. took us upstairs to look at the bedrooms and master bathroom; it had a tub and a large shower. Mr. said, "Dan, this is a real man's shower!" It was almost a room of its own, about eight feet long, could easily hold three or four people, and was almost big enough to be a bedroom, a damp one.

Dan called the kids in from chasing each other, and together they trooped up to check out the bedrooms. Greg said, "Hey, look, you guys, there are enough bedrooms for everybody!" Mart and Justin scrambled into the attic, with its winding stairway. Lots of windows up there too. The attic was big enough to accommodate a couple of sleepers. It ran the length of the house. Their voices floated down to us standing on the second floor. "Hey, look–all this writing on the walls," Mart, almost five, said.

Justin, seven, called down, "It says, Make Love, not War. I saw some more like this in the basement."

"And all these stick people drawings–how come *those kids* got to write on *their* walls?" said Mart. "And here—is this a giant sunflower?"

Greg looked at the drawings, then said, "This sunflower and stuff is like pictures I saw of Haight-Asbury. Do you s'pose they used black lights?" He was thirteen; how did he know about that?

We went to the living room, and Greg stood by the immense picture window facing west, calling, "Hey, you guys, look at this huge window! Wonder how they got it in here. And look, this whole wall, it's all windows!"

I wrinkled my nose at the jungle pattern of their living room drapes, but they could be replaced. Such big walls called for big paintings, so these owners had huge paintings of ships under sail. Awful, awful, awful. I hoped to God they wouldn't offer those to us.

"What about these nice paintings? Do these go with the house?" I asked the owners. Fortunately, they loved their paintings and would take them along. I visualized burning them in the immense yard if they didn't take them.

Dan and I and the kids went home to talk this house over, and our agent had the good news that someone had made an offer on our old house. Mother-in-Law gave all the credit to St. Joseph. We had to scramble to get ourselves packing, but we did it.

The first thing I did on moving day was hang my own paintings—landscapes of the Hudson River, farm scenes, bright abstracts–to make the house feel familiar to all of us, even before the furniture arrived.

A swarm of young children came into the yard to gawp at us, our furniture, the piano and so on. One kid—there were nine from his family–said to Mart, "This is our park. What are *you* doing here?" The same children climbed into the movers' truck while the men sat on the grass to eat lunch. Then the men stood, walked to the truck and said, "Okay, kids, beat it!"

Immediately kids ran from inside the truck like rats deserting a sinking ship. That mover got it right; they didn't need to be told again. I learned that neighborhood children played in our yard much of the time. Our "new" house had been for sale for a year, and the owners never chased them away—perhaps that would have interfered with cocktail hour.

The morning after we moved in, I discovered at breakfast that the electric stovetop didn't work. At all. Fortunately, a kind friend lent me an electric frying pan to boil water for coffee and tea, and make simple meals like spaghetti with sauce or beef and beans.

To add to our moving day chaos, my mother called to tell me she was coming out from New York to help. Her "help" involved her emptying cartons humming or whistling to herself as she put pots, pans, dishes, cups in places where I had to spend weeks looking for them. After she went back to her home in New York, it was a welcome surprise to discover my spatulas in the broiler or spices in the dining room hutch. As my father often pointed out, housekeeping was not her strength; he continued to blame her lack of homemaking skills on her college education.

Another of her helps: A writer friend overseas had called weeks ago to ask me to look over her completed manuscript of a social science work; she said, "I'm sending you my only copy."

I begged her, "No. Don't send it. No, no, no. Never let your original out of your sight." I knew it might get lost or tossed; moving unearths rubbish and buries treasures.

She got huffy and insisted. "You're being silly, Anne! It will be perfectly safe with you. I know you, and I trust you!"

She did *not* know my mother. I never knew when Mother might decide to eliminate what she thought was clutter. She often threw out piles of paper and clothing without asking me. This time she knew I was busy with movers, kids, meals, and so on.

And so, my friend's manuscript disappeared without a trace, somewhat like one of Thomas Carlyle's original manuscripts, though it was his maid not his mother who burnt his only copy to a cinder.

The day after the movers left, the dishwasher quit. So we started out with almost NO appliances. The washer, dryer, and refrigerator we brought in ourselves, thank God.

However, once we moved in, and my mother got out, I felt lighter. I had that "I'm on vacation" feeling. Sunlight poured in the windows in every room.

The children were all in school, including Martin in kindergarten a block away. However, I came home one school day, to find a police officer ringing the doorbell. Martin let him in and was talking with him. I heard the officer say, "The people next door said someone from here threw eggs at their windows. Do you know who that was?"

I soon learned it had been my second-grader, Justin, and his new school friends. I had several dozen eggs in the basement refrigerator; I hoped to do a lot of baking once I had an oven again. But when I looked out that fall day, I saw splats of raw eggs, lots of them, drying in the warm sun on the neighbor's windows.

My first thought, was, "Oh, no! not another neighbor problem! We just moved in!"

I went over and rang her bell. An older woman answered, her face a study in unhappiness.

"I'm Anne, your new neighbor. I'm afraid the boys have made a mess of your windows. I'm terribly sorry."

"Yes," she said, "I'm sorry, too. The family that lived in that house, we didn't get along with their children either."

"I will get the boys to clean off the windows," I said.

"That isn't necessary," she said in a sad voice. "My husband and I can do it."

"No. These boys need to learn."

I went home, realizing I was new in this neighborhood and knew no one. I had to line up the offenders. Justin knew only one name. I looked the family up in the phone book, and went to their house a few blocks away. I brought Justin with me.

Fortunately, the mom was home, and I explained the situation. She immediately said she would help, got her son away from the TV, picked up the phone, and said, "I know these other kids. Their parents wouldn't like them doing that, either."

She made some calls, and soon she had rounded up a not-so-merry band. Armed with buckets, rags and soap we all marched to my neighbor's house. The boys grumbled, but they came.

I got out a ladder to get to the top windows; the dried-on egg yolk was reluctant to come off. With much scolding, she and I got the boys to clean off most of the mess. The elderly man who lived there came out to watch, said nothing.

As we moms worked, the background chorus of "Why do WE have to do this? When it rains, it will all come off, etc.," continued without letup.

Mrs. S sounded as fierce as I did when we said, "You have to. You made the mess. You *have* to clean it up! Keep going."

Buckets, soap, Windex, rags, more water, paper towels, a huge garbage can. The wind picked up. I worked frantically and so did Mrs. S. After a while, I stepped back. It wasn't great, but it sure looked better.

"What do you think? Can we knock off?" I said quietly to my colleague. The boys or course, continued to whine as we prodded them to keep going. "You're not done!"

I was exhausted. I still needed to start dinner and it was getting dark. We agreed it was "good enough" and let the boys go home.

Once inside my house with dinner underway, the doorbell rang again. It was the same police officer. "Just wanted to check on how it was going. I talked to your neighbors. They told me the boys cleaned up. Ma'am, nobody does things like that."

"I couldn't let them get away with that. They're second graders."

He thanked me profusely, and left. I was wiped out and didn't want to chat.

Our troublesome neighbor from our former home tried to get our new address from the others on our old street, I found out; I had begged them not to give it to her, and they agreed. With her out of my hair, I could feel free.

And then, one day a few weeks later, I saw a car parked outside of our hedges; I recognized the black Ford Falcon of the neighbor we moved to escape. She parked there for a long time. I felt shaky. I had been afraid of her before. What brought her to drive over here and park by our house? And who had leaked our address?

Then I saw a patrol car park behind her car, and a policeman stopped to speak to her. Perhaps he thought she might be in trouble, sitting there in the middle of a street with hedges along both sides. As he returned to his squad car, she drove off.

I didn't see her car again after that.

TURNING POINT

One evening before dinner, Dan uncorked a Pommard wine as he said, "Hey, Annie! The chairman called me in today. He wants to send me to a seminar at the Aspen Institute." As the children milled about his chair, he swirled the wine in his glass, breathed it, rinsed it 'round his mouth, filled two glasses.

"And you're invited, too!" he said. "The wives *all* go, the chairman told me. We can take the kids. Rent a house! I already asked; he said, Sure!"

My heart sank. Another command performance for Wife of . . . compounded by "Children of." As I'd discovered in Paris, "Five Children of" was trickier than "one or two of." For me, it felt like being on a lake alone in the water with five life preservers; I could get my arms and legs into four of them, but that fifth ring drifted out of reach. For instance, in Paris when six-year-old Justin wandered away at the train station...and I hadn't noticed.

And while ours were good kids, being on display for two full weeks would strain good behavior of even model children like Jesus' cousin John (later John the Baptist). Would *he* ever shoplift candy bars? Although he and Jesus looked well-behaved in paintings by Caravaggio and Leonardo, those were photo opps. Not two weeks among high flyers from ARCO, Coca-Cola, and the Ford Foundation.

But Dan's enthusiasm, as always, was unstoppable.

And so it came to pass that one Sunday morning, after taking the train from Chicago to Denver, we all headed for the Rockies high ahead of us.

We had the rented station wagon, the map, our luggage, the readings, the children, my mother, and my fear of heights. Dan insisted on driving because he said he was "the best driver in the world, bar none!" Note that his having only one eye meant he had no depth perception, and that all his previous driving took place in the Flatlands.

My mother rode shotgun in the passenger seat. I sat behind her to manage the five (squabbling) children. We had stocked up on books and games for them, like those enclosed puzzles where you try to roll ball bearings into tiny eye holes in a clown face or shake microscopic balls into holes on a two-inch golf green. But on long drives they seemed to prefer punching each other or engaging in "Stop it! Stop looking at me!"

"Me? I wasn't even looking *near* you!"

"Were too, you liar! Mother, make him stop."

"All RIGHT! Knock it off, you guys," I said as I always did.

And Dan said from the front, "Settle down, now, settle down," as he always did. Mother rolled her eyes toward heaven, to which we were closer than usual. With our station wagon climbing to crags and peaks, Dan turned to the children: "Hey, we're going to cross the Continental Divide, you guys!" Then, "Oh, oh, look, comin' up on Loveland Pass. This is where that plane crashed. See? I think it was right here? It was carrying a college football team." At that time our only route went through Loveland Pass.

"Dan? Wh … where are the guard rails?" Mother pointed to the highway rim. She and I had assumed we'd have rails or low stone walls like we had on Storm King Highway in upstate New York. And these roads were far more hazardous. As our car rose higher, I saw Mother peek out, then squeeze her eyes shut. Her window gave her an unimpeded view of the sheer drop below.

I heard a quiet, "Oh, Jesus, Mary and Joseph!" as she dug frantically in her purse and pulled out a crystal rosary. My spouse jovially asked, "You're not scared, are you, Mother?" and roared laughing. When she turned her head away from the view, I saw her lips move as the beads slipped through her fingers.

Sitting directly behind Mother, I could see how close to the edge our tires came. In a plumb line thousands of feet below us, ant-sized cars and trucks moved safely across the floor of the gorge. How I longed to be among them, instead of in a station wagon with this affable madman. Despite my begging "*Would* you stop turning around, Dan! Keep looking at the road!" he would turn fully around to address the children as he barreled along.

"And look, team," he chortled, "see those blocking ramps for run-away trucks? That's for when their brakes and gears fail, and the truck goes out of control on the way down the mountain."

"Can we see one, Dad?" Matt asked, but Dan busied himself with his tour guiding. "Isn't this just sensational? Look, look over there: snow! Snow and it's July! Come on, let's stop and you can play in it."

"No, No," I said. "Please. Let's get to Aspen." Where it's safe. And flat.

Dan pulled into a lookout. "Isn't this glorious?" The children ran across the highway to a huge patch of snow to caper about. The boys made snowballs with their bare hands. The younger ones squealed as snow covered their pants and socks. Mother and I stood by the car, our backs to the edge of the precipice, while Dan climbed down from the lookout "to get a better view."

I went back in the car and tried to calm myself by looking through the Aspen material I had received weeks earlier. The "welcome" letter had said up-front that "wives of attendees were expected at the discussions" each morning. (Which explains Mother's presence on these heights—so that while I mulled wisdom of the ancients, she would take our children to the pool.)

The letter went on, wives were not to "speak or comment aloud during the sessions." As it turned out, we wives sat on a raised tier behind our spouses. Urged to study the readings as well, we wives could "discuss them during cocktail hour and dinner." The seminar would "expand executives' horizons and help them reconnect with their values" rather than stay mired in the details of corporate life. It would "lift their sights above the possessions that possess them."

Including wives ensured that executives would break free long enough to "consider issues beyond their desks and business magazines." Comments from prior years included: "We became much closer during this time" from wives and husbands.

H'mm. We'll see.

As we rattled along the brink, semi-trailers whipped by going the other way or overtook our car, disappearing fast around the next sharp curve. When our two youngest, Mart and Justin, fell asleep, I went through my copies of *The Federalist*, Rousseau's *Social Contract*, Marx and Engels: *A Communist Manifesto*, and then lighter fare such as Pericles' *Funeral Oration*, Aristotle's *Politics*, and Machiavelli's *The Prince*.

"Dan, did you finish reading *The Prince*?"

"No," he said laughing as he negotiated another pass. "All those readings? There are 34. I counted! Way too much. For anybody." I had at least skimmed through them, underlined, made some notes. Previously, when I suggested he take some readings with him on business trips, he told me that at the discussion table "I'm going to wing it!"

At the picnic area near the Continental Divide, we stopped so the children could see how water would run east and west down the mountain from the same spot. Dan and I found this interesting, but the children really needed to run free after their long hours in the car.

That evening, our first event in Aspen was a cocktail party at the home of the Institute's leader, Joe Slater. His spacious deck looked out on the valley. Elegantly attired and drinks in hand, we made the rounds to greet Dan's fellow participants. As we stood in a group by the railing admiring the aspens below, one man, Alan, said he was a "returnee" and asked which condo unit we were in. Dan said loudly, "We rented a house! We brought our kids."

"And how many kids are we talking about here, Dan?" Another executive, Mason, looked wary.

"Five. We have five. But I'd like to have ten. Anne's mother's looking after them. She came, too." That meant eight of us in the rented house. Still, Dan's sisters had nine and seven children, and his cousin had twelve. I had privately decided that five was about right. For Me.

Mona, a remarkably pretty and really pregnant woman with long dark hair and huge blue eyes, joined us to say, "Oh, we have three little boys. I only wish I'd known. I would have brought ours, too." Her husband was part-owner of a West Coast football team. They and we seemed to be the youngest couples by far.

Another man, Ben, came up to introduce himself. A trim, athletic-looking union leader, he told us he was here as a "resource," and that the resource men (or facilitators), were there "to keep the discussion going." Then he pointed out, "It's interesting that although Betty Friedan's book came out eight years ago, Aspen is under attack for not allowing women to participate. At the discussion table, I mean."

"That darned book has caused a *lot* of trouble," the man from ARCO said. "At our house we call it *The Feminine Mistake.*" He actually said, "darned." Must be using his party manners.

Hearty laughter from most of the men, including Dan. Ben looked thoughtful.

"Aspen's getting heat, too, for insisting that men bring their wives," said Alan, who was also a resource person. "When I've been here before, some executives asked to bring girlfriends. That's never been accepted. Though one man did get his girlfriend in, this spring."

Mona's husband chimed in, "I hear there was quite a fight over that."

"Yes, and in the end, they stayed in the same condo!" Alan said as the others chuckled.

Mason, a first-time participant like us, said, "Interesting. I hope they can hold the line on keeping this just for males."

Ben looked slowly at each face around the circle, then said, "I think the time will come when they will have to allow women to participate." He took a sip from his Liebfraumilch. He met my eyes and smiled. I thought he was really attractive, much more so than the other men there.

"But having wives and husbands fighting at the table could get really unpleasant!" Mason said.

Shocked, that he expected husbands and wives to fight publicly here, I said, "Why expect them to fight?"

"People can be courteous in public," Ben said. The other men grumbled, "It would never work," and "Might get acrimonious," as dinner was announced.

Together Ben and I went in to the Four Seasons with his wife and Dan.

The next day, Monday, we settled into our routine: after breakfast each morning the wives went to the Health Centre for an exercise program. The goal was the "sound mind in a sound body" ideal of ancient Greece. After that, we settled into the discussions from 10 to 1, then lunch at the Four Seasons–Meadows, after which the men went to the Health Centre to become sound.

The rest of the afternoon was ours to study, bone up on Aristotle, sleep, play tennis or swim. Then it was time for cocktails and dinner–"when the wives could put their two cents in," as one man generously put it.

While I was in the seminars seated in the tier behind the men, my kids were in charge of my mother. Or supposedly, she was in charge of them. She took them to the outdoor pool each day. There was a Coca-Cola dispenser at the conference building and Cokes were free. At home, our kids were never allowed to have soft drinks, but with Mother in charge, they helped themselves. This was a "great luxury," oldest son Greg told me, but they never mentioned this perk until after we got back home.

The cottonwood trees were active while we were there, with their fluffy balls that Greg said were "like a snowstorm."

All five of the kids went with us on horseback rides a few afternoons when the conferences had free time, and once we drove farther into the mountains to Wapatui where the Huskie dogs—a multitude—howled when it was supper time. Their owners served us potato salad and burgers cooked out in the open to the musical accompaniment of the many howling huskies. I asked for the recipe for the potato salad and was given a copy. It started with

"Peel 100 lbs. of potatoes...."

The recipe was written for the huge number of tourists. I broke it down and shared it with the other Aspen wives.

Few of us knew that before the first session, moderator Bill Swenson had met with the resource men. Saul, an author and writer for the *Village Voice,* had brought his wife and 18-month-old daughter. Ben told me later that Saul began the session saying, "I want Sarah to attend *not* up in that second tier but *here* at the table with the other participants."

After a heated exchange that included Saul's pounding the table, Bill said, "The Institute has never done anything like that, Saul. It's not our policy." Bill, formerly with the State department, had to take an undiplomatic stand.

"Then, if she can't sit there, I'm leaving. *We're* leaving," Saul had said, walking out.

Although the first discussion (Arthur Miller's *Death of a Salesman)* took place on time, it seemed subdued to me. Saul's chair was empty; his table tent sign, forlorn. I watched in silence from the second tier with the other women as the resource men and Bill talked about Willy Loman who "had given his whole life to the company."

The rest of the men sat, chins in hand, or looked down at their texts around the open octagonal table. Looking at the other women sitting in silence, I wondered if the men below us were out of their league with this stuff. Most were senior-level executives, and ordinarily they dominated any conversation. Or, maybe Dan wasn't the only holdout on doing the readings.

I was also uneasy because the night before, Dan had asked if he could use my texts since I had underlined and written comments. I said, No.

He pressured me long and hard, insisting: "You don't have to talk and I do. And I'm the one the bank sent here." As I handed them over, I felt angry and said so. He tried to mollify me with, "You can use my copies. They're good as new."

During the next session, I noticed the man next to him leaning over to glance at my notes. Dan had asked me not to tell anyone he was using mine. I felt resentment simmering in the back of my mind. But it was part of Dan's job to be here, I told myself.

The next morning at mid-break as I poured myself some of Four Seasons' excellent coffee, moderator Bill came over. Earlier, his good looks and smooth manner had made me dismiss him as negligible, a diplomat. So he surprised me by saying, "Anne, Saul wants Sarah to sit at the table with the men and talk. And I've agreed. However, I can't have her sitting there by herself. I need one other woman to sit there with her. Would you be willing to do that?"

Me? Me who felt woozy from the high altitude, coordinating the children with my mother, having them stop by at breaks so they could tell me about injustices perpetrated by Mother and various siblings, and trying to look like I had it all together?

I said, "Well, I *have* done the readings, Bill. But please check with the others to see if anyone else wants to do it."

Except for Mona, the other women were far more senior than I, and I had assumed that they would be eager. In fact, one woman had just published a book on Russian education.

How wrong I was. When Bill came back from polling, he said, "I can't get anyone to sit there." Amazed, I said, "Of course I'll do it." The next morning at the Women's Health Center when we settled to bake in the sauna, I learned some had done a few readings. None had done all. And yes, every one of them had graduated college.

"I thought the readings were my husband's job," one woman said and others agreed. Further, the wife of Mason, the bank president, said, "Look, I'm just here to relax, get a massage and enjoy myself." I also learned from some of them that the companies who paid to send us here would receive reports on the men's participation. It cost many thousands to send anyone to this Executive Seminar, so their bosses wanted to see results.

Wednesday morning, with me on the bench among the guys and Rousseau up at bat, Bill lobbed an easy question to Sarah, lounging in her seat next to Saul. "Sarah, what about *The Social Contract?* What was Rousseau trying to do with it?"

Leaning across the table on her right arm and resting her blonde head on her bicep, she said, "Ya know, I didn't really get around to that one."

In the complete and lengthy silence, I felt myself perspire. (Betty? You listening here, Betty Friedan?) And though I cast my eyes down on the text like a nun observing "custody of the eyes," Bill turned from her and said, "Anne?"

Arrgh. *Why* didn't he call on the man next to her? She sat halfway down the table from me. I took up the gauntlet for us wives: "Rousseau's quote, that 'Man is born free but everywhere he is in chains,' was his attempt to make people conscious that all authority, legitimate authority, is based on an agreement. And that people unite their individual energies and form an association that defends and protects each with the common energy of all. That's what the social contract is. He dropped this into the pre-Revolutionary climate in France ..."

As I spoke, I looked into shocked faces around the table. Where before the men around the table sat quietly, now every man stared at me. Was I saying something wrong? Unclear? I finished up my thought, and silence settled around me like snow drifting in through an open door.

I saw the men look at me, then look at each other, and I felt unforgiven. Should I have said, "I don't know"? I also realized that so far this week, not one of the executives had said a word in the discussions.

Only the resource men (Harry—a school principal, Ben and Saul—writers and activists, Alan—formerly a Dean at Harvard Business School) had done the talking along with Bill. So that was why we had "resource" people. So Bill didn't have to talk to himself.

And though all the executives had their books open in front of them, and looked attentive, they sat without speaking and seemed out of their milieu. It reminded me that when I stopped by Dan's office, I noticed that senior executives seemed uncomfortable or even angry when they were away from their own work area—out of their milieu, making social conversation.

That must be what was happening here. Rousseau—with no balance sheet or actuarial tables to anchor his words in reality—was heavy going for them.

After I talked, the men made small efforts to participate, offering brief comments, "Very insightful," "Relevant to today," and the morning wound down. I was not called on again, and neither was Sarah.

That evening at cocktail hour, Ben and Harry came to me to ask, "How did you feel sitting at the table this morning?"

I couldn't say, "The real question is, how did *you* feel about my being there?"

But I did say, "The reaction made me wonder. Does it upset the group dynamics to introduce new faces and voices?" I felt I had to sidestep saying directly, "The way everyone stared at me made me feel unwelcome. Some of you looked shocked."

Mason and other men had joined us to listen, crowding Dan to the side. They seemed intensely curious but didn't answer my question or say what they felt. And instead of my feeling good about participating, I felt uncomfortable. And no one said a word about Sarah. She and Saul were not there for dinner.

My talking that morning contrasted with my corporate wife role as hostess for Dan's bank. When bankers from the Quad Cities and their wives came in for the annual correspondent bankers' banquet before Thanksgiving, I hostessed and worked hard as my "nice" self to make them comfortable, drawing them out about their hometowns, and the fun they had shopping in Big Town U.S.A., our Chicago. Here at Aspen, those skills were not called for. In fact, I thought the guiding principle here was "Silence is Golden," along with "Little wives should be seen and not heard."

After dinner as Dan drove me, Ben and his wife, Mary, to our housing, I said, "Ben, what was going on this morning? I feel like I should write a note to Bill about having Sarah and me at the table. I felt we didn't belong."

Ben seemed agitated, and said irritably, "Would you wait on that, Anne? Please. I have an idea. Don't do anything just yet."

Privately, I felt like the Ancient Mariner, but said nothing further.

The altitude was making me dizzy and each night; I would startle awake several times. Just walking short distances exhausted me. I mentioned this to Saul who empathized. "When we were in the Peace Corps, we lived high up in the Andes. The height made me sick to my stomach, and I heard it was called 'altitude sickness.' It didn't bother Sarah, so not everyone gets it."

"What were you doing in the Andes?" I said.

"Our assignment was to teach birth control to the Peruvians."

"Peru's a Catholic country. That must have been a tough sell."

"They couldn't accept the idea," he said. "It didn't help that Sarah and I are Jews. And I thought eventually they came to hate us."

"They may have thought you attacked their culture."

"But, Anne, these people were starving! And they kept having children."

I found Saul really easy to talk to. However, he had bought heavily into the 1960s' "natural is best" philosophy. For instance, using deodorant was against his creed. This made him difficult to be near. And he needed the extra-strength variety.

I had noticed that the seat next to him was the last to fill each morning, but hadn't connected it to his personal hygiene. Then Ben told me he had taken Saul aside and said, "Saul, either you take a shower twice a day, or get some deodorant and *use* it. Otherwise, people will avoid you."

I found myself spending more and more time with Ben, having lunch and joining him for dinner. Dan liked having him and Mary as part of our group, though Mary didn't seem to have much to say. He was nice-looking, highly intelligent, and made insightful comments. But more important, he treated me as an intellectual peer and listened to me when I talked, exotic behavior that fascinated me. It felt wonderful to have someone pay attention, to listen.

No one in my early life or education had treated my ideas with such respect. I had accepted this meme of the Irish Catholic culture, where responses were usually "Who do you think you are?" rather than "What an interesting and different idea."

Parents often told their children, "I didn't compliment you because I don't want you to get a swelled head." Most bright young people in my world never really knew where they stood even in class. No one was made aware she or he was top of the class or that they had an "original thought." They were conflicted about their intellectual achievements; everything was swept under the cultural rug. (Andrew Greeley has commented on this meme at length. In *That Most Distressful Nation, The Taming of the American Irish*, Andrew Greeley points out that Irish-American children grow up not knowing where they stand in the family or elsewhere, and that they lack confidence and are rarely praised. He also writes that he observed that Catholic kids were just as bright as Jewish kids but hadn't the self-assurance that Jewish kids had.).

The altitude continued to be a problem for me. Drinking coffee made it worse, but more than the altitude, I had an inkling I was falling in love. With Ben.

I was shocked: how could this happen? With all the talks I had given in Chicago high schools on marriage and family life, I had believed that only the Unhappily Married had affairs. And besides I had five children, so I couldn't possibly have energy for . . . could I?

This feeling was a bellwether. I never thought about whether or not I were happy in my marriage; it was my job and my choice. And suddenly I was flooded with delight by Ben's attention and admiration. At the morning meeting, I would look up to see him smiling into my eyes, and I filled with joy. I thought he was wonderful, brilliant, and his seeking my opinion and saying, "You are a very bright woman!" thrilled me.

Though Dan seldom noticed what went on with me, that night he said and said it more than once, "You know, I think Ben is in love with you!" We were in the living room with my mother and the children all around us. He sounded amazed, astonished. That hurt more than an accusation. It sounded like "Why in the world would he, or anyone, fall in love with you, of all people?"

I laughed it off, "Oh, don't be silly."

But he was right. So, it was not just me feeling this electricity. I woke often thinking about Ben, thrilling to know I would see him again soon: breakfast, or a discussion where he would look up suddenly and catch my eye. This feeling seemed to happen and wash over me suddenly.

And if my oblivious spouse had suspicions, how obvious was it? Our two couples spent more and more time together. Had Mary noticed if Dan did? I didn't get much of a "read" on her. And since each day's schedule allowed free time in the afternoons, Dan and I often went somewhere with our children, and not other participants.

The next night Bill Swenson and his wife, Bunny, invited Dan, me, and the Arnolds for dinner with the current Aspen Scholar-in-Residence. Conrad had co-written one of our readings, "The Port Huron Statement of the SDS" in the '60s, to protest everything including the war. Before Conrad joined us Bill said, "Conrad sometimes doesn't turn up at dinners where he's expected."

However, he did turn up; I sat on his right and Mona on his left. I thought afterwards that the Swensons chose us two couples thinking younger, attractive women would keep Conrad at the table. He seemed pie-eyed and sat there saying, "Far out!" and "Wow!" about every topic from Mona's pregnancy to my choice of beverage (wine). The Port Huron Statement had indicated a somewhat more extensive vocabulary.

At first I thought he was really agreeable, then I realized he must have smoked a substantial amount of weed before he joined us. Bill seemed irritated as far as he would allow himself to show it. But ever the diplomat, he kept the dinner conversation percolating about football (for the Arnolds), children, and gingerly, politics since the Arnolds and I surfaced as Republicans (Nixon was President). Dan had no interest in politics.

Conrad mostly sat smiling pleasantly, then excused himself before dessert ("Gotta run!"), and after that Bill pointed out his concern: "Conrad hasn't been contributing to the seminars as we had hoped he would when we gave him this year at Aspen." Apparently, Conrad larruped along, vacationing for the whole year. He hadn't written a thing. He was also a resource, but clearly an empty one.

Dan said, "Well, I can see how that could happen. This is a beautiful spot, Aspen. Our kids are having a ball." He lay his arm across the back of my chair and lit a cigar.

Bill's wife, whose real name turned out to be Eleanor ("But please call me Bunny. Everyone does"), said, "Well, it is lovely, but there have been some break-ins in this area."

"Yes, we never had to lock our doors before. Never. And now everyone is putting in locks and bolts," Bill said.

"You've seen the hippies around town, I take it?" Bunny said.

"You mean those people who smoke by the dam with their bare feet in the water? We saw them when we drove in," I said.

"Those are the ones. They lie on the grass there during the day and roam through town, break in, steal.... They need money for drugs," Bunny said.

"And cocaine is now a serious problem here." Bill looked thoughtful. "I think the time will come when we move the Institute to another spot." A few years later, such a move did take place to Wye in Virginia, leaving Aspen to the pot smokers and cocaine users.

The next morning at break as Ben and I stood drinking coffee, I felt dizzy. At first I thought it must be the altitude again. I was in a daze much of the time. My heart raced; I felt breathless.

Dan and I often went somewhere with our children in the afternoons. One afternoon we decided to drive to Vail with the children and my mother. Ben's wife Mary, had overheard us planning at lunch and caught up to me later to say, "I've always wanted to see Vail. I'd like to join you." This didn't seem like Mary; she was usually subdued, and seemed almost worshipful toward her illustrious husband.

"Mary, you'll be crowded in the car with the eight of us," I said. She hadn't seemed pushy before; yet she was extremely so now, out of character really. When I told Mother, she said, "What in God's name does she want to come along with *us* for?"

"She's my friend, Mother. I said she could."

"But the station wagon will be jammed! Can't we be by ourselves?"

Mary really insisted, again not at all like what I had seen of her, and when we got to Vail, she stuck pretty close to my side. When she stopped to window-shop while keeping me in sight, Mother sidled up to me to say, "She's really got a nerve! So pushy!" Another time, Mother muttered, "Can't we get rid of her somehow? Is there a bus she can take back? I've had almost no time with you."

Mother was often rude, so I paid no attention. I was lucky she had come with us to keep an eye on the children. I could never have handled them and attended the discussions. The kids mostly kept out of her way when she visited us. She was never a cuddly grandma type, and I was surprised that they all got along as well as they did for this visit.

Towards the end of our excursion, it dawned on me: If Mary came with us, then I couldn't slip away for an assignation with Ben. She must suspect something. Was she tagging along to keep tabs on me?

I felt awkward. To dodge Mary, Mother suddenly pulled me into a jewelry store. Her interest in jewels was nil, but now she browsed the counters, glancing out the window. In the distance I saw Mary looking nervously around the plaza, then turn and approach the store. Mother picked up a silver aspen leaf and bought it for me, "to remember your time here," as Mary entered the store saying, "There you are!"

On the drive home Dan asked point blank, "Why did you want to come along, Mary, exactly?"

Looking flustered, Mary said, "Well, I've always wanted to see Vail. I heard so much about it." Mother sitting next to me, jabbed my hip with her forefinger.

"By the way, where's Ben this afternoon?" Dan said. "Would he have liked to come along?"

"I have no idea where Ben is. Or what his plans are," she said.

That night at dinner, Mary was more quiet than ever. Dan, I and Ben talked about Saul's book with Chuck and Mona. (Saul and Sarah never came to any dinner. They didn't want to leave their little girl.) Ben said, "There has *always* been a generation gap. In fact, the kid who wrote *When Push Comes to Shove* lives across the alley from me. We talk about this. What's new is that people are listening."

"How much of their demands stem from people like Saul being raised by the 'Don't thwart your child' interpretation of Dr. Spock?" I asked.

His eyes shone and got larger as he looked at me and I drowned in them, hardly hearing him say, "Well, they do expect their demands to be met. Not just listened to."

This kind of thinking in the '70s paved the way for the Me generation of the '80s and for the sense of entitlement that followed

Mary watched our verbal ping pong and I imagined her trying to weave an invisible security fence around her spouse.

"So what happened to 'Children should be seen and not heard'?" Mona said. "I don't understand these sit-ins and lie-ins,"

Ben had told me he had lunch with her. "She's very bright. Everyone comments on her looks, but she's intelligent, too." Ben got around. I thought, *he really likes women.*

"We're not much older than Saul," I said trying to paddle along as though I were not ready to wrap myself up in his arms in front of the entire dining room, "but we aren't SDS types. Does Dan's working at a bank mean he's sold out?"

"Look," Ben said. "I grew up in the garment district. My parents worked there, and I quit high school to work. I joined the garment workers' union and I've been there ever since. I've been a socialist since puberty." Every word he said rimmed with gold, throbbed with brilliance. *What* was happening? My body was betraying me!

"Are you saying you *grew up* protesting?" Chuck narrowed his eyes.

"Right. And when we went to a strike, we planned the violence beforehand: whether to use pipes, blackjacks, how many broken noses, broken arms, whatever, it was orchestrated down to the last detail."

Violence! I quivered at the vision of men believing in ideals so great they would beat each other bloody!

"The SDS aren't like that," I tried to surface. I trembled, imagining Ben reaching for me across the table. I struggled to say, "But they don't let people respond. There's no dialogue. They want the attention not on solutions but on them."

He penetrated me with his eyes. My head swam. "Wanting that spotlight makes people do strange things," he said. "I've had women I didn't even know show up at the workplace accusing me of fathering their children!"

Dan guffawed. "Really!"

"Yes, they attributed a pair of testicles to me that I never had." He shrugged, looked away and sounded rueful. Then he turned quickly to Dan and said, "So can we learn something from Conrad and Saul, do you think, Dan?"

"That's why they're here, isn't it?" Dan said, setting his wine glass down carefully. He located a fresh cigar in his breast pocket. "But so far, they're not getting through to me. Come on, little girl, it's time we headed for bed."

Oh, no!

That night, Dan sat on the edge of our bed and held his head in his hands. "Why does everyone want to get *your* opinion on things? They don't seem to want mine. I can't understand it. "

Then he shook his head. "And Ben, I'm sure he's in love with you!"

"What makes you keep saying that?" I riffled through the next day's readings so I could hide my burning face. "By the way, Chuck and Mona got a call from family that they were needed at a dinner tomorrow at the White House. They'll fly out in the morning."

I took great care in setting out tomorrow's readings.

"Mom!" Justin's voice. "Greg's got my toothbrush! He's scrubbing Mart's head with it!" I ran to administer justice.

Since Sarah had gone to Bill and asked *not* to sit at the table—I hadn't known this—Bill had asked me to step down as well, something about "no need for you to have to sit there." I was disappointed and protested, but quite firmly he said, "It's better not." She and I now sat together among the tier of wives. Dan, of course, had wanted my copies back now that I would not be at the table.

With all the people washing around us, more than ever Ben and I were never alone. We exchanged looks across the room, stood together at the buffet at lunch and started to talk but were always joined by Dan, Mary, or both. We sat in the heart of a crowd at dinner.

Mary and I worked out together each morning at the Women's Health Centre. When I started back to our housing, often Ben happened along and we walked together. Dan would catch up to us in his most Friendly Bear manner, and the three of us would walk under the aspens together, talking politely of the latest discussion.

People, ideas, readings, workouts, family filled every minute: in the pool with my children ("Mom, mom, look at me!" "Mom, watch this cool dive I learned yesterday!"), at discussions Ben and I catching each other's eyes when he spoke ("Aristotle's *Politics* differs from Rousseau's work in that. . . "), through evenings at concerts (Claudio Arrau, a young people's orchestra) and at art exhibits (massive abstracts by artists-in-residence). My head spun. I was exhausted. I had no time for me, let alone for a tryst. Everything was sliding from underneath me; it all felt like too much everything.

And on the last day, we breakfasted together, Ben, Mary, Dan and me. Ben stood up and said, "I want to talk to Anne." He and I went to a bench outside as airport limos gathered at the entrance, Dan loaded the station wagon for our return trip—not through Loveland Pass this time—and the others stood about making farewells.

Ben sat to my left and took my hand. "We're in the '70s now and the current thinking is, 'If it feels good, do it.' I feel powerfully attracted to you. But I have been faithful to Mary. We had two children together. Our youngest is twelve now.

"And my friend, Jan, he's head of another union, tells me I should have a girlfriend like he does, a dancer. Now that I know you, I think about that—a lot. He says his wife doesn't know. I think she knows."

Far away I could hear, "Mother!" "Mom!"

He squeezed my hand harder. "Mary is my friend. Acting on my feelings for you would be wonderful, I know it. But what we would lose—would be trust. Mary's, in me. And Dan's, in you."

Now my mother, "Anne! We're leaving, dear."

"You're in Chicago, I live in New York. And we're committed to our marriages, for better, for worse. But know this (he gripped so hard it hurt): I love you." Tears stood in his eyes. I felt numb; I didn't want to let his hand go. And I choked.

Voices of my children called me back to my life with Dan.

HOME FROM ASPEN: ART AND THERAPY

A few weeks after we returned from our Aspen trip, Dan brought home a letter to the bank chairman, from Joe Slater, the director of the Aspen Institute. The chairman was the one who had sent us to Aspen; he sent for Dan and gave him the letter. In it, Mr. Slater wrote he wanted Dan's wife to come to New York for an interview because she had had been recommended as a possible moderator for next summer's Institute.

"Dan's wife." Me! I was thrilled by this recognition. Further, to my knowledge, no woman had yet moderated, let alone sat at the "big table" with male participants.

Dan was quite upset by the letter and couldn't settle down; he paced through the house saying, "There's some mistake. I'm sure it's *me* Slater wants to go to New York. I cannot understand why *your* name is on there and not mine." Yet we had been there together for all two weeks, and he heard me talk about Rousseau and interact with other participants.

He got angrier as he paced. Finally wildly angry, Dan called Slater's office several times to straighten out his "mistake." After the fifth call, the secretary told him Slater had left the country and couldn't be reached.

I felt insulted that Dan thought it *couldn't possibly* be me Aspen wanted-ed. I did want to go. Dan's objections made it impossible. I would have had to approach his boss without Dan's knowing. His boss had sent us to Aspen to develop Dan for the ranks of senior officers. And given the Institute's policy of excluding women from active participation, my being recommended was extraordinary.

I regretted not becoming a moderator for the Aspen Institute. It would have been a real stepping stone into a world I longed to join, and perhaps I would work alongside resource Ben the next summer. A delicious prospect.

I didn't realize then that with this letter, the spotlight that always shone on Dan had shifted. When we were at Aspen, the focus often settled on me at the lunches and meetings. But this letter tapped into Dan's deep wells of fury at not being the center.

Aspen's interest in me changed our marriage for the worse. Dan was angry at me for having been recommended. In fact, he was so angry that from that point on when we disagreed, he put his hands around my throat and squeezed to silence me when we disagreed. Or he would force me against a wall and lean his forearm across my throat.

Each time he was rougher. I became frightened to discuss bills, permissions for the kids, whatever.

I slowly began to realize I would have to give up my dream of a good marriage. My parents had been so unhappy together that I wanted to prove to myself that a happy marriage was possible. I had prayed diligently for years that I would find a good husband, and when Dan came into my life—through my brother "fixing" us up for a football weekend–I was convinced this was "God's plan." Back then, my belief in the power of prayer was unshakeable.

Yet the affirmations of my intelligence and the respect from Ben, from a former Dean of Harvard Business School, and from the others, revealed to me who was behind my corporate wife façade. Rising to the surface of my mind came flotsam and jetsam of an awareness—how limiting my environment was, how people surrounding me never saw this side. Yet it had always been there. I thought of these people as my "familiar circle."

Could I step outside that circle, make changes? If I did, it could be only slowly.

Was I strong enough? It would mean going it alone.

Dan's disparagement of me worsened after that letter. "What could *you* ever do? I love you, Annie, but you could never hold a job!" He told me

I had been so "sheltered" that getting a job would be impossible for me, that I was "too mentally ill" to work. "and besides, you never get the ironing done.".

Dan said this so often when we argued that I began to doubt myself. He would add, "I love you, but you have no contact with reality." Hearing this sabotaged my confidence. I felt despairing and my thoughts began to drift toward killing myself as a way out. I had a stash of pills left over from various prescriptions–Dexedrine, antihistamines, lots of aspirin–and I started to think I could use them to end my life. Even a big bottle of aspirin could do it.

I grew up thinking I had no options. There was only one right way to live, and the Catholic way was it. For a Catholic, a divorce was out of the question—a mortal sin that would send me to hell, therefore unthinkable.

Worse, because my younger brother had spent his high school years in a psychiatric clinic in New York, Dan and his family were quick to assume I also had a mental disorder.

A faint light inside me began to glimmer into hidden corners of my awareness. And as I turned toward what the light exposed, people around me, the "circle," brushed aside my new perceptions. Some asked would I take on "room mother," "picture lady," or PTA secretary. When I refused, I heard, "After all, your children are in school now," the caller, a mom of seven or ten, would tell me. I still refused.

One bright friend in our social circle said of my time at Aspen, "How exhausting it must have been for you at Aspen to have to sit there and be brilliant. I would hate that."

That fall all our children were in school, and I was not expecting another baby. And as the weather got colder, I thought I didn't need to turn on the heat if I were the only one in the big house. It was 1972 and I was losing weight and diminishing myself and my presence. I tried hard to be there for the children when they came home from school.

"Equal rights" was merely a murmur, and feminism in my world poked its head through the *status quo* only to be stepped on and shoved back down. What had gone wrong in my life stole over me only gradually—like fading sunlight. My family of young children occupied the front of my mind—yet pain lurked in dark corners of my awareness.

Family life with its usual turmoil sped my days along, but in the dark of night, time stretched out and I was alone, haunted by my nightmares. In those, I was murdered, night after night, drowned in the Chicago River, thrown from a cliff, or hanged.

As the days wore on, I had less and less energy. Every shopping trip felt like I had climbed a mountain to get there; back home I had to put away the bags of groceries. If the kids were around, they helped. They liked to go through the new supplies to help put away, at the same time as they sampled the grapes, mixed nuts, crackers, and other snacks.

I startled awake many times each night. I had nightmares, and often a voice would wake me, scolding, "What happened to the promise?"

Ever since Dan and I married, I had worked hard at being "nice." I was desperate to get along, to succeed at my marriage, but I didn't realize that the price of belonging was to stop being my real self. So many times I heard "How would *you* know?" when I offered an opinion. Despite my excellent education and my family's political experience, my opinions were often scoffed at. I spoke up less and less often.

The self I brought to the Midwest had not been acceptable as she was. I was told I "talked funny" being from New York. I once thought we were all alike across the U.S. But I was soon to learn East Coasters differed greatly from Midwesterners.

For instance, strangers in the Chicago suburbs usually said "hello" as they passed each other. If a stranger in New York greeted me on the street or in the subway, I would have called a cop. Chicagoans' flattened "A's" grated on my ears, and the way everyone pronounced names of Illinois cities like Cairo (Kayro), Vienna (Vyenna), and Missouri's New Madrid (MADrid) set my teeth on edge, and reminded me how far from home I was.

My feeling I had failed was ever-present, and Dan continued to tell me it would be my fault if he ever got fired.

I lost more weight and had almost no appetite but I continued to put one foot in front of the other as I managed the household, the children, the bills, the neighbors, repairs, and so on. My heart rate was high; my family doctor said it was tachycardia. He gave me a thorough checkup and said there was nothing *physically* wrong. I knew the source: it was terror.

My weight went down so low that my nice corporate-wife clothes no longer fit. They hung on me, and a friend asked if she could have some of my "fat" clothes, since I could no longer wear them. My doctor told me if "you lose one more pound, you are going in the hospital on intravenous."

Christmas was coming, and my sister Elaine now living in Oregon invited all of us to spend the holiday with her and her family. I wanted to go; Dan was afraid to take time off, that he might "come back and find (his) desk out in the hall." We argued about it.

In the end, we went. This was one fight I won, though Dan was antsy about work. He was head of a technology division, where his new multimillion-dollar computer system was up and running, the system he ordered despite the chairman's veto. Dan called often to check on it while we were out there.

Elaine and her doctor husband lived in a hilly suburb near the Rogue River. Robb loved the outdoors, so their surroundings gave him the chance to fish, hunt, and row his flatboat on the Rogue.

Being with blood kin revived me as I hoped, Dan and Robb drank together companionably, and our children–all eight–played and swam happily. Mostly.

Elaine and I did chores together, like in our growing-up years. As we washed, dried, sorted, and folded laundry, we talked as sisters do about our families. I could see she was concerned that I had lost so much weight, so the tone changed from female bonding to something painful.

As my sister filled the washer, she turned to me with tears in her eyes. "I know you are going through a really hard time. What I want to say is, *please* don't get pregnant. I'm worried about you. I know Dan wants ten children, but now isn't a good time."

I stood there in mid-fold, stunned. I had no idea this was coming. I remember suddenly slumping against a wall, needing to breathe.

She went on, "I know you see divorce as a terrible sin. But that doesn't mean you can't get one. And–you're in no condition to take on another baby."

My Catholic sister! We'd had the same upbringing and schooling by nuns and priests. I was shocked and not ready to hear she thought divorce was an option. Yet here was encouragement to divorce.

We had both urged our mother to get a legal separation many times. She always answered, "No, these children need a father."

Did she mean *our* father? He was seldom home. And when we walked along Broadway, and our dad passed us in his convertible, he acted like he didn't see us. We would wave and call him, but he ignored us. That, along with his never giving us rides anywhere, was just the way things were.

We had no idea that other families were different. At his funeral, my sister introduced herself to a city councilman, who said, "I had no idea George had children!"

As it turned out, Dad had another family on the other side of town. None of us knew. But separation, let alone divorce, was out of the question for my mother.

So my sister's advice shocked me. But it did pry open a door in my mind. I realized I had needed to hear exactly what she said. She got through to me and for the first time, I began to see a glimmer of another way out of my life, a faint gleam like a Holy Grail in my future.

That afternoon Robb sat and talked with me while Elaine and Dan took all eight kids to an indoor swimming pool. When Robb finished asking me about what I thought was the basis of my marriage, I told him, "Dan needs to think he's superior and puts me down a lot."

"You are depressed," he said at the end of our talk. "I want to get you some help. I have a Chicago friend from med school who can recommend a psychiatrist."

He talked with Dan about it the next day, and Dan hit the ceiling. That night, when we were alone in bed, he forcefully argued, "Robb wants you to talk with a psychiatrist. We don't need any damn psychiatrist getting involved. I *don't* want you talking to one."

"But I want to," I said. And I knew I had to. Feeling better than this constant dragging sadness was my goal. I had to try.

"And just how do you think you will pay for it? I certainly am not going to pay for any appointment with a psychiatrist."

I remembered I had a little money saved.

"'Cause *I* won't pay for it." He continued to argue and I knew we were headed for yet another wrangle. But I was so wiped out, I closed my eyes. Many times if I didn't agree with him, he kept arguing until out of sheer exhaustion, I said, Yes, to whatever he demanded, just so I could get some rest.

This time, since we were in the house of someone else, he didn't raise his voice. And after a spate of talking to himself, it got quiet enough for me to fall asleep.

I knew I would carry through on this, even though both of us knew executives who bribed their wives to avoid counseling. Sable coats, luxury cruises, and costly jewelry were rewards for these wives who agreed to forego counseling. Therapists often encouraged wives to examine their unhappiness, consider their options, and allow the possibility of divorce if all else failed.

"The unexamined life is not worth living," Socrates told the world long before psychiatrists began putting in their advice and stirring lives up.

Robb did follow through with his recommendation, and once Dan and I were back home, Robb called with the name of a shrink. I promised to contact this doctor.

And I continued to keep thoughts of suicide at the back of my mind and cuddled my secret thought of divorce like a beloved pet. And yes, I had heard many times divorce meant a lonely life. For me, though, the loneliest time had been when I was married.

Not everyone understands why women need to talk at length with other women; it can be about everyday problems or larger troubles. However, to be in therapy is not the same as talking things over with a woman friend. Perhaps that was the original therapy—centuries ago women gathered at the well to fill their buckets and chat or knelt at the riverside to wash clothes in the company of others. They could sort out spousal problems as they pounded their husband's work clothes clean with rocks.

I continued to feel profoundly sad and down, and I continued to lose weight. I made an appointment with the psychiatrist my sister's husband located, as I bore in mind that Catholics were never to seek help from psychiatrists. That would break with tradition; we were supposed to talk over problems with our priests, usually in the confessional. Unfortunately, priests—men who did not marry and weren't supposed to have families—usually had no experience to call on when abused wives needed help. At best they could tell these women to "offer it up for the poor souls in Purgatory" or endure "to keep the marriage intact. Pray that he will see the error of his ways."

For those with alcoholic spouses, the usual advice was "Your husband works hard to support his family. He deserves a drink now and then."

"Now and then" was a euphemism for the daily six-pack or pint or more of bourbon. Such "words of comfort" brought little solace, but no priestly counselors existed who might give practical solutions, like "get out while you can."

In today's world, most therapists I have talked with acknowledge that wife beating is pretty much incurable. The conventional wisdom is, if the abusive spouse attacks a second time, it's best to leave. Leaving an abuser takes guts especially if there's nowhere to go. Often the one abused has no guts left.

For Catholic wives, there were no solutions, only continued suffering. Locked into the Catholic system of thought, they had no way out. Turning to the Church usually meant no provision for shelter needs. Rectories had no places for escaping wives to stay. It would give scandal should the housekeeper see a Father welcoming a runaway wife. In my experience, I knew these well-meaning older women loved nothing more than sharing a story like that with their network.

I knew enough not to reach out to a priest, especially since priests we knew saw my spouse as a "fine man and a wonderful Catholic" and often told me so. Then, too, I had kept everything inside me. Deep in depression, I felt I was wrong for even reaching out to a psychiatrist for help. It was a mortal sin even to think of it, let alone follow through.

The night before I was to meet the psychiatrist, I woke with a start and a powerful sense that I had to end my life. I rose quietly and went into the hall. My children and my husband were asleep. It may have been two a.m.

I stood on the carpeted stairway above the landing where stained-glass windows looked out on the rooftops of North River Forest. I was on my way to the basement to drink insecticide. I didn't think of my pills. I had to end my life. I had lost my way. There was nothing left.

I stood there. I hadn't pulled myself out of this quicksand. I should have. It was time for me to take myself out of life.

I could take whiskey with it. The insecticide would go down easier, maybe.

I had to do it. Powerful forces drew me onward.

My heart was pounding hard against my ribs. I was in terror. My hand on the banister shook. I often had nightmares of being murdered by strangers in hangman's hoods who strangled me, threw me from cliffs, drowned me in the Chicago River. But I was wide awake now—and in the middle of those nightmares. Those strangers—were they ME? Was I punishing myself, killing me?

I never saw their faces. But now I was about to do their job.

I was frightened and trembling.

Something made me call, "Dan! Dan! Help me, please!"

By some miracle, he heard me and ran out into the hall. I said, "I'm going down to kill myself. I need you."

He put his arms around me and led me back to bed. Greg came out, too. Dan sat next to me, soothing me by saying, "Maybe you'll feel better in the morning. I'll make us some martinis, and that will help you feel better and get back to sleep."

Alcohol was always a solution in his family. I took a few sips and lay down, then slowly I fell into sleep.

The next day, I found the psychiatrist's office on Michigan Avenue, and rang his bell. He sat and talked with me, taking notes on a legal-size yellow pad and puffing on an unlit pipe. He probed gently, asking the standard shrink question: "What about your father? What was he like?" and so on. I thought, *What good will talking about my father do? He wasn't about to kill himself.*

I didn't like the personal questions, but I tried hard to feign polite interest.

Toward the end of our time, still chewing on his pipe stem, Dr. H said, "How long have you been thinking about it?" His tone was gentle.

"Thinking about ...what?"

"You know. About killing yourself."

"How do you know?"

"I just knew. I think it would be good if you came back tomorrow to talk with me again."

On the way to the train, the sky didn't seem quite so dark as it had on my way in to his office. And I did go back the next day for a much longer session. We followed this with three sessions a week at first.

While this dark time was far from over, this small first step started me on a different journey. Months of depression followed my struggle to rise. This doctor did listen and made no judgmental comments. His listening heart was a change from the denial that surrounded me when I tried to talk to the "familiar circle" about the pit I was mired in.

As time when on, when I described Dan's behavior, the psychiatrist would counter with "I can't make any observations about anything that happens outside this room. I can only deal with what goes on between you and me."

This approach maddened me. I was perfectly clear about what was said and done, but the psychiatrist was "not a witness" to my life, as he put it. After a long time, Dr. H was concerned that I remained depressed.

At one point when I felt terribly low, I told him, "I went back on Dexamyl."

"Would you like to go out and buy yourself a hat?" he said.

"A hat?"

"Yes. Lots of women feel better when they get a new hat."

"I don't usually wear hats, and no, that wouldn't help. This isn't a 'new hat' situation."

In fact, he advised me to tell Dan I would have to leave him if there was no change in our relationship. He even said, "If you don't tell him, I will!"

I wouldn't dare have him try to tell this to Dan. I knew he would enrage Dan, but I would bear the brunt of it. Since our Aspen adventure, Dan choked me when I disagreed with him, so I usually took our arguments outside so neighbors could hear and see if his shouting and strong-arm tactics got out of hand. I felt a lot safer that way.

I asked Dr. H to arrange for therapy for us as a couple, and he agreed. I thought I could start talking about my wanting to leave by telling Dan I wanted to try "couples therapy" first.

While I found myself telling my troubles to a man who was skilled in psychiatric and clinical approaches, I realized I needed more: I needed a woman's ear. And fortunately for me, my sister was available and vital to this process. She had sorted things through with a shrink herself; she was sympathetic to my situation in a way that the male psychiatrist could not be. He did have children (three) but seemed removed from their daily care and troubles. Women listen and say, "I know how that feels," or "That must have felt really bad."

I needed to talk out my daily life with someone who knew, understood, and assumed I was telling the truth of what happened. My spouse was seldom home and when home, busied himself with his work. He liked to spread his papers around his desk so that none of us could approach closer than five feet away. Matthew decided in second grade that

"I never want to work in an office and have a desk job like Dad." (And Matt never did.) Dan was just inaccessible.

What happened in my psychiatric visits was far removed from my daily pain. When Dr. H said, "I can't deal with your family issues. I can discuss only what goes on between us in here," I thought he was telling me, "It sounds to me like you are not a reliable witness to your own experience."

Thinking it might help make my situation clearer, I asked if I could bring my children in to meet him. "That way, Doctor, you can see what I'm coping with."

"Absolutely not! This therapy is for you only. I do not want to meet your children."

He sometimes mocked me for being afraid of my husband, but after we began Couples Therapy, he apologized.

If I talked about a problem with my mother-in-law, for instance, when she said, "All politicians are from the gutter, including your father," he said, "It seems to me there are lot of people you just don't like."

I had hoped he would say, "That's an odd thing for her to say," or "That must have hurt."

He so often said, "I can't deal with anything that does not happen in this room." I figured this meant that anything I related about the outside world was suspect—that he assumed I developed a fictional Other World when I left his office.

In later years, talking with social workers and psychologists, I heard practical solutions to ordinary issues with my children and other relatives. Freud, the Godfather of Psychiatry, encouraged his disciples only to listen, make murmuring noises, and take notes. Strange to think Sigmund Freud had six children of his own. I have read that when one of his boys fell and cut himself, Sigmund would say, "Why did you let that happen?"

This psychiatrist told me I would "have to change 85% to get better;" this thought disheartened me—what was so awful about me? I asked early on, "Doctor, if I have to change that much, could we focus on what's right with me? On my strengths? What do you think those are?"

He nibbled on his pipe for a few moments, then said, "Well, the fact that you asked this question means you are bright."

"Anything else?"

I had the distinct feeling that I had asked the un-askable question. Our task was to focus on all that was wrong with me, so we could fix me. Surely there were parts of me that got me to cope with my children as well as the myriad tasks of being a corporate wife. Couldn't we build on this? But it was time to end our session.

What I got from this exchange was a feeling that I had embarrassed the psychiatrist. Still, it was important to acknowledge he had helped me past the suicidal phase. Early in our meetings, he said, "Committing suicide is entirely up to you. It is your choice."

His approach clearly put the responsibility on me. No one else could stop me if I wanted to go.

Our family doctor had said, and my husband agreed, "Anne would be much happier if she were pregnant again." A sixth child? That was their solution to my troubles?

I relayed this suggestion to my psychiatrist. He said, "It's entirely up to you. If that's what you want, then I would be happy for you."

I said, "I don't." I knew my sister was right. Now was no time for yet another baby.

As it was, it was hard work to keep breathing. But it was also important for me to recognize that this expectation was part of my faith—the Catholic view that a couple should have as many children as God sends. I privately suspected the Church wanted to populate everywhere, no matter what the cost to a family. Or particularly to the mother of so many children. I really thought I couldn't manage any more than I had. Five is a lot of voices to listen to, tears to dry, and mouths to feed. Another pregnancy would distract me from dealing with why I was so deeply unhappy. But here again the shrink pointed out, "The responsibility is yours."

While I continued to teeter on the edge of the "only way out," I also found myself feeling a small measure of happiness. This came when I was at art class: To distract myself I had decided to take an art class in the local high school at night. I thought it could help me to get a few hours away from my stove and sink. The kids usually had homework, and I could leave after dinner. I thought Dan wouldn't object mostly because he was away during the week. I knew he saw painting as "something women did."

And so that first night I went to class, we had dinner early. As we dug into spaghetti and meatballs, six-year-old Martin said, "You guys, listen. I want to tell you something Joshie told me. There's this armless, legless man who drops out of trees onto Cub Scouts, and he, he eats them."

The others passed food, poured milk, started in on him:

"Oh, come *on*, Mart, you don't believe that, do you?" 14-year-old Greg said, helping himself to more bread.

Mart's eyes were wide. "Well, yeah, I do. Joshie says they talked about it at their meeting."

Matt (12) said through a mouthful, "Mart, that's impossible."

"It's true. I know you don't believe me," Mart said, "but it's true. All the man leaves behind is this little pile of bones. And bits of their uniforms, buttons."

"So, OK, how does he get around to do this? With no arms and legs?" said his eldest brother Greg, helping himself to more noodles.

"He pulls himself up," Mart said, "by biting his way up the bark of the trees with his powerful teeth."

The others looked at each other, lowering their eyebrows. "*Sure,* Mart."

"Right." They kept on eating.

As I headed to the car, I saw Mart going around the house, sidling, his back to walls.

Art class was a world away from my daily life. Here the teacher, a kind man with white hair and shabby clothes, chose our subject, and we all sedulously followed his "Dip your number six brush into your Indian Red and a dab of Cerulean." In the end, all our paintings were similar, not quite self-expression.

Then little by little, I began to feel more like my old (once frisky) self, at least in class. My playfulness, frowned on by my in-laws and spouse, returned one night when the teacher left the room. I ran over and switched his painting for mine. When he came back and walked about, he stopped at my desk to exclaim, "Why, this is wonderful! Beautiful job, Anne. I can't tell you how pleased I am that you have improved so much."

The others were snorting and choking with laughter. When I confessed what I had done, he turned bright red and ran from the room. When he returned, he said, "I praised my own work! I'm so embarrassed." I felt bad for embarrassing him.

But I'd do it again.

Another night, as I cleaned up after class, my paint palette flipped out of my hands and landed upside down on the floor. I lifted the palette to reveal a splattered, colorful design beneath. As I stood there admiring this waterscape of paints, our teacher came up behind me to say, "What a beautiful abstract you made!" We smiled at each other, co-conspirators playing at art fantasy. And not "Clean this up at once!"

When our term ended, he suggested I try a class at the Oak Park Art League. So one night, I climbed their creaky stairs to the studio, not knowing what to do. Other people were chatting as they set out their equipment. A burly, good-looking man came in a few minutes later, in work clothes. He sat changing his steel-toed boots for loafers, and glancing at me, said, "What are you working on?" (Not, "hello, my name is ....")

"Me? Nothing. I mean, yet." I tried shrinking into the wall behind me, but he kept on talking.

"Well, let's pick out a subject, and you can get started." Was he the teacher? He didn't sound like he would ever say as the earlier teacher did, "Copy me as I paint this stroke."

Suddenly I was to pick out something I would like to paint? And paint it? Having heard for years from my spouse that I was not capable of making decisions, here was this stranger telling me I could choose a subject and work on it. He handed me a few copies of the *National Geographic* and said, "Find something you like." As he walked away to look at another student's painting in progress, I felt I had been thrown in the deep end of a pool.

I walked around the studio to look at what others were painting: a locomotive in oils, a small girl at the shore in acrylics, still life of lemons on lace in acrylics, a watercolor of a basement window overgrown with weeds. All these night artists had day jobs—driving a truck, designing graphics, architecting, or working as a nurse, office manager, or full-time mom. They laughed, talked among themselves, talked *to* themselves, saying out loud to no one in particular, "This is going just *awful*." Or, "I can't paint. I shouldn't be here."

And no one responded. Apparently, no one was supposed to. The chatter and scrape of chairs and easels, water running, coffee perking made a noisy, happy buzz like the kitchen at home when the children and I put a meal together for a holiday. The old paint-spattered floor squeaked as our teacher, Joe, walked from one artist to another. He stood next to or behind each to comment or pick up a brush and add a lick of paint or two. I heard him say in his rumbling voice: "This is coming along. Keep going."

He wasn't much of a talker. Once I heard, "Set this aside for now, and get going on something else." That turned out to be his way of saying, "Nicely done. Just put a matte around that."

I stumbled into the unlighted storeroom, dragged out an easel, filled a container with water, squirted colors onto my palette tray, and mostly wondered, "Do I belong here?" I didn't know much about watercolor painting, just that I liked it. What I found was that once there, I didn't think about what might be going on at home, the squabbling, whining, fighting about doing the dishes, who had sneaked off to watch TV, or hide in a bathroom–normal routines. I found a photo I liked and started in to lay out the design.

At the end of class as I washed my brushes, two women stopped by the sink to say, "Anne, after class we usually go out for a beer or some wine and a sandwich. Would you like to come?"

I refused, politely. It was already ten o'clock. Out to a bar, *now?* My husband expected me back home in bed.

CONTINUING WITH THERAPY

As I went about my corporate-wife life, I took the train to see my psychiatrist while the kids were in school. When we socialized in the corporate world, I continued to look for people I could talk to about things I loved, like books or going to plays. I still missed my college friends from New York keenly. All had jobs in Manhattan, as I once had, and three had entered the Ursuline convent, a semi-cloistered one where they were not permitted to write letters, accept phone calls, or go home unless a parent died.

Dan had set upon the fast track at work and came home too tired to talk. And when I took my children for checkups to our family doctor, he pointed out that for me to be a "really good mother, a woman needs to de-educate herself so she can be in touch with her children's feelings and thoughts."

Try as I might to conform, I couldn't de-educate myself. Dan traveled much of the time to Stockholm or Reykjavik or Munich on business. For the most part, I was on my own with five young children, and I had drifted closer and closer to serious depression. My doctor brother said, "I know what you need: you'd feel better if you got a job. A job and your own car."

I continued helping Dan write his talks and reports and meeting with candidates for jobs as his direct reports. I also took part in the role executives' wives played—wear black, drink little, say nothing controversial–and for me, Dan added, "And don't say anything funny!"

After we came back from Aspen, Dan and I arranged a twice-yearly get-together for alumni of the Aspen Executive Seminars. One Aspen group weekend, a CEO said to me, "I'm setting up a Women and Minorities Diversity program. I would love to hire you to run it. You'll be perfect!" I knew I would relish the job, with my youngest in first grade now.

But I'd need consummate tact to get Dan to agree. So I waited until the next night to tell him. I was fixing spaghetti and meatballs for dinner. As Dan pulled into the driveway, Justin (eight) came to the kitchen. It was his turn to do "Before Dinner," and as he got out knives and forks, he said, "You know how I always wanted to buy a guitar? 'Cause I love your Elvis records? Well, I think instead I want to buy a panther."

"Let's see. . . did I put in oregano?" I muttered to myself, opening the spice cabinet. As Mart (six) came into the kitchen, Justin went on, "I figure it would be easiest to keep him up in the attic, back in that storage area? What should I feed him?"

At that point, Dan came in the back door, greeted everyone and poured himself a glass of red wine.

"Justin, you dork," Mart said, "panthers only eat steak. And that's really expensive." He spoke in an extra-loud voice; as the youngest, he had already had the habit of making sure we all heard him.

As Justin set cutlery all on the right side of the plates, he said, "You don't know anything about panthers, Martin. And besides, you aren't part of this family. You are adopted, so shut up.

"Mom, I also need to find out about when you need to start using a whip."

As Dan lounged against the sink, I said, "Dan, I wanted to tell you that Peter Schmidt asked me Saturday if I'd be interested in heading up his Diversity initiative. I told him I'd think about it."

"You *what?*" He shouted, banging down his glass. The boys melted out of sight at once. "You are not going to accept that job! I *will* not allow it! This house and the children are neglected enough as it is!" He put one fist against my throat and with his other hand backed me into a corner. I couldn't breathe. He weighed 100 pounds more than I did.

After that, I didn't pursue it. But the violent arguments with Dan had worsened.

More and more, I felt frightened that my life was out of my control. My nightmares got worse and I lost 35 pounds in just a couple of months. When I sat down, I had to sit on a pillow because I had no fat. As I washed dishes or vacuumed, I thought about hitchhiking down Route 66 to Kansas and waitressing at a truck stop. I could steal another woman's driver's license.

My mother-in-law had disapproved of my being in therapy at all, saying, "Dear, we Catholics deal with problems in Confession. The priests are our psychiatrists. And you have a good sense of humor. That means you can't possibly be depressed."

"My brother thinks I am. He's a doctor, a surgeon, and I value his opinion."

"That brother of yours doesn't seem to know much! Whenever I ask him about my symptoms, he says, 'We didn't cover that in med school.' And besides, dear, psychiatrists just want you to fall in love with them. I know. I went to one once. That's what that psychiatry stuff is all about."

I decided to keep on with my therapy anyway. At the same time, my life with Dan escalated to a point where he broke my nose in an argument. Although I had always believed I *had* to stay for the children's sake, living up to this was harder and harder. I knew I couldn't go home to the East Coast; my father made that clear at my wedding. I had so wanted to make this marriage work.

Divorce was never an option for a Catholic like me. And yes, I had absorbed a great deal of Church doctrine, studying St. Thomas Aquinas at length in high school. He emphasized that "Love was an act of the Will, and one chose to Love." So I felt terribly guilty because I couldn't "choose to love" this man I lived with. He was my assignment from God, and I couldn't handle it. I had thought often about dying, and how it would release me. It felt like the way out.

I began taking long walks in a nearby graveyard while my children were in school. I felt envy for those who slept beneath the fallen leaves.

I never felt lonely as I walked the little bricked paths. In German, their headstones professed vigorous confidence that "Our Redeemer liveth," and a sure knowledge that the souls designated in graven letters are at rest at last. The weight of these inscriptions—and even their surnames—seemed to press them still deeper into the earth: Nikolas Hakendorfer, Johanna Fleischfresser, Grunhilde Jarzomkowski.

I felt them surround me as I walked among their resting places. I saw them returning from a shadowy world, their bodies transparent, wrapped in shroud-like garments, to possess their small plots of land, moving gently, quietly past me, at peace with themselves and each other. As a child, I was terrified of passing through cemeteries, but now I found their inhabitants not at all forbidding. Though they resided at such close quarters, here there was no rancorous neighborly dispute, no petty envy of the more opulent markers or tombs. The atmosphere of acceptance soothed me.

Meanwhile our lives went forward with school events, gymnastics meets, my art class, and Dan's traveling. He had just been invited to a conference on computer technology in Madrid in November. He asked me to go with him, and I thought the trip would be a chance to talk to Dan about therapy together—couples therapy.

Then one night after I had another bout with Dan, I called my brother in New York who said, "I'm frightened for you, Anne. Leave. Now. Take your credit card. Go to a hotel."

"What about my kids?"

"They'll be fine. Just get out. Now."

But that night, I didn't.

MADRID

I was packing for my flight alone to Madrid via Paris. It was 1973 and Dan had flown to Paris earlier that day for a conference on computer technology to bring Spain up to speed on computers. The Franco government had contacted Dan's boss and asked for an expert to lead them into the tech world. At that time, Fascist Spain was cut off from innovations such as electronic data processing, and Dan's banking world was already buzzing about electronic funds transfer.

Our host in Madrid had invited all speakers' wives, and I thought this trip would give me time alone with Dan to get him to agree to try Couples Therapy. I hired a friend's daughters to stay with the children in our absence.

As I packed, Martin, five years old, came into my bedroom. He brought his Tigger hand puppet to me.

"I want you to take Tigger," Mart said, looking serious. "He can guard you and keep you safe on the plane." Mart knew I dreaded flying so far away.

I teared up. He loved his little puppet and slept with him each night. I hugged it against me and said, "Mart, that's so thoughtful! I would love to have him with me."

He tucked Tigger in the top of my suitcase, with his little head sticking out.

"I'm afraid Tigger might get stolen or lost over in Spain. I'll travel to a lot of places, and he might get away from me. Please keep him safe here?"

As I gave Tigger back, Mart's little face crumpled and quiet tears slid from his closed eyes. I wrapped my arms around them both.

"I love Tigger, too," I said. I'd have loved to take him.

I flew first to Paris, then boarded a train for Hendaye on the Spanish border. I knew almost nothing about Franco's Spain; all news coverage of Spain was held closely inside the regime. Years later I learned that Franco had hoped to join Spain to the Axis Powers—Nazi Germany and Mussolini's Italy—as another fascist state.

Late at night I disembarked at Hendaye alone. I was about to cross the frontier, alone and in the dark.

My suitcases are heavy. I look to the November stars high above the six-foot high coils of barbed wire on either side of me. I am the only one walking through the Spanish frontier now, and there are no porters at 2 a.m.

I set one suitcase down and carry the other forward thirty feet or so. Then I set that one down and go back for the first. When I have the two together I sit on them and rest. Through rolls of barbed-wire, I can look into the glittering eyes of the frontier police. They wear brown uniforms and carry rifles with fixed bayonets. They silently watch me drag my luggage.

I have detrained from Paris to cross the frontier into Franco's Spain on foot. There is no other transportation.

Before I left, Dan told me how much he looked forward to being with me without our children. And while we are alone, I need to talk to him about our marriage.

This is a long walk—up one corridor and all the way back along more barbed wire. As I lift one heavy suitcase, I recall it contains the three pounds of *Fodor: Guide to Europe*. Fodor has promised me a deluxe hotel with every modern amenity. I hope that includes someone to help with this luggage.

At the far end of the barricades, the seated guard asks for my passport. The passport photo taken three years ago shows me with four of my children. There is a light X across their faces. The guard says, *"Donde?"*

I am looking at the ground and falling asleep on my feet. I do not notice he points to the children. I muzzily assume he wants to know where my suitcases are. I bend, touch the suitcases, say, *"Aqui."* I know almost no Spanish.

He looks grave, slaps his hand on their pictures. He now barks, *"Donde! Donde! Los niños!"* The guard behind him steps forward and after a time, we three sort out where my children are without my having to open the luggage. I may now proceed to the station and catch the train for Madrid.

My train pulls into Madrid just after dawn. Dan will fly in from Paris later today, so I go directly to the Mindanao Hotel in the old part of the city. Here I surrender my passport as all visitors must. Inside our room a huge bouquet of fresh-cut flowers greets me, and on the vanity table sits a large gold-foil-wrapped box of chocolates, the dark kind. Despite their luscious aroma, I have no appetite.

"Every modern amenity" seems not to include toilet paper. However, a large brass handle on the wall presents itself, with *"Servicio"* inscribed above it. I twist the handle.

Nothing.

I try pulling it. It comes off in my hand, and from down the hall, I hear a muffled shriek. Is that the maid, shouting she will be right with me? My Spanish is quite poor. I place the handle carefully inside the laundry hamper and lie down to think.

Several hours later, the phone beside me rings. In urgent *Español,* a woman implores me to . . . something.

I ask for "English, *por favor.* My Spanish is not good."

She slowly pieces together, "All . . . the ladies . . . are . . . waiting . . . for you."

Most men taking part in this information services conference have brought spouses, and the *Ministro de Informacion* has arranged a Ladies' Program, she continues. "Surely, you have a copy of the Programme!" At this moment, "we are to visit a *Fundacion,* a favorite project of the Generalissimo, an Orphans' Hospital."

I remind my caller that I had written in advance that I would not take part in the Ladies' Program. I had planned to attend my husband's talks at his request.

Haltingly, she tells me, "You are to attend the Ladies' Program whenever you are free. All the ladies are to attend."

"Yes, but right now, I want to sleep."

"That does not matter. You are to attend."

I gently lay the phone down on the pillow next to me, so as not to disturb her further. I fall back to sleep.

The conference is to open at an elegant luncheon above a small pastry shop in Old Madrid. As I climb the narrow staircase to the second-floor banquet room, I mull in dread how I must arrange with Dan to have our Talk.

Candles burn in silver sconces along the linenfold mahogany paneling. Sumptuous crystal chandeliers reflect in the dark polished wood above our heads as I introduce myself to Arne Groot from Amsterdam. We companionably sip sherry near an oval table set for about thirty, several goblets at each place. Arne shows off his English like a pleased child as he says, "This Amontillado is quite excellent, is not it?"

I nod and glance at the pyramids of fruit built on gleaming epergnes. I see the imperious head steward direct his platoon of waiters using discreet coughs and finger snappings. From above his fine aquiline nose, he surveys the room and everyone in it like a Mother Superior.

Arne holds his glass to the light from the chandelier above us, then catches sight of a woman just entering the banquet room. She heads directly for us, crossing the room with the bearing of a general. Tall, imposing, hair beautifully coiffed, she speaks before she reaches us: "Aah. There you are."

The pinpoint pupils in her Delft-blue eyes impale me as she says, "And where were *you* this morning?"

"Me?" I ask.

"Yes! We all went to the *Fundacion* today and we *missed* you. *All* the other Ladies made an effort to be there. Except you."

Shocked by the force of her manner, I murmur, "I am sorry you missed me."

"It seems to me," she continues, "I remember our interpreter telling us that she called you. And! That you were in bed." A pleasant smile, as sweet and cold as sorbet. Her manner reminds me of my mother-in-law.

"That Ladies' Program, you know, is really quite well-arranged. It shouldn't be passed by, even by you." Another smile. "Now. What are you planning to do tomorrow?"

Arne steps between us to introduce me to his wife, Britta, formally, and I note she is quite a bit taller. Unimpeded, she continues at me: "There are no general sessions in the afternoon. The Ladies are scheduled for the Prado. Everyone should see it. I myself have seen it many times. When else were you planning to go to the Prado?"

I mumble that "I will go between sessions," and quell an instinct to ask her what Prado means, since she seems to think I'm ignorant.

"Nonsense! We have an excellent interpreter. She speaks all the official languages of the conference. It's much, much better if we all do things together, don't you agree?" Smile. "I'll go find Sofia now and tell her to expect you on our bus."

Directly behind me, the faint creak of a highly starched collar startles me, and I turn. A wizened waiter in a shiny, immaculate tuxedo a size too large holds an ornate silver tray. Glasses holding amber liquid march in rows of four across it. Arne and I each take another glass and the tray moves on, deftly offered left and right throughout the rapidly filling room. A second waiter moves in the wake of the sherry, with heavy silver bowls in each hand. Black olives arrayed in neat rows in one, salted chicory nuts in the other. The waiter's moist dark eyes match the olives. He turns back once and gives me a tiny smile.

Too late I realize the olive has a pit, and I sense Mother Superior can see me palming it. As I debate whether to wash it down with more sherry, Dan comes toward us, addressing Arne.

"Isn't this great sherry? Terrific. Terrific! Oh, hi there, sweetheart. You know, Arne, I drink a lotta sherry back in the States, but it's not this stuff! I guess this is that *fino* I read about in Fodor. Say. Listen. Do you think we could get bigger glasses? These little dinky things . . . hey, waiter!"

Another tuxedoed Madrileño passes us, armed with bowls filled with almonds lined in precise formation. Grabbing his sleeve, Dan repeats his question. The waiter pauses, regards Dan in silence, glances at Mother Superior who watches us intently, looks down at his sleeve, raises his eyebrows. Without a word, the waiter gently raises his arm, frees it, moves on.

"Oh, well," says Dan, "I'll just have to take two at a time. So, Arne." Arne chokes, swallows, as Dan continues, "Hey, I read that talk of yours on artificial intelligence, and I want you to know that I think it is first-rate! Really terRIFic! What did you think of mine?"

"The one on the ego-less programming environment?" Arne asks.

"Yeah, yeah, right. A lot of people think it's marvelous, but that's just . . ."

Dan breaks off as a British couple comes into the circle, and Britta returns as I spot an ashtray into which I slip my olive pit. Two heavyset Bavarians enter the group, and Dan, grabbing their hands, says easily, "Hi, there! Say, let's get some introductions going here. This is Mike Crawford from IBM/London and his wife, Wendy, and you can just call me Dan."

"Ja. So!" One big German beams affably. "Und you may call me Herr Oberlander, und this is my associate, Doktor von Schaufenbuel. You are Americans. We watch often your 'Bonanza' at home in Munich!"

He greets Britta and Wendy as Dan signals the waiter for more sherry. The rest of us stand in silence looking away from each other. Then Arne asks, "Has anyone heard yet from IBM/Tel Aviv?"

"Say, I hear some of their top guys are supposed to be here," Dan says. "They're into some really sophisticated stuff over there. By the way, I'm giving a talk for them next month. Did anybody here ever stay at the Hotel Daniel-Tel Aviv? I was wondering about the food there."

The Germans look sour and say nothing, while Mike says: "None of my Jewish friends at IBM would willingly go into a fascist state like this one."

Dan: "My invitation indicated they just want to get up to speed on information technology."

Hoping to bring up something neutral besides television, I say, "Did any of the IBM/Paris people get here yet?"

"Oh, the French!" Arne seizes on this. "You *know* how they are. They probably haven't even yet responded."

"The French!" says Doktor von Schuafenbuel, "They are why we can never have a workable united states of Europe. They are...," shaking his head, "impossible to deal with."

In the midst of this prickliness, an ascetic, distinguished-looking man approaches. At once I feel great respect for him. The group falls silent as Doctor Luis Petit-Hinojosa looks directly at each of us, greeting us individually. His intelligent blue eyes are remarkably kind. "I hope that the next few days will be helpful and productive. For all of us," he says in slow, precise English. "Unfortunately, the Generalissimo cannot be here in Madrid to meet with us as he had planned, but he is following the conference with intense interest."

Even Dan is silent while Dr. Hinojosa continues, "The Generalissimo has offered us this dining room, his favorite, for us to meet in, and he hopes we will enjoy it. I much regret that our bullfighting season has just ended. I think you would have found bullfighting refreshing and . . . exhilarating. Especially after the talk sessions."

With a few more gracious remarks, he inclines his head, then moves on to the next group.

We stand quietly for a moment, then Dan says, "Say! Speaking of bullfighting, one of our IBM guys has a great story. One of their salesmen got appendicitis over here last year. You know, that's a big fear these guys have: getting sick away from home and American doctors and all. Everybody knows American medicine is the best in the world, and I'll drink to that!"

The others glance around warily as Dan goes on even louder, "So anyway, there isn't time for this guy to get back to the States. Or even to London. That's the second best place for medicine. This is an emergency, so the hotel doctor recommends a surgeon here in Madrid who's supposed to be their best. The doctor insists that the surgeon is so good that he leaves only this little tiny scar. Like that," Dan holds his right thumb and forefinger an inch apart. "Beautiful work. Guaranteed. So, OK, he goes ahead, and he has this operation, see."

Arne and the others have stopped drinking to listen.

"And when he comes to, he checks for the scar right off. And sure enough, it's this little tiny thing. But there's this big bandage around his head, see, so he rings for the nurse and asks her why the bandage."

The men seem fascinated, while Britta looks around bored.

"So the nurse tells him that the other doctors assisting decided that the surgeon did such great work that they voted to give him Both Ears!"

Dan and Arne guffaw. After a brief pause while they look at each other, the British couple joins in. The Germans continue to smile politely, sure the punch line is imminent.

We are summoned to lunch. My nearest table-mates are men from the Ministry of Information, one of their wives, and a man from Brazil. Multilingual chatter patters around me. Four languages only are allowed at this conference, and the man from *Brasilia* fulminates about Portuguese: "It is not an official language! I have prepared my talk in Portuguese!" Tears start from his eyes and his voice rises to a falsetto as he tells us, "This slights Spain's oldest friend! And nearest neighbor!"

He waves his hands, points out that "*French* is an official language! Yet no one from France has come!" He will go to the Consul-General in the morning, he shouts, and "I will deliver my talk in Portuguese!"

The slim, fashionable woman to my left is clearly enjoying herself. She grins at me often, especially during a course the hosts are proud of, she tells me. It is *cocido*. She smiles. "You . . . like?"

To me, perhaps because I'm not hungry it tastes like it might be a Ken-L-Ration meatloaf, but I have had my share of nationalistic discourse. I manage to smile and nod.

"You have . . . you have . . . you have children?"

I hold my hand up to show how many: five.

She crows triumphantly, shows me six, pointing to her smallest finger: "*Nena!* One month!"

I like talking with her, but it exhausts me. I try the man on my right, who stares off at the ceiling, favoring me with his elegant profile. He and I negotiate our language congruencies: some French, a bit of English. He tells me he is called Señor Ricardo de Calle de la Loup, and that he works directly under Dr. Hinojosa.

There is a Rioja wine to accompany our luncheon; Sr. Street-of-the-Wolf lifts his glass. I lift mine, expecting a toast. Instead he stares carefully through it at the chandelier. He sniffs the bouquet thoughtfully, then looks across at Dr. Hinojosa who watches him closely. Senor clears his palate with a crust of bread, tastes the wine, rinsing it 'round his mouth, chewing it slowly. Another sip . . . he pulls a face of distaste.

All the waiters behind our chairs watch attentively. He gives a faint negative shake of his head to the host, lifts a slender forefinger. Mother Superior comes at once to his side. Their sibilant exchange is brief. At a snap of Mother Superior's fingers, the phalanx of waiters steps forward like a chorus line to remove the offending beverage.

Far down the table, I hear, "Hey! Where're ya going with my wine? I haven't even tasted it yet!" I'm glad I sit this far away. The men around me glance at each other, look down, say nothing.

I ask Sr. Street what is wrong with the wine. He sniffs disdainfully, says with finality, "That wine . . . was impossible. It could never stand up to a cheese!"

I want to take a quick sip before my glass disappears but the waiters watch me. Dan continues arguing with them, so I will carry our American standard alone, not give in to my wish.

A new bottle, a *Valdepeñas* this time, appears at Sr. Street's elbow. He tastes it. He smiles. This wine passes the test. It will meet even a strong cheese without compromising itself. We can all relax.

He turns to me then with a charming though haughty smile. He tells me Dr. Hinojosa has "great hopes for this conference. There are problems with . . . accessibility to data" in the ministry.

I had so hoped he wouldn't talk about systems. So often over the years when Dan wasn't available, his business associates assumed they could talk just as easily with me about his technology expertise.

My French isn't up to "user-sheltered programs" and "embedded logic." I sidestep and ask if he anticipates that over time, Franco's successor will want to gather data in much the same way and for the same reason as the Generalissimo.

Sr. Street turns, faces me directly. "We do not discuss the successor to Franco." His tone is icy.

Brief silence. Surely what will happen when Franco passes on must come up? The Generalissimo is in his seventies, but the subject of age, too, must be taboo.

"Your United States has been quick to point out surveillance in a police state as unconscionable," Sr. Street continues. "Yet what about your Mr. Nixon's White House Enemies list? And those tapes, what kept him from burning them?"

I feel I must choose my every word with care as he goes on, "In this country that would never have happened. That your *Presidente* feels he must resign! If he believed what he was doing was in the best interests of the government, for the . . . general good, then to resign is unthinkable.

"You see, Anna, the real problem is that your *Presidente* was, as we say here in Madrid, not working close to the bull."

There must be something we can talk about. I look around the table, now getting cleared for dessert, and see a sherry glass. Poe's "Cask of Amontillado" from high school English comes to mind. Has Sr. Street read it, I ask? He mistakes my meaning, looks horrified. He tells me he thinks I have told him since I arrived I have consumed an entire cask of sherry. My working in French is like swimming underwater.

Sofia, the Ladies' interpreter, rises and passes out packages like a delighted child offering gifts. These, she explains in French, then English, then Spanish, "are the work of Spanish artisans. You are to open them now." And I realize that the more I hear her talk despite Britta's praise for her language skills, Sofia speaks none well.

Arne sits across from me, and I see him puzzling over an enormous dark green leather ashtray with two silver buttons on the side. He and I decide it must be an electric ashtray. The rest of our time at the table I see him playing at pressing the buttons, then watching carefully. Nothing ever happens.

All the gifts are handsome, most often enamel-and-brass letter openers or scissors. My package contains a set of military hairbrushes, heavy with olive-green leather and chrome. They look like curry combs. Since we have no horse, I'll give them to Dan or one of my four boys. I don't dare leave them in a Hotel Mindanao waste basket. The Generalissimo will know the instant I check out.

Much later that day, I return to my room to bathe and dress for the "gala dinner at 10 p.m." I open the tap and the water spills into the tub with force. Hot, comforting, healing steam rises. I inhale deeply.

Our phone rings. It's Wendy: the gala requires "full evening dress," she has just realized, and she and Mike have brought none from London. "Mike has no tuxedo; we both want to know if you will wear a long gown?"

I look up from the phone to see a large wet stain on the carpet spreading rapidly towards me from the bathroom. The tub!

Barefoot I run to watch the bath water cascading down the sides of the tub, lapping gently at the doorsill, spilling over to inundate the bedroom rugs. I wade in, turn off the water, throw all the thick towels I had planned to wrap myself in onto the floor. They submerge. I feel guilty and frantic. I grab both bedspreads, throw these on the tile floor. When all are underwater I return to the phone to ask Wendy, still waiting to find out about my dress, to call *Servicio* for me.

The maid arrives quickly, walks in, sees the wet carpeting, the soaked towels, the bedspreads she must account for. Arms upraised, she shrieks at the ceiling, "Agua! AGUA! A-G-U-A! Madre de Dios!" Sobbing, shouting, she runs into the hall. Doors bang, other voices shout back.

Returning immediately with mops, buckets, piles of cloth, more towels, she never stops the torrent of words in which "norte-americana" and "Dios" predominate. She works furiously, clanging buckets, jabbing mops, viciously banging handles against doors and walls. Her hair falls in her eyes, and punctuated by sobs, her soliloquy gathers speed and resonance.

At first I try to help, grabbing for a mop handle, but the look in her eyes terrifies me. I suspect I have infringed the class barrier. I go in and lie on our bed to finger the few pesetas and bits of lint in my hotel bathrobe pocket.

The sounds of finishing up come from inside the bathroom. I stand in the doorway, offer what I have from my pocket (sans lint). The sun of her smile warms the room after her cloudburst.

She leaves beaming.

Much later that night, I and the Crawfords and Groots and Dan find ourselves together at a banquet table. Britta wears daytime business dress, as do Wendy and I. But hundreds of others at this dinner have obeyed the summons to appear in formal attire. Consequently, the staff has hidden us in a brightly lit area where waiters keep trays and serving carts. I groan to myself as we sit; I like Wendy, and Britta's English is superb. But what a pain she is, even in short bursts.

Looking off to the other tables, I see women in glamorous long gowns, bosoms frankly exposed in the candlelight. Arne mocks the formality, and says, "In Amsterdam we never have dinners like this."

After a silence, Dan sets his wineglass directly in front of him, and says, lowering his voice. "Now that we've started the conference, I realize what they really want is background on sophisticated systems. They plan to collect data, lots of it, on private citizens."

"As I talk with the members of the Ministry, I realize they think this is completely justified," Mike says.

"But under their Bill of Rights," Arne says, "the Franco government can abolish freedom of speech or movement. Even residence. Or associates! They have themselves legally absolved in advance." He shrugs and takes another sip of the excellent wine.

"And they call that the Charter of Privilege!" Mike grimaces sarcastically.

Britta's eyes snap dangerously, and she all but spits out, "This is so like the Occupation. It's as fresh as yesterday that my father and brother lost their lives to the Boches!"

At midnight we have more speeches to listen to; I see women drooping over their dessert, dozing, allowing their heads to sag back, eyes closed. The Minister for Information speaks at length, extolling international understanding and brotherhood.

Afterward, the six of us head for a disco in the hotel basement. It is 1:30, merely the shank of the evening for Madrileños. Inside all I sense is texture; I cannot see even my feet. The music guides us as we stumble to some low seats. As we sit, Leon Redbone's "Witch Queen of New Orleans" surrounds us. Apparently it's light enough for the band to recognize and salute us Americanos.

Gradually my eyes adjust to the absence of light. Ahead I see an elderly man in evening dress slumbering in front of his untouched drink. His chin slumps on his chest. Wisps of hair stand out straight from the top of his head.

Didn't I see him upstairs? The waiter gently prods the sleeping man, but when our wine arrives, he dozes off again. I hear The Guess Who's "American Woman, Stay Away From Me" in the background as we chat about computer crime (in English, thank God).

"Come on, swindling the computer is like a little kid playing with an electric train," Dan says loudly. "It's just amoral."

"What do you think motivates a programmer," Mike asks, "to outwit a big corporation and bilk it of millions?"

"Because it's there, like Mallory said?" Dan asked.

"No! People resent the big men at the top. For one thing, corporate heads refuse to spend the time to learn to use computers. I know; I try to get them to Executives Only sessions. They refuse," Mike says, annoyed.

"Programmers are a breed apart," Arne says. I want this conversation to continue, no matter how dull. I don't want to be alone with Dan, to confront him, and yet I must.

"Yeah," Dan says, "this is just their way of tipping the power pyramid on its side. And besides (he laughs affably), there are no legal precedents, so it's actually a perfect crime."

"And no witnesses," Mike says. "The evidence can be programmed to destroy itself."

"Sure! It's a sweetheart of a setup," Dan says. "And most corporations won't report these robberies. They don't want to look stupid.

"And the guy who siphons off the money," Dan continues laughing, "he just has to be brilliant. Hey! Anyone can rob at gunpoint, but screwing a computer! God! What a great way to retire early."

At this, the lights come up full in our faces. Nearby, a rock group has come in and starts wiring up their gear. The men are in skin-tight jumpsuits. The lead singer, a husky, rough-skinned blonde, huge shoulders bulking out of a yellow sequinned dress, sounds like Neil Sedaka. They look at us with loathing.

At the first burst of their amplified sound, the old man starts up with a cry. The waiter goes to him at once to help him find his way to the door. The tufts of hair still stand out from his head as he walks away confused.

We can't stay here and talk, and my heart sinks as we all part company. I hope Dan drank enough to fall asleep at once.

The next morning we wake late, because yes, Dan had had more than his usual amount of alcohol, and we rush to the conference table. At each place stands a stack of prepared speeches, handouts, diagrams,

Gantt charts. I sit behind Dan with copies, noting that his are in English. All this plus the gifts for our children and the military hairbrushes will make closing the suitcases on the last day a real problem. I will need to find someone heavy to sit on my suitcases if Dan reacts to my news as I expect he will. Sr. Street is sleeping, but at the lectern stands Dr. von Schaufenbuel; definitely the best candidate. How should I phrase my request, my German being only slightly better than my Spanish?

Von Schaufenbuel speaks of trends in data processing, particularly capabilities of integrated circuit technologies. Listening to anyone read aloud a speech is hard enough, but sitting there with the translation in front of me ("meta-level problems"), I feel his guttural sounds drill into my spirit. Still, anything to fill the time until I am alone again with Dan. Who now steps to the podium. He had wanted me there to listen to him. And so I settle in to "applications of codifiability, smart terminals with bubble memories, Boolean logic, serial *vs.* direct access philosophies, areal density, misprioritizing, and inter-and multidisciplinary skills requisite for heuristic problem solving."

At last, the interpreter steps up to share the microphone with him. A question gets repeated in Spanish, French, and German. Then the answer, the same. During the coffee break, Arne comes over to tell me how wonderful Dan is. "A great man! So knowledgeable, your husband. And intelligent! You know I barely understand him, so that means he is brilliant!"

He complains next about the Austrians, who have gone to El Escorial instead of attending. I had noticed that the social functions, the sumptuous lunches, the gracious late-night dinners, the tours are all well-attended. But our conference sessions are not.

"And what can one expect?" Arne sips the excellent coffee from a porcelain cup. "The Viennese can never be serious. Too fun-loving! After World War II when their entire city had been razed to the ground, what did they rebuild first? The Opera House! Not factories! Opera!"

Nationalism again? I ask, "What did you think of the talk by Dr. von Schaufenbuel?"

Mike joins us as Arne says, "Too much ground to cover. I don't think even the Spanish knew what they wanted us to accomplish. They have been living behind closed doors for too long as far as data processing is concerned. It will require more than this conference to update them."

Dan bursts in, "Their objectives should have been made clear before we got here. Everyone prepared talks on different subjects. If these people really want to develop a national data bank on their citizens, that wasn't made clear. And it's not what we came for."

"We will cover what we can," Arne says evenly.

I speak up, "I had a few moments last night with the Minister for Information. When I told him I thought it was wrong to collect data on private citizens, he looked flabbergasted. Part of it was that I spoke up at all, being a woman, but he said, 'But this is a great convenience! Don't you understand? What if someone should fall ill? And no one knew about it? This is a protection for our people!' And he walked away from me."

"Yes," Mike says, "some of the Minister's men said just now, 'You must remember that the Generalissimo has brought our country great peace.'"

"What I'm hearing," Dan says, "is that they've trumped up excuses for this civil espionage. If there's another conference, I don't think our people should be involved."

As the others walk back, Dan leans in close to me, grabs my upper arm to squeeze fiercely and says, "What in God's name did you say that to the Information Minister for? Now you've made him think I can't control my own wife!" He looks furious.

With Arne signaling to him from across the floor, Dan says, "Don't do that again, and don't tell any jokes tonight at dinner. Just let me do the talking." Wearing a broad smile, he catches up to Arne.

The Ladies' Program

In the meantime, the Ladies have been lunching at a magnificent paella restaurant, and I join them there. This is the afternoon the Ladies are scheduled for the Prado. Aboard a yellow bus with Corinthian leather seats, we arrive at the entrance. The lack of patrons entering and leaving make me suspicious. As we park, our interpreter, Gloria remembers, "The Prado is closed due to it being that feast day of a saint." Some discussion here about just which saint in Spanish and French, but she throws up her hands, pointing out "So many feast days! They cause the Prado to close frequently."

Gloria and Señora Petit-Hinojosa deplore the end of bullfighting season. "How you all would have loved it!" Gloria tells us. Señora then offers an alternative with Gloria's help: about sixty-nine kilometers outside the city, she has a summer home. Would we like to see it?

We would. She is delighted, happy as a little girl about sharing it with us while our spouses update her husband for the Generalissimo. As our bus lurches along the outskirts of Madrid well above the speed limit, I talk with the women from Austria in French. One is a remarkably pretty, dark-haired girl who earlier had avoided talking. She travels with her father on all his business trips, she tells us. She entertains for him at home, her mother being dead these many years. She answers my questions politely and patiently, but without interest. She seems to prefer looking out the window at the peaceful afternoon with its cobalt blue skies.

As I work to make conversation, I hear Britta Groot behind me saying in English to Wendy, "When *I* first went to Paris, *my* French wasn't very good either."

I settle back to look out the window myself. We pass scrub pines and dry sandy hills. Yet the clarity of the air sharpens my perceptions, and I think how wonderful it would be to bring paints and brushes out here.

The bus halts near an old railway sleeping car pitched out lengthwise from the side of a rather steep hill. Sturdy metal structures support the extended end. Sand surrounds the car and in the distance, I see a few low trees with platforms built around them and benches underneath.

The protruding end of the railway car holds the entrance, and the Ladies climb down from the bus. They stand looking at the six-foot ladder that they now must mount to get inside the car. The Ladies are concerned about their stockings. Gloria tries to raise their spirits by saying, "Eet will be eenteresting, no? Our adventure, no?" She no doubt hears Britta on the sidelines saying "How FUNny! Why, how very funny!"

We climb the short ladder and step inside. And then I see why the car protrudes as it does. The Hinojosas had chosen this hillside for its view of the surrounding country, lovely, hilly, and visible from every window. We walk slowly, visiting the club car first with its wonderful overstuffed easy chairs. The all-inlaid paneling combines various woods to form floral designs around the words "Spanish Railway System" (in Spanish).

With the fifteen of us in there, it feels crowded. We move on through the dining room, with its tables and chairs of solid mahogany. Next, individual sleeping areas; each of the four children has one. Several others are for the parents and their guests, all neatly made up and with the magnificent paneling. The tiny kitchen lies at the car's end, with its electric generator and water supply, now shut down for the winter.

From the kitchen's back door, we step directly onto the hill; this is the embedded end. Most of women seem amused, but only Britta says so. Her laugh sounds like glass breaking, and today she laughs often.

Farther up the hill is a small shelter where the three Hinojosa boys keep their sports equipment. Bicycles hang from the ceiling above a huge bin of fencing masks and bibs. Foils are mounted on the walls, and below them sit golf clubs and soccer balls. When we ask our hostess about the giant sunfish painted swimming across the floor, she tells us, "My eldest son painted that." She smiles affectionately as she looks at it.

"Is there no place for your children to swim?" asks Britta.

"No, too far from the ocean," our hostess says through Gloria. This reminds the Ladies that they are thirsty, and our hostess "regrets that there is no water with everything closed down." She goes back inside and comes out with a bottle of Fanta cherry soda, which the Ladies share.

The wind is rising and the sun has moved low in the sky. The air has turned chilly. The others start down the hill to the bus that waits by a stand of low trees. The driver sits on the front steps of the bus reading a thick, leather-bound book.

Señora waits for me and we, the last to leave, walk together slowly down the hill. She asks me in bits and pieces of French, English and Spanish if it is "not true that old railway sleeping cars are collectors' items in the United States? Are they not valued highly there?"

Usually vivacious, she looks at me with eyes filled with hurt and puzzlement. I assure her, "Yes, in the U.S., they are greatly cherished." She has shared an intimate part of her family life with us. And the Ladies were merely amused.

As we walk, she tells me, "Dr. Hinojosa likes to come out here on weekends, even in winter. Sometimes by himself. At home in the big city apartment with all the servants, we have much official entertaining. Our boys and even our daughter like the freedom of being here — with no servants. And the city is no place for children to run free."

She tells me our conference means a great deal to her husband and his work. She hopes it will resolve some of his difficulties. "Before it started, he worked until five in the morning. And he is now exhausted."

When Señora comes down to the bus, the driver having ignored the Ladies twittering nearby, immediately rises, puts his book away, stands at attention.

She and I sit together on the ride home. We don't talk much, but I feel little need to. I hear Gloria halfway back in the bus say to Wendy, "Is great honor, no? For someone . . . from nobility to show us their private summer home. She is *hidalga*."

And farther back, I can hear Britta sitting with the Austrians, bursting into peals of laughter, "But how amusing this was! Don't you think?"

I had read in Fodor the section devoted to what the women of Europe were like: French, German, Scandinavian, Italian. He also included notes on to what degree they are pickup-able.

But there was nothing about the women of Franco's Spain. I wonder if he ever met any like Señora.

That evening the conference participants and their escorts are scheduled for a flamenco club in Madrid's Old Quarter for dinner. One female dancer seems to find Dan particularly attractive, and the men on both sides of the table laugh openly about how she smolders at him, and how intense appears her interest. Dan, puzzled, often shakes his head. "What are you all talking about?" He asks me to explain what's going on, yet her attraction to him is so strong I can almost taste it.

As each dancer takes a turn in the spotlight, the other dancers say loudly to her what sounds like "cal-may! . . .calmar." The entire restaurant becomes engaged in this magnetism. I feel mortified. I also feel like calling out to her, "Yes, take him! I'm going to leave him!" Yet in front of these business associates, I must maintain my nun-like silence.

She gets more and more impassioned as she seems to throw herself towards him, and the men from Brazil, Portugal and Spain seem especially delighted. They signal to me that I should encourage him to go along with this. Would they want their wives to as well, I wonder. But the rest of the evening passes without incident, and we fall into bed without talking.

The last morning, I'm even more conscious how attendance at the conference has dwindled. At dinner each evening, the other participants would glow over trips they have taken that day instead of meeting as the Generalissimo had required. They rave about Alhambra. The Royal Palace. Escorial. The Alcala. Toledo. "And the food! Fascistic countries are all alike: The food is marvelous!"

As the final session ends and attendees pack their briefcases and notebooks, Dr. Hinojosa comes to me and Dan. Earlier, he had asked each participant to be there at the last session. Now he asks, "Do you think the United States would sponsor a conference similar to this one?"

Dan looks at him, "You mean *in* the United States?"

"Yes, of course. Preferably on your East Coast. New York City or possibly Washington."

Dan starts to answer at the same time that I do. We step on each other's words. "Yes . . . well . . We can't commit our State Department to anything like that right now."

"Without talking it over with them first, that is," Dan finishes up.

"Well, Dan, what about your firm, then?"

"I'd have to discuss that with my superiors," Dan says.

"Your superiors." Dr. Hinojosa smiles sadly.

"But since most of the participants would be coming from Europe," Dan says, "why not a more central location? Milan, for instance. Or," he turns to Mike who joins us, "how about London?"

Mike, in a more junior position than Dan, gives him an agonized look. He also demurs. As soon as Dr. Hinojosa was out of earshot, Mike mumbles, "I wonder where he ever got our names in the first place?"

"I can see why *I* would be asked; I do have 500 people reporting to me," Dan says. "And our bank was the first to get into this technology."

"But these fascists need to interact with much more senior management," Mike says. "Especially for this! His contacting you and me makes me wonder about the quality of the Generalissimo's intelligence."

I feel bad for Dr. Hinojosa, but relieved that it's over. To hold a conference on setting up a database with information on every citizen—health profiles, personal problems and financial status—in the United States seems unthinkable.

Dan's conference broke up with the people who arranged for it expressing disappointment at its results. We made our farewells. It was my view that those who set it up didn't quite know what they hoped to learn. Spain was still a fascist state under Generalissimo Franco–closed to the outside world.

I thought that though they hosted us elegantly, they had a great deal of research ahead, and they needed higher level experts than those they had invited from the UK, Austria, France, and, of course, us. Dan's expertise was in banking technology, not in gathering personnel data.

On the train leaving Madrid Dan, no longer under pressure to perform at the conference, can listen to me better, I hope. As he opens a book and stares from the window of our private compartment, I say to him, "Dan. I have to talk to you about something: I can't keep on, the way things are between us."

"What? What are you saying to me? What's wrong with our marriage? It's fine! (He slams his book down.) *You're* the one who's always so negative. We have a wonderful marriage! Everybody knows it. Except you."

"Dan, I want you to go to Couples Therapy with me." My voice shakes. He's bringing up Our Wonderful Marriage as he always does. My plan is to offer therapy before I bring up divorce.

"Wait a minute! Is this some dumb-ass idea of your sister's?"

"I really want us to get Couples Therapy."

He grabs my arm and squeezes it hard again. "Is this because of that flamenco dancer? Is that what this is all about? I want you to know (He jabs his forefinger into my clavicle with great force) I *did not* go home with her. And you know that. I could at least get some credit for that. You just don't appreciate what a really wonderful marriage is all about.

"Everybody knows what a great husband I am. Just ask my mother! My friends! I am an Ideal Husband. No one is a better husband than I am."

"You know how much weight I've lost. This is why. I have been dreading telling you this."

"Yes—and that's another thing . . ."

"I really want us to go to therapy together."

"Can't you get it through your head? *I* don't need therapy! Just because you are not happy in such a wonderful marriage is living proof . . . that you're Insane!"

So often my being "insane" has caused me to disagree with him.

"And besides, if you're thinking of leaving, you could never survive without me!" he continues. "Someone like you can't possibly hold a job! Whatever do you think someone like you could do?"

He glares, and I tremble as I often do. His rages are fueled by great energy. Suddenly he lunges, grabs my throat in both hands and starts choking me.

Just then, the conductor opens the compartment door to see our tickets. Dan jumps back, picks up his books, ruffles through his papers. I hand the tickets to the conductor, relieved to have finally managed to get out the words I so dreaded saying. And someone, a stranger, has just seen Dan choke me, tarnishing his image.

I settle back in my seat and look out to the clear sky and ahead to what the outcome of this will mean: No more trips as an executive's wife. More fights. Ostracism by all those, like Arne, who see Dan as a hero.

But also the kindness of friends, and I hope for a lawyer who will understand how formidable Dan can be. And at the end of it all, eventual safety for me.

I remember the unopened box of Spanish chocolates I had packed in my suitcase. Suddenly I feel hungry.

That was a huge step for me. From that time, I stopped losing weight. I did not gain, but I saw this as a victory. I wouldn't have to enter the hospital as Dr. H had threatened, and I wouldn't get the intravenous feedings.

In Paris, Dan saw me off on the plane to Chicago, then went on to Amsterdam for more meetings. I had to return alone to get back to our kids. But I had accomplished what I set out to do: get Dan's agreement about Couples Therapy.

AN UNEXPECTED PASSING

When I entered our front door after flying home from Europe, I saw the babysitters' suitcases sitting next to the door, all packed and ready to leave. I thought this was a signal they had had it. As it was, two of the children had the flu, and I, the mom, was much needed. One boy was on the couch, vomiting into a big steel bowl in the living room. In a daze I paid the sitters, did what I could to soothe the ill kids and get back into my Mom role.

The phone rang a few minutes after the sitters left; it was my doctor brother. He asked, "How was your trip?" He seemed to be choosing his words with care, and this was odd.

I told him I had just arrived, the kids were sick, and I couldn't really talk for more than a few minutes. "Did you call for any special reason?" I said.

"I was thinking about you and just called to see how your trip was," he said.

That was even more odd, but I hadn't time to puzzle it over. He and I never called to chat, but voices called me upstairs. He hung up shortly after.

That night while I slept, the phone rang by my head. It was my sister. She was flying back to our hometown in New York. "Dad died last night," she said. I could hear her sobbing. And she went on, "And you have to come home for his funeral. It's tomorrow morning." She was yelling. "At ten o'clock! My flight is delayed! It's raining and I'm in Seattle!"

"I can't be there tomorrow," I said. I was groggy with sleep, couldn't process what she was telling me. How could this be? Our dad was only sixty-two. "I just paid the babysitters," I said. "They're gone!"

"Get somebody else. You have to come. You have to!"

"Dan is in Amsterdam. I can't leave the kids alone. Two of them are sick."

I held firm despite her insistence that my place was with my kin, not my kids.

And now I understood why my brother had called earlier: My father died as I flew home from Spain.

In the morning, having fed the children, gotten the well ones off to school and the sick ones comfortable, I went to talk to Dr. H. At the start, he said, "Your brother called me yesterday. He wanted *me* to tell you that your father died."

"Why in God's name couldn't he tell me himself?" I said.

"Search me!" Dr. H said. "He must think you are too fragile to talk to."

"My sister called at midnight to tell me. She wanted me at the funeral Mass this morning back in New York. It's going on right now."

The circumstances of my father's passing were all over our home-town paper. He had been the mayor, and he died suddenly. In bed. With his girlfriend.

As soon as he died, his girlfriend had the presence of mind to call the police and not a doctor. They responded to a trouble call about Dad at once, checked his vitals, dressed him in his work clothes and propped him at his desk at his construction company. With the stage set, they then called the coroner who could pronounce him "dead of a heart attack while working late."

One detail that reporters included in their front-page story: No one could find my dad's shoes, so the officers set him at his desk in his sock feet. When my mother saw the story, she said, "Why couldn't they find his shoes?" That fact upset her more than his death. The news articles did not mention his girlfriend; I'm sure the officers kept that out of the police report.

No one ever did find his shoes. But more than shoes were missing: his death occurred the night before he was to testify in a bribery trial involving $40,000 cash alleged to have been given to him. Despite detectives, my uncles, and bankers searching every bank in the state, there was no sign of the $40,000.

Had he taken it? From that day to this, no clue to the money's whereabouts ever came to light. I had my own suspicions. I grieved for the woman who had three young children to raise with no father, and no other resources. She and my father had never married–so this young family was not acknowledged anywhere, certainly not in his obituary.

COUPLES THERAPY

The kids often told me "Dad never listens."

"He doesn't listen to me, either." I agreed. And that hurt.

Our telling him didn't seem to matter to him. However, some time after we returned from Aspen, Dan was reprimanded by his colleagues–managers on his level, that he "didn't listen" and that he "bullied people." One complaint involved his grabbing a subordinate by the tie, and pulling his face close as he said, "Don't you ever disobey my orders again!"

His boss, a senior vice president, had said, "You're not paying attention. You don't listen." Dan told me this one dinner time, and then he said, "I do too listen. I'm an excellent listener."

None of us seemed to get the message across to him.

We did go to Couples Therapy together, and Dr. H pointed out to Dan that he didn't seem to hear what we were talking about.

"I'll go see an ear specialist," Dan said, as he made himself a cup of coffee from the doctor's coffeepot on the desk.

"That's all well and good," the doctor said, "but I'm talking about paying attention."

Dan reached down and took a notebook from his briefcase. He began jotting a few words; I assumed he was transcribing what Doctor H said.

The psychiatrist turned to me, and said, "Anne, tell us what you like about Dan."

Oh, no! I was put on the spot. I couldn't think of anything to say.

"Well?" Dan sounded irritable.

"I … I think you are good with our kids," I said, but knew I was lying. They were often afraid of him. I couldn't think of anything positive right then.

Dan surprised me by saying, "I sometimes get the idea they are afraid of me."

The doctor said, "Of course, children are sometimes afraid of their parents. You, Dan, are a big man, and that can be scary."

I had a sudden recollection of Justin coming back from having lunch with Dan. I heard screaming in the family room and ran in. Justin was alone and crying loudly.

"Whatever is it?" I said, with my arms around him. He was nine.

He said through his sobs, "Daddy makes me feel crazy!"

"He makes me feel that way, too," I said.

When Dr. H asked, "Have you ever hit her?" Dan said, "Oh, I slap her around once in a while, but everybody does that."

Here the psychiatrist looked at him for a long minute. Then he said, "No, Dan, everybody does *not* do that."

"Of *course* they do!" Dan said as Dr. H rolled his eyes at me in silence.

The doctor didn't ask Dan what he thought of me. He did ask Dan to draw two circles that represented what our relationship was.

On his pad, Dan drew a large circle, and said, "There."

"I see only one circle, Dan. Where's the other?"

"They're both there."

"Is one just on top of the other?" the doctor said.

"Yes! That's how close we are!"

"Dan, there isn't any room for Anne to breathe. The circles are supposed to intersect."

"No," Dan said. "You've got it all wrong."

The doctor drew two circles that intersected in the middle, with individual space inside the remainder of the circles. "Here. This is the way a marriage should look."

Dan looked at it, and said, "I like my way better."

Then the doctor said, "I'm afraid our time is up for now."

"For our next appointment," Dan said, "could we make it a double session? I want to get this process over with as quickly as possible."

The doctor agreed and set it up for the following week. As we went to the door, Dan said, "Doctor, about how long do you think it will take to get Annie back to normal?"

Doctor H looked at me for a long minute, then said, "At this point, I can't really estimate."

I remembered the children and me and our talking to Sarah, the school therapist, months ago. She told me when I talked about moving far away from him, "It's important for the children to see what Dan is like for themselves."

At this time, Justin had recurring nightmares about chemical equations that he couldn't resolve. He knew he was good at chemistry, and later on, he found his future in chemistry, but he would wake sweating in terror. Then one night when Dan came in to pick up another child, he said to Justin, "What the hell's bothering you, anyway?" and Justin said, "You. You bother me."

Where he got the courage mystified me; his father was a really big man. But Justin's nightmares seemed to subside after this.

During the two-hour session with Dr. H that next week, as Dan stirred his coffee with his ballpoint pen, suddenly the psychiatrist said, "I have to stop. I'm completely exhausted. Please leave."

"Hey! We are paying for two hours!" Dan said. "Our time isn't up!"

The psychiatrist did look wrung out. He just ushered us out.

We didn't have two-hour sessions after that, and a few weeks later, the doctor ended our session saying, "You two don't belong together. You are not at all suited to one another."

One day that same year, Dan's boss's wife surprised me with a lunch invitation to her country club, and I drove out to Barrington Hills on a lovely summer day. I hoped it was for something nice, like working with her on one of her charities or her literacy committee.

Alice and I seldom spoke over the years; we saw each other only at company functions, dinners where everyone was on their best behavior. A pretty, beautifully dressed woman with a tinkly laugh, she was well-liked throughout the company. Her husband was a senior vice president, so I felt flattered by her invitation.

As we settled in to an elegant lunch of salmon salad, she got directly to why she invited me. "Dan doesn't pay attention to what's going on around him. The chairman is very concerned. We are all hoping Dan will listen to you."

"I have a hard time getting through to him myself..." I started, as my heart sank below my knees. I had hoped for something nicer than being asked to deal with Dan's personality. This not-listening trait of his hurt me often; he paid so little attention to what I said. I had long ago decided to stay in this marriage no matter what. I was determined to suc-ceed at it. But I gradually recognized that his not hearing me meant I was in the marriage by myself.

"You can't tell me anything about him I don't know," she interrupt-ed. "He's just like my brothers!" She smiled winningly.

I thought, *No. He can't be. Or she'd know I can't get through.*

"Anne, I know you can talk to him. My husband asked me to get to-gether with you because no one has been able to make a dent with Dan."

She leaned toward me and her tone became urgent. "Anne, his job is at stake. I'm here to warn you." She looked intently at me, and I dropped my eyes and began creasing and uncreasing the hem of my linen napkin.

I thought, *Oh no, more work for me—to keep my husband in his job.*

I cleared my throat, said, "I'll . . . do my best."

"Dan's spending is out of control," Alice went on. "He ordered a new company-wide computer system that the chairman had vetoed. Dan's signature is binding. Millions of dollars the directors don't want to spend."

As Alice spoke, I remembered Dan pontificating at dinner that "the chairman doesn't know what he's talking about. Our system is obsolete; we've got to stay current. Buying the next generation of computers is mandatory."

She watched me turn my fork over as I thought *I've got to eat. I can't lose any more weight.* I tried a small bit of salmon, choked.

Alice went on, "The chairman told my husband, 'We can't afford Dan.' And the Directors agreed. Everyone has tried to tell him. No one got through so far."

She reached over and gently squeezed my hand. "I *know* you can do it," she said. "Now, what about some dessert? The *tiramisu* here is to die for."

I felt myself freezing inside despite the warm day. We finished lunch shortly and went to her nearby home. It looked so settled and peaceful surrounded by low hills. She asked me to come in for a moment to see her husband, now home from work. He and I had always gotten along well and now as we talked briefly, his eyebrows rose in that quizzical expression that meant, "Did you get the point?"

Energy seemed to seep from my hands and feet as we said goodbye. I had a message to deliver, a last resort. Many colleagues had tried to get through to Dan, and now it was up to me: I had the ball. Time for the Hail Mary pass. And I was no Roger Staubach.

I headed for my own home sick at heart. This highway was one I often drove, but that day I lost my way. I had to retrace my route twice before I pulled into my own driveway. I knew in addition to Dan's "not listening" that he intimidated subordinates and had been accused of bullying them. I saw him do it with the children.

When Dan got home a few minutes later, he poured us both some Merlot. I shooed our hungry kids out of the kitchen as I said, "Dan, I want to tell you about my lunch with your boss's wife."

He and I stood leaning against the kitchen counter, wine glasses in hand, as I started to recount what Alice told me. I ended with, "She said that so many people have tried to tell you you're in danger . . . of getting fired. It's because you don't listen."

At that, he straightened up and shouted, "She did *not* say that! You have no contact with reality! You are distorting the whole thing. I should *never* have allowed you to meet with her."

I shook in the face of his rage, as I did so often. One small boy crept into the kitchen, looked at us both, then melted out of sight. While I held on to my grasp of what really took place, I began feeling I had failed in some way I couldn't figure out. His behavior was again at odds with his frequent words, "I love you!"

He ranted, "You always get things wrong. Everybody at the bank thinks the world of me!" He went on, now yelling how mentally ill I was, but I knew the children had to eat. It was time to get dinner on the table with his bombast for counterpoint.

My Hail Mary, a desperate move, got intercepted.

Soaking alone in the bathtub that night, I asked myself, *If I don't take the pills I hid—would divorce be worse than what I'm living with? Divorce or pills, either way, I will go to hell.*

I had begun to realize that I didn't mind being with my children so much; however, I was gradually recognizing—and not wanting to—that What I wanted and needed was to get away from my husband. And this led to massive guilt feelings and loss of appetite. Whenever he came into a room where I was, I wanted desperately to get away, and did. As my feelings sank even lower, I thought ending my life would be easy. Divorce was only a faint gleam and pills were immediately at hand. I could escape my life.

But what effect would my dying have on my children? I couldn't leave them behind with Dan. He often said, "These children don't need supervision." When he was in charge, they would avoid him, wait till I returned, then pour out a litany of injustices to me. what I wanted and needed was to get away from my husband. And this led to massive guilt feelings and loss of appetite. Whenever he came into a room where I was, I wanted desperately to get away, and did leave the room.

Dan had learned about my stash of pills from the doctor and that I wanted to take them to get away from my marriage. One Saturday after lunch, he came to my room and sat next to me on the edge of my bed. He took a package from his pocket and handed it to me, saying, "Open it. It's a gift."

It was a box from Tiffany's in their trademark aqua. I opened it to find a large, polished gold-color metal box with jeweled florets on its cover. Dan said, "I thought this would be a nice thing for you to put your pills in, you know the ones you want to take to…. Well, anyway, I wanted you to know that it's all right if you want to do this. It might be good for the children if you were gone… They will be all right. We can get along without you."

I had been holding my breath. I didn't realize it until my chest hurt. Had I heard him right? My eyes fell to this elaborate pillbox in my hands, and I watched my tears splash on its top. Tears didn't affect the metal.

My spouse was taking my job from me—dismissing my importance to my children and to him. I felt annihilated—my husband who so often said "I love you" was crushing the life from me.

The sun on the trees outside my windows glared on the green leaves. Everything seemed sharp in the brightness of that sun on the grass, the hedges….

He said it again. "We'll be fine without you. These kids don't really need supervising."

The smell of his Old Spice after-shave made me feel sick. I couldn't talk. His tone was soothing as he went on about how much he loved me, how this would be best for everyone—if I were gone.

I felt dizzy. The ground seemed to slide from under me. I sat there in a daze.

The next day, I took the box with me to the psychiatrist. As I handed it to him, I said, "Dan gave me this. It's for my pills. He said it would be (my voice got hoarse), it would be OK if I were . . . gone. He and the kids would be all right without me."

The doctor held it on his knee, looking down, saying nothing. I leaned closer.

Why wasn't he saying anything? I saw his lashes were wet. He didn't look up at me but cleared his throat to say, "You do know that some people would think this was hostile, don't you?"

He did look up then to meet my eyes. His look was so bleak it went straight to my heart. He was grieving for me, where till now I had been only numb. Seeing his tears, my own eyes burned. Tears I couldn't shed yesterday began streaming and puddled in my lap.

I didn't understand Dan's behavior, and I couldn't figure out what was happening between us. He presented himself to other people as the perfect husband. Dan told everyone who listened that he did the dishes, made meals, did the laundry, washed the diapers, made simple repairs, shopped for groceries, and took care of the children.

Women would corner me at parties after he had told a group of them how much he helped. They would say longingly, "How I wish my husband was like yours!" What he told them sounded fabulous, and it was. He didn't do all those things even when he was home, and he was away so much.

If I dared to call his bluff and tell any listeners, "But he doesn't do all that. And he's gone so much of the time," he would put his arm around me affectionately and say, "Annie doesn't know what she's talking about! Of course, I do all that."

In today's terms, Dan would be considered a Narcissist. This was still the 1970s when Narcissism had not been identified as a disorder. I later learned from several therapists that deflecting any criticism is typical of Narcissism, a disorder now considered incurable. Had I known this then, I would have felt less drowned out. But knowing it wouldn't have given me weapons to deal with it. Physically, he was heavier, taller, and stronger than I was. Hitting him back got me nowhere. He just laughed at me.

These days there's more literature about this disorder than in the 1970s, but still there exists little about strategies to cope with it. Those married to a narcissist feel flattened by the barrage of blame-shifting, accusations of mental illness, projection of the narcissist's own insecurities, and rageful envy of their spouse's accomplishments. In response, the spouse strives to placate this controlling partner, hopes that will bring peace, but feels his or her self-confidence evaporating like air leaving a balloon.

What narcissists want most of all is to look good in the public eye; they believe rules don't apply to them, and will do anything to protect their image. For this reason, narcissists fight savagely against any divorce action because it makes them look bad.

Today's politicians and CEOs often have this type of personality. They cannot accept criticism and they provide frightening examples of people who can't see how destructive they are, laying waste to others–especially to their families. In the wake of these people are children who end up in mental hospitals, prison, or who commit suicide.

The Gathering Storm

"There's a cop at the door," Greg called, after opening the front door.

"He wants to speak to Mom." Then Martin came to get me from the kitchen. I went out and said. "Yes, Officer?"

"Is Mr. at home?" Showing me his badge, the cop said, "I have a ticket here that needs his attention."

Apparently Dan had ignored a moving violation ticket he got five months before.

"How much is it for? I'll pay it." I opened my wallet.

Greg stepped in between the officer and me to say,' "Mom, Mom, you can't do that. Dad has to handle this one."

This sort of problem happened over and over—overdrawn accounts, late night calls from collection agencies, bills I hadn't known about like dues for the University Club, an unsecured loan for $27,000 that had to be renewed every quarter, and hadn't been. This one had gone past the extension time—all these troubles took a lot of energy and time from me. I hadn't known about them. Dr. H said, "One definition of depression is Depletion."

That was it: Why I felt so exhausted. I felt licked before I started so many times.

Another time well after I started talking to Dr. H, he said, "As you get better, you are going to have to realize that there is something very wrong with Dan."

What was this? After all this time, he wasn't telling me as he did formerly that all that went wrong was somehow my fault. Earlier, when I tried to relate what I was coping with, Dr. would say, "*Why* do you believe what Dan tells you?" as though I were the one at fault. Dr. had never talked about what Dan's part in this tangle was. I was the one who had to change, Dr. often said.

My therapy sessions with Dr. H continued when the kids were in school. Sometimes I wrote to my sister for hours about how I felt. Talking with the psychiatrist wasn't enough; so I wrote to Elaine about getting myself through making breakfast for everyone, then going to my bedroom and lying on the floor exhausted. I lay there until it was time for the younger kids to come home for lunch. I had no energy and didn't know why. Gradually I realized with the doctor's help what was wrong: I was deeply depressed.

At the same time, a builder came to the house each weekday to remodel the screen porch into a family room and make the kitchen work again–the stovetop, oven, and dishwasher had died before we moved in. He was an architect, not a people person, and he had questions for me, since I was the only one there.

He would knock on my bedroom door to ask as I lay there, "How deep do you want the cabinets in the kitchen? Eight and three-quarters or nine and a half? Why don't we put a fish tank in the family room for the kids? What length should the apron of the fireplace be?" and so on.

I stood up to answer him, but whatever I answered was received with a sort of sniff that indicated I had made the wrong choice. Then he'd sigh. Sometimes I said, "I have . . . no idea."

"But you *have* to have one. It's *your* house," he said.

I could hardly think. I was on a series of medications designed to lift depression. What he asked seemed so distant, so unimportant. I wanted to answer, "Don't bother me. Let me lie on the floor. Go … away."

I didn't, of course. I did say, "I'll be down in a few minutes," but it didn't register. If I went into the bathroom, he waited outside the door until I came out after washing my face, brushing my teeth, combing my hair. He ambushed me with a fusillade of decisions I wasn't up to making.

"Do you want maple wood, cedar, or ash for the shelving?" he'd say.

If I said, "What about pine?" he would counter, "No, no, no. You can't do that! Too soft." Wrong again. My father-in-law had recommended this builder because he was in the parish. My in-laws insisted on working only with people who were Catholics: builders, doctors, dentists, etc.

I couldn't figure out why this man seemed so sour; was it me or something ethnic? We both were Irish. If he brought in another man to work alongside him, they never talked–no banter or jocularity like when men worked together in my hometown.

It seemed odd, but right then everything seemed odd. I was in a zombie-like state. Part of it was the meds I was on. The doctor changed these from time to time, because I seemed to be in a stupor much of the time. I still shopped for food methodically, tried to plan meals and get them together somehow. I didn't want to eat, but the family needed to. Everything was an enormous effort, and I had to sit down every few minutes.

The builder was there all the time, and even sat in our dining room to eat his lunch. His wife drove over with it every day, and they would argue out in the driveway. I was too tired to wonder why he didn't bring it with him. I didn't want to talk to him.

I envied my husband who could go to work and the kids who were in school. They left me alone all day with him.

One time when the rest of the family was at the lake, I had come home to see my doctor on a Saturday. As I drank coffee in my bathrobe, I heard scraping at the back door. I thought I had my house to myself. It was the builder stopping by to measure something. He didn't have a key and was picking the lock. I grabbed some clothes and let him in.

I couldn't escape him; being home alone was a luxury, and yet here he was barging in on my privacy. On Saturday.

Somehow he conveyed that I was wrong just for being there when he didn't expect me.

As part of my therapy I kept a journal and made notes about others who shared the doctors' waiting room with me. Clients for two other psychiatrists beside mine came to this room to wait for their turns at the psychiatric mill wheel.

One morning I waited across from a man with a muscular build and five-o-clock shadow. He wore a yellow dress with a black plastic purse and low-heeled pumps. His white hair was styled in a Dutch-boy bob. He wore a cloche, and I wanted to stop and suggest more becoming colors, but there seems to be a code for us mental patients: "No talking to each other, and avoid eye contact."

This man waited patiently for me to return with the key to the Ladies' Room before he took it and went in. This was the '70s; perhaps he struggled with transgender issues. M*A*S*H was popular TV fare, and Jamie Farr was getting laughs as transvestite Klinger, but only as a ploy to get a Section 8 discharge.

This man's face told me he was not playing this for laughs. I felt bad for him.

A girl wearing a head scarf and sunglasses came into the waiting room with an older man; I guessed—her dad. When one of the other shrinks came out, the man stood and said loudly, "Doctor, this is Barbara." She kept the sunglasses on and said nothing.

I shivered; this guy was running the show. I figured he'd go in with her and do all her talking. She was probably depressed, and I could see why. I pegged him for a bully with maybe incest as part of the package. I really didn't like him.

I usually had only a few minutes to wait, but I noticed two short, ugly men who sat together; I assumed they were a couple because they weren't talking. Also, as I left after my session, I saw them go in to my shrink together. They looked like Munchkins.

In the '70s, psychiatrists' fees were high and S&H stamps were popular. I made a small table-top sign for the shrinks' waiting room. I glued S&H green stamp logos on it, and lettered: "We give S&H Green Stamps."

I left it under the lamp on the magazine table. I hoped other depressed people saw it and smiled. More likely they might think it was "hostile," yet even a year later, it was still there.

As I continued to feel really cast down and despairing, Dr. H decided it would help me to attend a therapy group in faraway Evanston. I begged for one closer to home, but he was adamant. His group met weekly at 8:30 in the morning—meaning I would have to leave my house before 7:30. Of course, I had to get my kids up, dressed, breakfasted, and ready for school before I left. All last-minute emergencies, "I need milk money!" and "Where's my permission slip?" had to be handled. Dan usually left the house before these small crises erupted. Or he was traveling.

With my kids sorted out and on their way, I had more than an hour's drive during rush hour. I was told to be there on time. Being late meant I was "resisting." Doing as I was told had become my only way to cope, so I obeyed when the psychiatrist insisted I attend "group."

After seventy minutes of driving I found the student center at Northwestern University, and bumbled about trying to find where the group met. I hated asking the scruffy, smelly students leaning against the wall and sitting on the steps. My mouth dried as I said, "Do you know where a...a therapy group meets?" identifying myself as a Mental Patient. I felt like I was wearing a visible strait jacket.

At last one student understood what I was talking about, "therapy group meeting." Avoiding looking directly at me, he pointed the way to the basement.

I entered a dimly lit room where people sat in a circle on an orange shag rug, no chairs. They slumped against the wall or lay on some large, soft pillows. My psychiatrist was already there, the only one wearing a shirt and tie. The other men wore soft clothes—jeans, collarless shirts. The women wore slacks or pants. As I slid down the wall to sit, people helped themselves to coffee perking in a far corner.

I got as close to the door as I could in the deepening silence. I knew nothing about "group." This doctor alleged it would help my serious depression. I didn't understand why getting to know a bunch of strangers would be helpful. The last thing I wanted was to meet new people, let alone talk to them about my closely held pain.

Inhabitants of this therapy world referred to going to a psychiatrist as "*seeing* someone" or "*talking* to someone." It sounded harmless enough but I knew these words were code for "person with serious mental disorder needs to talk to someone who understands crazy people."

Dan, despite my begging him not to, had told many of his friends, relatives, colleagues, and most of all, his boss, that I was "seeing a psychiatrist." Consequently, whenever I was with them at company dinners, for example, they chose their words with care, a look of alarm on their faces as they avoided my eyes. All the in-laws spread the word until I became a present-day leper without a bell.

Our insurance agent, for example, had gone to grammar school with Dan. When I went to his office to talk about my doctor bill coverage, he looked to either side of his door before shutting it. Was he making sure no one was nearby? Or maybe he was checking to see if the security guard was close.

In answering my questions about insurance, he lowered his voice and leaned forward, as though this material were terribly hush-hush. "Now how often did you meet with this psychiatrist?" he whispered.

We were discussing prescription costs, permissible deductions, reasonable and customary coverage, and so on. Not state secrets. Perhaps he expected me to go into a psychotic break? I felt like an extra in the movie "The Snake Pit"—alongside Olivia deHavilland.

After much hemming and hawing, he said, "I'm sorry to tell you there can't be any reimbursement for these doctor bills. Or your prescriptions. None."

That was odd. Dan and I thought we ought to recover at least *some* funds, so I argued with him. "I can't really talk about this," he said. After that, he leaned forward over his desk, almost curling himself up on the surface like a frightened animal, and waited for me to leave.

Really, couldn't he have told me this bad news on the phone? He and his wife belonged to our parish, and my "condition" had been spread abroad by my mother-in-law. I had broken the unwritten commandment, "Thou Shalt Not Seek Therapy. Offer It Up."

I had often been admonished if I complained of pain: "Man is born to trouble as the sparks fly upward," from the Book of Job. We were supposed to suffer; that was our lot in life, and the big payoff was to come when we died and went to heaven.

I knew Jews did not believe in heaven, and began to think they had a point. We Catholics were not into enjoying life, but rather enduring it until we could get to heaven.

One parishioner stopped me at our local grocery to say, "You've been seeing that psychiatrist for over a month now. Are you almost finished?"

"Not quite," I said, and under my breath, "Not that it's any of your business."

Most of the time, what I did was cry a lot when I was alone. I was not running screaming through the streets naked. If I did that, perhaps I could live down to everyone's expectations. But I hadn't the energy for even that.

When I got home from the insurance office, Mother-in-Law called. I never wanted to talk to her, but I tried hard to keep the peace between us. This time she wanted to argue about my needing therapy. She said, "You *can't* be depressed. *I* know what depression is. That poor Mrs. O'Connor with seven children is depressed, but you, you have a sense of humor! That means you are not depressed."

Like depression was something people laughed off. So now I had to defend feeling depleted in the face of everyone's denial. Even my doctor brother told me, "All you really need is a job. Get a motherly housekeeper for the kids."

He had another bit of advice: "It might help you feel better if you slept with a few other men, just to put Dan in perspective." I choked on that. Was he volunteering? I didn't want to ask. He was my brother and I loved him, but I sadly realized he didn't have a clue as to what had driven me so low in spirits.

Just running the house, managing the children, shopping for food, doing the wash (never the ironing), and serving meals already took a great deal of energy. Getting into bed with another man–aside from the rage this might stir up in my spouse and the danger to me–was over the top unthinkable, impractical, more exhausting even to consider.

The psychiatrist said, "That husband of yours leaves you with an awful lot, the five children, that big house. You do realize it's a form of control?"

Actually, I *didn't* think of it that way. It was just my job; I was a corporate wife and had to do it. I still had a lot to learn about what "normal" was. My expectations for a happy marriage had never been high.

And I knew that some of our friends envied me: the big house, the executive husband, the façade of all is well. What happened when the door closed was never out in public. No one wanted to believe me. When I started to complain about being hit, for instance, to our family doctor, he cut me off, saying, "Have you any other questions about the children?"

My mother would say, "I have to get you off this negative topic. Did you know your brother is taking his wife to Club Med?"

With Dan's frequent travels, I was usually the sole parent and I had the children's activities to deal with. Greg had basketball, and two of the boys, Justin and Matt, were on different gymnastics teams. That meant attending several meets to cheer them on. Beth and Martin often sat with me. I remember sitting on the hard wooden benches, my now skinny bottom getting sore as I waited for 15-year-old Matt to do his routine.

He was a champion on the trampoline. I often held my breath as he performed. "Tramp" could be dangerous. I can see him still, standing in a shaft of sunlight, tall, handsome, his arms raised in the traditional salute to the judges before starting his set. The gym fell silent, the judges gave their signal to begin, and he mounted. As he began lofting high above the tramp bed, his teammates shouted, "Show 'em, Doodles!" and "Hit it, Matt, hit your set!"

He was oblivious, graceful, focused on his routine. Long months of practice gathered into this moment as he twirled, bounced, flipped, and came fluidly, elegantly into his dismount. He stood, arms raised again as applause and shouting roared around him.

On the ride home, Martin said, "I will remember this night forever," and Matt said, "It was perfect. I only wish…Dad had been there."

At home Matt would take his silverware at dinner to show us how the moves went, using their names, "This is the Barani, and then here's the roundoff," and so on. His siblings' responses were the usual, "Oh, shut up, Matt!"

"Would you cut it out?"

"Would you just pass the bread, fag," etc.

I would tune in with, "Don't call anyone a 'faggot'!"

Did they get on each other's nerves? Weren't they kids? For instance, when Matt was a freshman in high school, he and eight-year-old Mart shared a room. Martin had a beloved hand puppet, Tigger. He took him everywhere and slept with him. At this time, Mart had made a little home for Tigger next to his bed. It started out as just a small house from a shoe box, but over time, he added a garage and driveway, a swimming pool and a playground with a swing set. He was proud of his layout.

When he asked me to look at what he'd made, I also saw a Tigger-sized bathroom complete with towels and a mirror made from aluminum foil. The towel racks were toothpicks, and then I noticed that Tigger's towels looked familiar. They had been neatly cut from our best hand towels in the guest bathroom.

Here I drew the line. Yes, it was creative. And yes, Mart had to pay for new guest towels out of his allowance. And next time, "ask before taking something already in use."

But more trouble arrived when Matthew came to tell me, "Mother, Martin is driving me crazy! Tigger takes up more and more space in my room. When I come home in the dark, I step on his sandbox or his drive-way. And Martin howls! You've got to do something."

So I got Mart to cut back on all the real estate when we talked about how hard it was for Matt to stumble in the dark on Tigger's garage or his pool. He could get hurt and things Mart had spent time creating would get crushed.

After a long discussion, he agreed; the outbuildings and pool were packed away.

And Tigger stayed at his villa over in the corner.

ALL SORTS OF THERAPIES

Meanwhile, getting back to "group," Dr. H cleared his throat, lit his pipe, and said, "Well! Why don't we begin by introducing ourselves to Anne?" He seemed falsely jovial, not like the kind man I'd been talking with for so many weeks. And so they offered first names – with a lack of energy that told me how unwelcome I was. As they talked, glancing at each other and not me, the interloper, I sensed they had been together a long time. I was glad I lived so far away. I would not like to run into them at the drugstore or the gas station. I imagined myself doing just that, and asking, "So. How's that OCD/impotence/hostility to your dad going?"

Because what had we in common other than disorders?

I didn't want to get up and get coffee, partly because my shaky hands might spill it. It would also mean I would need to find the bathroom later. I couldn't imagine anyone here being helpful. I was sure they would send me to an exit door that would shut behind me and lock. I began closing in on myself, sinking inside, thinking how was being here going to help me, exactly?

Apparently the deal was to sit in silence until the pressure got to someone who blurted something, anything. I was damned sure it wouldn't be me. Getting coffee and fuss-budgeting about sugar, spoons, white-out masquerading as cream, and so on, took quantities of time. The session was to last ninety minutes, and that stretched ahead of me like a prison sentence with no chance of parole. Cold sweat gathered in the small of my back. Would people attack each other? Dr. Shrink had said it would "feel like family." ("That bad?" I said when he brought it up.)

OK, *that* bad. And not only that, but I had to *pay* to be here.

I knew I was their first new member in two years, an outsider, and as they looked me over, they offered feeble, toneless greetings.

"Hi, nice to meet you,"

"Dr. H told us you were coming today."

People got up to help themselves to coffee perking in a far corner. I was as close to the door as I could get.

Later that morning, they spoke of meeting the following Sunday morning for coffee, their usual routine, away from the therapists. My spirits were low to begin with, but at this, they sank further. I was not included, fortunately.

I couldn't get my mind around why they would want to socialize. It shocked me. All of them were also in individual therapy. To me that meant not-quite-normal. Wouldn't Sunday morning gatherings be like breakfast at a mental hospital? Didn't they have friends, obligations, family gatherings, church services?

That first session, I was sure people were feeling "on display" with a new member, me. And I felt so bad that I had to sit there among strangers because Dr. H thought it would do me "good." I couldn't wait to get away.

The two "parents" of this "family" were Dr. H, and a female named Dr. Emmy. I figured they were there like lifeguards to help if anyone got in over his or her head. Why were two needed?

I looked Dr. Emmy over without seeming to stare. She was plump, wore a wrinkled pants suit, and I saw a run in her pantyhose when she sat down. I had expected her to have dressed neatly to show us what it looked like to be "together." Actually, I thought she looked like she didn't care.

My psychiatrist looked neat, like he could handle problems. As I got to know more about group therapy, I came to realize such groups appear to be inhabited by more grotesques than a Dickens novel. They may well have thought the same of me. Some seemed as though they did not want to "get better."

What they really wanted was a forum for airing grievances against parents, spouses, partners, siblings, politicians, and anyone slighting them in line at the liquor store. The others usually endured these tirades in silence, waiting for their turns to hog the spotlight, or they said aloud, "Who does that remind you of?" or else, "You must like that or you would leave."

These expressions were bandied about whenever someone got close to having a genuine feeling. Such questions threw the speaker off track and annoyed me. These therapeutic clichés distanced me from what was going on.

If I didn't like someone, I wanted to dislike them for their very own selves and not because it reminds me of my mother/Sister Evangelista/ some babysitter I once hated.

So after I had been in the group awhile, sometimes I said, "Can't he just keep talking?" instead of taking us into the archeological digs of childhood.

As I recalled the first session of group, nothing much seemed to happen, meaning no open fights. Some complained about siblings, parents, etc., but I was sure they felt "on display" with me there. And I felt so bad that I couldn't wait to get away. Minutes crept by on hands and knees. When the time was up, I bolted outside, past the layabouts still smoking on the steps. When I talked again with the doc, he said, "Unless you have a fever of 102, you have to be there every week."

I would rather spend the time cleaning our bathrooms, but I went along. For a time.

After the first few sessions I learned that one assumption the group made was that if a woman gets hit by her partner, she "asked for it." So when one member, a lawyer, brought up hitting the woman he lived with, they murmured this. He went on, "I feel so bad seeing Doris's eyes all black and blue." He seemed close to tears.

The others agreed that she provoked his blows because she "liked being hit."

Being new to the dynamics of "group," I took a chance and said, "My husband hits me. I don't like it."

"Why don't you hit him with a frying pan?" one unmarried man said.

"Because he is much taller and weighs a hundred pounds more than I do," I said.

Some murmuring followed.

"I don't provoke the hitting," I said, thinking *I want to stand up for myself.* I saw that the group found it easier to blame the hittee than to confront a hitter who had so little self-control. I found it puzzling that the two psychiatrists didn't make any suggestions or ask questions.

I sat there, asking myself, *Why did the two of them let their clients paddle along in these mental lagoons without suggesting a course correction? What was their function, anyway? We paid them for these sessions. Were they just there to listen to grievances, drink coffee, accept fees, wait for the session to end, but not make judgments?*

It took me a long time to realize that psychiatrists are not counselors; they don't offer practical advice the way social workers and psychotherapists might. Their main job seemed to be to listen and murmur "Mmm." It frightened me to get so little response.

Later on, when I consulted psychotherapists—*not* psychiatrists, I found their suggestions regarding daily-life-type problems eminently practical and useful. Freud would never accept this helpful approach.

Back to group: Sometimes the shrinks here made what I thought were veiled accusations. For example, I mentioned I had a nightmare of an iceberg that I lived on alone.

Dr. Emmy said, "And I suppose you didn't do anything about it?"

"No. I did. I painted it," I said. "I could bring it in here," I would have liked to hear her say something kinder, perhaps "That nightmare must have felt bad." But she didn't have the emotional tools to say even this.

A few weeks after that, she was later than usual. She was often late. No one told her she was "resisting," but why was that applied to us patients or whatever we were, and not to the moderators. That day, Dr. H told us before she arrived that her teenage son had gone to Florida to live. Unfortunately, he had hung himself over the weekend.

When she came in, her face was red and puffy, and her clothes were more wrinkled than usual. One man, the lawyer, said, "Dr. Emmy, I am sorry for your trouble. But I have to say, this isn't such a good recommendation for a psychiatrist, now, is it?"

I was shocked and tensed up. Why wasn't the other shrink picking up on this rude comment? No one else said anything for a moment.

She snuffled what sounded like an agreement and said, "Fred and I thought he was ready to be on his own. We were wrong." More tears.

Why had she come today, I wondered. She handed our group the equivalent of a wet, messy diaper to deal with. Her blotchy face told us she wasn't handling it well. She should be at home. Or talking to her own shrink.

With ordinary people, this suicide would have been something we could talk about more kindly. But with someone I scarcely knew–a shrink–not possible. They're supposedly experts on feelings. And this was a tragedy.

Of the members here, only I had sons. One woman had a daughter. The rest had no children.

I went for my regular haircut; even in the depths of pain, I had to keep up my corporate wife appearance. My hairdresser was often candid about how happy she was to be divorced as she snipped away. However, this day she looked into my eyes in the mirror as she worked and said, "You may not need this, but I am going to give you the name of my lawyer. Just so you have it."

I thought at the time that hair stylists were only the source of information on where to get an abortion, not for divorce lawyers. This stylist was not raised by a Catholic family but by the Salvation Army. Catholics were shielded from Information about divorce. For them, it would be a serious sin even to think about. Hedged in by the spikes of potential sin on all sides many Catholics, me among them, made repression along with denial a habit of mind and a way of life.

Other than this hair stylist and my faraway brother, I knew no one who was divorced, no one I could talk to about the forbidden subject. I kept her lawyer's number in my wallet.

Then one day in the depths of despair, I called. His secretary sounded kind rather than devilish. My hand sweated around the phone as I asked for an appointment. I was extremely aware that this lawyer was Jewish. But were there any Catholic divorce lawyers? We knew a lot of lawyers, and some Catholic lawyers might advocate and arrange for a separation if the circumstances were dire enough. A separation meant continued interactions and much hope for reconciliation.

I needed a more clear-cut solution. Separation would mean involvement with the banished spouse who would live elsewhere. I couldn't deal with his coming into the house whenever he wanted to.

At the appointed time, I made my way to the office of this Prince of Darkness, on Madison Street in Chicago's Loop. I hadn't eaten since the day before and felt lightheaded as I sat in a big, soft, dark brown leather chair, the kind that's so hard to get out of. The secretary, a few feet away, called over to me, "Did he ever hit you?"

I was shocked. How could she talk so openly? What if someone overheard us? She was just doing her job, but this was so personal! I just stared at her, and asked for a key to the ladies' room.

After that, it was time to enter the devil's lair. As in the movie *Devil's Advocate,* I wanted to touch the doorknob to see if it felt hot, and did when his secretary's back was turned. (It was just warm.) She ushered me into an office with dark mahogany furniture, huge oil paintings, and windows that looked out over Lake Michigan.

Mr. G's hand as I shook it was warm, firm. He was shorter and rounder than I; heavy-set, and his eyes behind his rimless glasses were kind.

I was alert to note there were no horns, no odor of sulphur, no visible forked tail. Not even a fireplace. My terror must have been palpable to him. I trembled. I managed to squeeze out, "This is just . . . exploratory."

With a few questions, he established that I was a mom of five, a Catholic, and that no one knew I was seeing him, my spouse in particular.

He seemed comfortable telling me, "As a matter of fact, my wife is a Catholic. So I know what you are going through. And I have close ties to the Cardinal's office."

I felt myself begin to let go. I didn't have to explain my terror. And if the Cardinal could talk to him, perhaps this man wasn't all that evil.

We covered what steps I needed to take, and I found myself blurting at one point, "I have a feeling of dread, that I will be punished for doing this."

"I don't let my clients get punished, Anne," he said in the kindest voice. I know now that my Catholic guilt feelings had surfaced. Other people feel comfortable considering divorce, but I expected to be struck by lightning or hit by a bus on the way home. This lawyer had a handle on the guilt feeling and assured me, "That won't happen. I won't let it."

Talking to him was such a relief. What he told me meant this is doable. And yes, he would do his best to see that I got custody of my children, and child support. And our house.

The next months I walked the edge of an abyss deeper than those we drove by on our way to Aspen. My resting pulse in those days was 125 beats a minute. How much worse could being divorced get?

Life continued to swirl around me. Our son Matt tore a ligament in gymnastics practice. In the emergency room, I was greeted like an old friend by the staff. When the nurse brought out crutches, I said, "Not more crutches. Our house is starting to look like Lourdes" –that shrine where afflicted people left behind their canes, wheelchairs, and crutches when the healing waters of Lourdes in France allowed some sufferers to discard these supports. But Matt needed crutches to get home, so we took them.

Examining Matt, the ER doctor was furious. He said, "These coaches! They push and push the kids past their limits and then, this happens!"

Matt had to keep his foot in a bowl of ice periodically at home as it healed. He was good about getting the ice and cleaning up, but he had to miss weeks of his beloved sport. At sixteen he was a sight in the high school corridor, being almost six feet four inches crutching along to class.

Crutches for his sports injury also set him apart. He had started his sport when he was younger and smaller. Most gymnasts are compact; Matt was possibly the tallest gymnast on record. I had encouraged him, because he seemed to thrive on it. And I told my boys I didn't want them playing football; I feared the injuries; I had dated a guy with no teeth on either side of his mouth from football collisions. The head injuries scared me even more.

I drove him to school and back. Managing his backpack full of books, the crutches, and keeping his foot elevated was a challenge. He didn't complain much, but he didn't want me helping him to the school door. "I can manage!" he said.

His older brother Greg was a junior at an all-boys Catholic high school. That year a Chicago reporter heard a rumor that drug use was rampant in local high schools. The priests gave her permission to interview their students. That night at dinner, Greg said he told her: "Heroin is what I usually use. Otherwise, cocaine." His siblings collapsed laughing.

"She had no right to intrude," Greg said. "So we gave her an earful." Other boys had enjoyed putting her on. She sounded really young and inexperienced for a journalist. Apparently, the priests concurred in feeding her fabrications. So when the article came out, it was a classic media "Chicken Little" horror story.

We treasured copies.

At the Art League where my class took place, Greg had taken on weekly custodial duties. He was there every week cleaning, emptying trash, sweeping. On nights when we had live models, I noticed his raised eyebrows as he swept, dusted, cleaned the stairs. He had to be there while the building was open for our classes, and nudes posed on random nights.

Occasionally as I sketched our model, I would look up to see a man standing in the studio doorway, but our teacher, Joe, chased onlookers away. He said, "Go on. Get out of here. No observers when we have models."

Since I was in therapy and Dan had come to meet with my psychiatrist for Couples Therapy, Dan asked to have individual therapy with the same doctor. "I want Anne's psychiatrist," he said.

This was not acceptable to Dr. H, apparently not even ethical, and he suggested a different psychiatrist for Dan.

Dan made an appointment with this new doctor, then late that night, Dan pounded on my bedroom door and shouted, "I don't think this guy could possibly understand me!"

By now I was afraid of him; we no longer slept in the same room because I was sleeping so badly because of my nightmares. I sat with him and did my best to help. I had a strong feeling that Dan did not want to face what was inside him. I did not say that, since I feared it would enrage him. I did say, "Why not just try to meet with this new doctor? If it doesn't work, you don't have to go back."

After a while he settled down.

A few weeks later this new doctor advised him to enter group therapy also, so he could see how people reacted to him. Dan did agree to this and started meeting with his group.

Throughout the seventies, the mantra "If it feels good, do it!" justified all kinds of behavior—dope smoking, dropping acid, and particularly experimenting with sex.

The shrink who moderated Dan's therapy group encouraged him to date the women there. This was so 1970s—behavior like this was considered normal. His shrink had told Dan he was "too emotionally dependent on Anne."

Following this advice, one woman in the group, Sylvia, and Dan quickly became opera-goers, dinner companions, and then lovers. I knew because he told me. When I said, "Don't tell me about it!" he just kept on talking. "I don't think you realize just how close she and I are," he said.

I was pretty much occupied with family matters, so too exhausted to take part in any sexual merry-go-round. Friends confided about church discussion groups for couples that encouraged "getting a little on the side," therapy groups where members were encouraged to hook up, and key- and wife-swapping parties. *The Ice Storm* movie set in 1973 depicted these scenes, though with sad consequences. Its ending rather took the fun out of swapping.

As Dan got more involved with his group and his new opera friend, he decided to take her to a weekend get-together of the Aspen-in-Chicago group that he and I had founded. We had set this up after we returned from our time at the Aspen Institute.

He told me, "She's heard about this Aspen group and would love to see what it's like. So I Invited her. That's all."

When he returned home from that weekend, he told me, "I can't understand it. All the usual Aspen members seemed shocked that I would bring someone other than you to the weekend!"

I wasn't surprised at their reaction. I had warned him it would not sit well, but Dan couldn't understand why they objected. We couples, all alumni of the Aspen Institute Executive Seminars, had regularly gotten together for years for discussion weekends. Usually we met at an elegant local retreat where we discussed works like Aristotle's *Ethics, The Federalist Papers*, Barry Commoner's *The Closing Circle* (1971), and *The Limits to Growth* from the Club of Rome (1974). Mortimer Adler chose our readings; at the time he was managing editor of *Encyclopedia Britannica*.

He moderated most sessions, occasionally assisted by Charles van Doren, *the* Charles van Doren well-known for his earlier part in the quiz show "Twenty-One" scandal. He worked with Mortimer in those days and taught at Columbia University.

Between twenty and thirty people attended these weekends. While setting them up was a lot of work for me, they were fun, interesting, challenging. The weekends gave me a glimpse of a world I once belonged to, inhabited by kindred spirits who loved books and discussions as much as I did.

My psychiatrist early in my therapy told me I was "lonely for my own kind." My siblings, my father's sisters, and my college friends had been my kind, but since I married, I lost touch with people like that. I had left them behind me, and when I was again among similar people at these weekends, it felt like breaking the surface after swimming underwater. I breathed in a sense of coming home.

Having someone take my place at the weekend hurt terribly. I felt numb, exhausted. All the fight had gone out of me. I didn't realize it then, but Dan's actions were classic narcissistic behaviors.

Hardest to handle for me was Dan's sense that he was always correct. In today's world a classic textbook example of this behavior pattern has been provided by Mr. Donald Trump, who assured his audiences that he also was never wrong.

A New Challenge

O ne night Dan came home from work unusually quiet. He sipped his cup of hot tripe soup and said, "This tastes especially good tonight."

I wondered what was wrong. He usually came in bursting with talk and wanting me to listen to him.

Finally he spoke. "I got fired today."

My heart started knocking against my ribs. My lunch with his boss's wife had been six months earlier, and she had warned us. I sat with him at the dining room table. There wasn't much I could say. "While I was traveling," he said, "the directors called a special board meeting. They voted to let me go!"

They were generous: the board let him keep his office and secretary while he looked for a job. And he could keep his regular salary for most of the year.

In the days following as colleagues and relatives heard about his dismissal and asked why, he insisted, "There is no reason for it!" Yet he had never mended his spending ways at work. Extravagant client dinners, club memberships, car rentals when we had two of our own, first-class travel expenses—these all added to the staggering amount for that next generation computer system. All together these led the board of directors to say, "We can't afford you."

He wrote letters to the bank's senior executives telling them he was "deeply hurt" by his dismissal. He mentioned "Anne is very bad" in his letters to them. I was shocked that he would use my being depressed to garner pity for his situation.

I had done my best, and I hadn't made a dent. Over the years I had the idea that it was my job to keep my husband afloat, He often said so. I thought I had failed as a corporate wife.

Meanwhile, life with our children demanded my attention. For instance, the way they managed their time! Maddening. One would start writing a term paper at 11:30 p.m. when it was due the next day. As I got into the tub, late, someone would knock on the bathroom door with, "I've got to talk to you. I've been waiting all night."

"But I've been right here."

"It can't wait till tomorrow."

Or if I asked on Thursday who would be home for dinner on Saturday, the usual answer was, "That's all the way to the weekend. I don't know if I'll be around or not." Still, I needed to have enough food on hand.

At dinnertime, our phone rang almost constantly. Those were the days of no Caller ID or answering machines. Our rule (actually, my rule) was no phone calls during dinner. The children took turns answering the phone when it rang with, "Hi. I can only take a message. It's dinnertime. We can't take calls during dinner."

With all the talking, squabbling and laughing in the background, the caller often said, "Say, are you guys having a party? It sure sounds like it." And the caller was assured that, "No, it's just dinner. 'Bye."

Sometimes we let the phone ring. Many times friends stayed over for dinner. This involved making sure the other set of parents knew, and then adding more potatoes or noodles, extra bread.

Conversation reeled from what a pain Mr. Z was in math ("Yeah, I had him last year. He never liked me, either") to deciding whether it was all right to have parties here at our house.

"Teddy C. had one last Saturday and over a hundred kids were there. Out on the street, mostly," Justin said.

"I hear some of the kids broke stuff," Greg said. "I wouldn't like that to happen here."

"Or people thieving stuff," Beth said.

"What would they take?" I said.

"Kids like to put stuff in their pockets, like those little dinosaur paperweights you have or your crystal birds. Happens all the time," Greg said.

"If someone plans to have friends over on Friday or Saturday, somehow word gets around. Then everybody shows up," Justin said.

The Internet wasn't up yet, but Tel-a-Kid was alive and flourishing.

"Like at Markie's," Beth said. (Markie, their cousin, had a party when her parents weren't home.) "They had almost two hundred kids and they ended up out in the street. Markie didn't even know most of them. Then the cops came and broke it up."

A somewhat different scene sometimes occurred in our Chicago suburb; several nearby families were connected to the Mafia. Occasionally, if a teen's party got out of hand, "button men" in silk suits came to the party house and quietly dispersed the crowds. My children told me one of these men had asked who was in charge, and when a kid said, "my grandmother," the man said, "This is too much for your grandmother. These kids need to go home."

No police were called. The kids left quietly.

We did have parties at our house, but never more than twenty or so kids. I stayed in the family room, and various kids would stop by to say "Hi" to me as they collected more food or another beer. I could tell how things were going from the noise level.

Added to the mix was their sexual coming-of-age, so that potential pregnancy loomed. Most teens had no access to the Pill yet. Drugs became accessible. Kids would ask one or another of my kids to "hold" a package, and they refused. Two narcotics officers were assigned to the school and chatted with the kids between classes or outside.

Their physical size challenged me as the boys, one after another, grew to six feet four inches. Their language skills gave them more articulate vocabulary that made insults precise and hurtful. These verbal attacks may be the stuff of sitcoms, but they could mortally wound parents who felt shattered by them. Further, the teen's own personality was hidden, and their interests were private now.

Dan Gets Ill

And then a new blow threw me further off course. Dan had often mentioned a bothersome swelling he had noticed, but did nothing about it. His group therapist insisted on his getting to a specialist. While I had many times asked him to do just that, he didn't. This therapist had gotten to him. When Dan saw a specialist, he discovered he needed surgery for a possible malignancy.

I quickly checked into his medical insurance, and saw that he was several months behind in his payments! This was one bill he always took care of, or promised he would. Oh, no! He was already at the hospital being prepped for the surgery! I flew to his room, brought him the insurance form to fill out, had him write the check, and then mailed it as quickly as I could.

The surgeon discovered he had an embryonal tumor, one he was born with. Yes, it was malignant. Two doctors said it "could have activated at any time." The lead surgeon told me later, "It may have been triggered by his being fired and a sense that you may want to leave him."

And so, here loomed another boulder to block my path. I had almost seen that clear water lay ahead. When this new situation arose, I had a recurring nightmare: I was alone in a swirling fog, climbing a cyclone fence. I could not see where I was going. I had to keep climbing up and to the right. No land below me, no end to the fence, no top. All I had were my fingers clinging to metal links in front of my face. I kept going.

The song "Stand by Your Man" was still popular, even though it had come out in 1968. I had waited so long to get away. Now what? Of course,

I called my lawyer. Only he and my brothers and sister knew I planned to divorce. By now it was April 1975; I had first talked with this lawyer nine months earlier.

Again Mr. G seemed unflappable. He said, "All right. We will wait until he recovers from the chemo, gets back on his feet and is earning a living again. In the meantime, say *nothing*. Don't do anything to cause an uproar, anything indiscreet. And whatever you do, *don't* date."

And so I was back down in the mire, sucked into the patient-care scenario, waiting for the prognoses and learning the test results. Most of all, coping with having his girlfriend, Sylvia from his therapy group, sit across from me on the other side of his hospital bed.

I had reached a point where that didn't matter. To the friends and family who criticized me for not throwing her out of his room, I said, "If Dan is not going to live through this, I would rather have people who love him be with him. It's all right with me–her being there." Dan had stopped feeling like "mine" long ago.

At the time, I didn't think how great a struggle it would have been to get Sylvia to *stop* showing up. As the days went by, she was astonishingly intrusive and persistent. She brought me presents of homemade bread, plants, small reproductions of paintings, and free-form poems she wrote late at night after she left the hospital. She came in every day to bustle around, plump his pillow and fetch water and juice. He mostly lay there groaning and asking for more morphine; he was there for three weeks that first time, and then a follow-up week shortly after.

She told me, "I really like you! I want us to be friends!" And I was too numb for any ready repartee to come to my mind. I was barely keeping myself upright. Friends? How appropriate was that? I began to think she was ugly, but my feelings could have been distorting her.

A big part of Dan's care was interpreting what the doctors had to say. Dan didn't listen. While the morphine didn't help him listen better, his way of coping had always been to shut out anything he didn't want to hear. In this crisis it was even worse.

This time, I was not alone in realizing this trait of Dan's. The chief surgeon said to me, "Mr. D doesn't seem to handle reality very well. So should we go with fairy tales for him?"

"Please don't give me that burden. Please tell him the truth. I can't have people believing everything's fine when it isn't," I said. Thank God at least he was one person who saw through Dan's bluster.

As it was, I was taking Valium around the clock just to keep myself sane. Having to face people who wanted to be joyful over news that wasn't true would make my life more hellish than it was already. Getting Dan to see what was really going on was almost more than I could handle, but no one else could do it, either, including his doctors.

I knew the doctors had told us the children were too young to be allowed in Dan's hospital room. He was to be there for weeks, so I talked to the kids about getting to his room for a few minutes. Greg was almost fifteen, so he could be there, but not the others.

I and Greg went in the front door of the hospital and up to Dan's room to alert him to the visit. With his cancer, the immune system was too vulnerable for all the germs that little children might carry from school. They were forbidden to come in.

Then I ran down the fire stairs and let the four other kids in; I cautioned them to be silent and creep up the stairs, no talking. We got to the fifth floor and slipped into Dan's room. He was lying in bed, but grateful to see them. Hugs all around. Whispered chatting. One of the boys wanted to see how the bed could be made to lift the headboard, but I thought the nurses might hear us laughing, so I said No. We didn't stay long. And we didn't get caught.

I still had to cope with the daily meals, the children's everyday issues—Justin having severe stomach pains–the bills, and all the phone calls. These were always, "How is Dan doing?" Some called close to midnight.

No one called me to say, "How are *you* doing?"

When I talked with the surgeon afterward, he said he had made the "largest incision known to man." That Dan's "temp is up and there are noises in his lungs. He needs to take deep breaths and cough."

I watched Dr. Snyder pull out the drain and snip off a piece of it, throwing it–along with the scissors–in the hazardous waste bin. That alone told me how serious the tumor was.

A team of doctors managed his care, and the oncologist wanted Dan to know that his chances of surviving this type of tumor were one in five. When the doctor said this to both of us, Dan said over and over to me, "I only want to hear positive stuff! Not this negative stuff."

I had to be the one to tell him, "This is neither positive nor negative. It's reality."

I noticed that the doctors seemed to avoid talking to him. They found it far easier to tell me the bad news.

In Dan's hospital room, as he recovered from surgery, he stayed on the phone for hours. The lead surgeon came to me. "Mrs. D This has got to stop! He is pushing himself too hard. Unplug his phone. Or unplug him. I mean it. Less visitors. He wouldn't get off the phone even though *I* was in there."

"You mean he didn't give you a few minutes of his precious time?" I said.

"No. This has got to stop. He is pushing himself too hard."

Why didn't *he* tell Dan? Actually, he tried. He went in to talk to Dan, but couldn't get him to stop his telephone call. He complained about Dan to me, as though I were his mother and could get him to stop. I couldn't. I found over the years that most people hesitated to confront Dan, and it was far easier to ask me to tell him any bad news. These doctors were no exception.

I reminded myself that it took the entire board of directors where Dan worked to confront Dan and fire him. No single individual that I ever knew of could stop him from doing whatever he wanted. As I approached divorcing him, I was once again entering the bull ring with a formidable opponent, only now I had a powerful ally, Mr. G. Amazing to me that he was not intimidated by Dan. And he had my back and never wavered.

Years later, Justin told me, "Mom, you are the only one who ever stood up to Dad and told him he couldn't do what he wanted."

Dan was hospitalized for three weeks, then again for a bit later. I did ask him if he could recover at Sylvia's home. He refused, saying, "I don't want my parents to know about her." He also didn't want them to visit him, so they never came down to the hospital. This seemed odd, but it was what Dan asked for. And because he had been so seriously ill, he again got what he wanted.

Healing and Moving On—Telling the Kids

Dan's healing from cancer surgery was a slow process. As with so many men, his work was his identity. Having been fired by the board of directors, he continued on salary from his employer without assignments. He kept his full-time secretary and his elegant office two doors down from the chairman. As he gained his strength back, he actively looked for work consulting on computer systems, his area of expertise.

Dan's doctors had OKd his return to traveling. He was anxious to get back to his traveling lifestyle. When we had couples therapy, the psychiatrist pointed out that "Consulting involves moving from client to client without staying with one to see the results. And this always-moving-on mode suits Dan's personality."

Dan started his search for a new job, traveling to Seattle, Boston, and New York, while I stayed at home by myself dwelling on thoughts of feeling my life was at an end as I managed the household, bills, and children.

To Dan's credit, he found a lecturer position at Illinois Institute of Technology. A business reporter heard of this job change and set up an interview. Dan asked my advice on what he could say to the reporter.

I suggested, "I've accomplished what I set out to do, and I'm looking for new challenges." Dan gave the reporter the impression he chose to move on, never mentioning he'd been fired.

The reporter saw his "choosing" to teach as a heroic act. The upbeat article's headline was "Career Change at 38: Ex-Banker a Teacher." It was a full-page article about how wonderful he was to pursue teaching. I have a copy of it.

Since he was allowed to keep his office, salary, and secretary for most of the ensuing year, not everyone realized he had been fired. He still traveled as much as before, only now it was to interview for jobs in other cities to add income to his teaching fee.

My Holy Grail–the divorce–now came front and center. As Dan slowly healed, his doctors had a more hopeful outlook. Recovery looked much more possible than it had seemed at first. Dan got back to his work and traveling schedule, I again contacted my lawyer. He agreed to find a lawyer to work with Dan, and Mr. G and I went back over the settlement issues in advance of my approaching Dan.

The next hurdle: I still had to tell Dan. I knew I had to do it with other people around me, since one-on-one inside the house with him was dangerous. I chose a time when he was returning from a business trip. A weekend art fair was a good setting for it; my art friends could be around me when I confronted him.

My plan: I had earlier refused to co-sign for an outstanding loan. He had been bullying me to sign it. My signature was my bargaining chip so I prepared a note, "In exchange for my signature on the loan, I want a divorce."

Then I arranged for Dan to meet me at the St. Charles Art Fair on Sunday, where I and my friends were exhibiting our paintings. It was a beautiful fall day. I sat by my paintings display with my friend Dorothy next to me; she had known my plan to divorce. Our instructor Joe and others stood nearby. They knew the setup and why I wanted—needed–them around.

And there Dan found me in the midst of my art friends. "Hiya, sweetheart," he said and without asking, took charge of one of Dorothy's folding chairs and sat. He leaned over to kiss me and I backed away.

I handed him my note. I knew he wouldn't make a scene at that point, but only because he never wanted to look bad in front of other people. He read it with a reddening face.

He looked furious. He didn't look at me, said only, "I've got to get out of here!"

He all but ran to his car. I learned he went directly to his lawyer father. I heard that Dan's parents were wildly angry at me for lining up a lawyer on my own, and especially a Chicago lawyer with a national reputation. Any local pussycat would have been intimidated by the family. I needed clout, and with Mr. G I had it.

Unknown to me, the day after that art fair Dan called my lawyer for an appointment. The secretary misunderstood his name and scheduled Dan for noon that day. He must have told her it was urgent.

I was alone in our River Forest basement doing laundry when the phone rang. I was astounded to hear: "Mrs. D, this is Mr. G. I have your husband here in my office. He's sitting across from me. I put this call on speaker phone. I can't have any meetings you are not part of."

I could hear Dan talking in the background. My hand on the phone sweated so much I nearly dropped it.

"I want both of you to understand that you, Mrs. D, are my client, and I can't represent the two of you. My secretary wrote down a different name, or I wouldn't have accepted the appointment."

The secretary wrote Dan's name down as "Victor"—I wondered if he had yelled so much she couldn't get it right.

I began to feel sick. I leaned against the wall as I listened. I had no idea Dan would approach my lawyer. If he believed Dan, it would discredit me. And I hadn't yet given him my "earnest money."

But as Mr. G talked, I realized he had believed what I told him from the start. After he grasped that Dan was *my* husband, he had called me. Apparently he didn't think I was crazy. He did sound angry. Then I heard him ask Dan to leave and he said, "I'm hanging up the phone."

The following day, he told me that Dan said I was "seriously mentally ill," and "not to pay attention to anything Anne said."

Hearing that gave me the shakes. That was our relationship in a nutshell.

Now that Dan knew, the children had to be told. I asked Dan to work with me on this, but each time we agreed on a time to talk to them as a group, he withdrew. "I'm not ready," he'd say.

I was on tenterhooks with every delay in telling our kids. I felt we had waited far too long. Finally I said, "I'll tell them alone. Will you just be there in the room while I do it?"

I made sure each of them would be home for dinner on the coming Saturday. I made a special dinner, pot roast and mashed potatoes. Twelve-year-old Justin was at a friend's house in Oak Park and had promised he would be home by six. Everyone else was there, sitting at the dinner table, but no Justin. I called the friend's family. "He left," they told me, "half an hour ago. He told us he had to be home by six."

We called other friends. No one knew where he was. My stomach was now in knots.

Then the phone rang. Dan answered and heard: "This is the Racine Avenue Police Station in Chicago. Do you have a son named Justin?"

Dan said "Yes," and the chief went on, "Well, your boy is here with his bicycle. Will you come down here and get him? Please."

Justin got on the phone just long enough to tell Dan he had made a wrong turn on Madison Street, and kept going east instead of west to our house. For many miles.

Greg, sixteen, and Dan hopped into our microbus and headed east for Racine Avenue and Madison Street. The rest of us puzzled over how Justin would make a wrong turn on a route he had taken for years.

My special dinner grew cold and colder. The Grail, almost within my grasp, was receding like a tide going out as I scrabbled at the water's edge to bring it back.

The other kids knew only that this was a special dinner, not why I made such a fuss about it. Beth was due to go to a friend's house for a party. The friend who arranged it called, "Where is she?"

I took the call. I couldn't let Beth leave until we told them. I said, "We're having a family meeting."

The friend got snippy. "She has to be here!"

Justin, Dan and Greg came in and we settled into our meal. Justin said between mouthfuls, "I kept going on Madison thinking I'd see familiar streets. Then I got to the corner of Racine where some nice ladies called me over. They were beautiful and they were really dressed up. They called, 'Hey, little white boy, what you doing in this neighborhood?

"'We want you to come with us to the po-lice station. We don't want no trouble, nobody saying 'What you doing with that little white boy.' The ladies walked with me to the station and told the cops I was lost."

It took a long time to get everyone settled down, and fed. Then finally I could talk. Dan didn't want to say it, so I did:

"We want to tell you we are getting a divorce."

"Oh no!"

They cried, all of them. Loud, painful sobs. The room grew damp with sorrow.

I cried at how much they hurt.

Justin said, "I knew it! I just had the feeling you were going to tell us that."

For years afterward, he worried that every time we had a special dinner, it meant bad news. He would ask me, "Is this a special dinner? Is there something bad you're going to tell us?"

In the midst of our tears, the phone kept ringing. Finally, I answered. It was Beth's friend again. She sounded pretty mad. "I arranged a surprise birthday party for Beth. Everyone is here. Where is Beth?"

I said, "Beth doesn't feel well."

Her friend said, "She has to come anyway. Tell her to get over here! Now!."

Beth did not want to go. I wanted everything to be "normal." I insisted that she should.

This was a mistake on my part. Beth needed to be with her brothers at a time like this, and not those girls. She was mad at me for a long time because I insisted. She said later she mostly just sat there at the party. She couldn't be happy and her friends were mad. She couldn't tell them why she felt so bad.

Dan then gave me a gift, a scrimshaw and silver bracelet painted with a butterfly. With everyone in tears, it was hard for me to appreciate it.

Greg said, "We knew you were having problems, but we didn't think it would turn out like this."

I asked Dan to move out and he said, "I will. I'll move out on Thanksgiving Day." "Absolutely not," I said. "We'll have Thanksgiving dinner together as a family."

And so, he moved the day after. Greg helped move his things to an apartment in the South Loop, an elegant one.

We did have a traditional Thanksgiving together. The following day, Dan and Greg with help from the others rented a truck and began sorting through what he would take. I rearranged the living room furniture so it wouldn't look so bare. Everyone was really quiet.

I felt worst of all for Greg. Of all he children, he had been the child his dad had spent time with in his earliest years. Once Matt came along, Dan was gone much of time, but for Greg, Dan had been around and they had a bond. One evening I looked out into the family room. Greg was sitting by himself; it was dusk. He just sat there, and the look on his face was so bleak that it stabbed my heart that I'd had to hurt him so.

It was different for each one. For instance, when Dan was ill with cancer, the Sisters at school had said to Justin, "It must be hard to have your father gone so much at the hospital."

"No," Justin said, "he's never around much. It's just like when he travels."

After I Told Them

No matter what, I told myself, in 1973. I had to keep going. For instance, during the time after my husband moved out in 1974 but the divorce was not final, I had to handle an IRS audit. Dan had not filed a return for three years straight, and we usually filed jointly. An IRS agent called and asked me to tell Dan that "the IRS is starting a statutory action."

The agent said, "I'm going to disallow all his deductions for those years. Your husband still has given me nothing, in spite of my calls. It's been five months.

"And remember, Mrs. D, your name is on the returns. But they'll go for him first. Can *you* do anything for me? Tell him he has to get that stuff in? All I have is what you gave me."

"No," I said. "I can't. We never even speak. If I could get him to co-operate, we'd still be married. Part of the divorce settlement is getting those years of IRS returns filed."

"What about your children? Can they tell him?"

"No," I said. "I won't punish the children by making them tell him that the IRS wants to talk to him. And I can't help you at all. The man's intractable. I wish you all the luck in the world. You are welcome to wait in my living room and go out to talk to him when he's in the driveway to pick up the children this Saturday."

"I don't work on Saturday," the agent said.

I wished I could say that. I had asked and asked for Dan to file the taxes. Over and over, he said, "It's on my list."

The agent went on, "Has he filed for this past year?"

"I know he hasn't. Couldn't I just come to the IRS office?"

"Not in this case. I have to be on the premises."

Uh, oh. Home inspection—on top of the audit. Questions would include "What is this room used for?" I had to face it. That or run away. I obediently gathered all receipts, medical bills, invoices for home office supplies, and check book registers; I ran tallies for each year. In high school, I was really good at math, but now? I was rusty.

I did try again to get my former spouse to be there, but he refused. I had to handle this alone. The agent arrived—a tall, good-looking dark-haired man armed with calculators, files and an intimidating binder with our name on it. I settled him in the family room, which my former spouse had indicated was his home office. The agent took it all in, raised an eyebrow, and said, "Nice fireplace."

Strike One, I thought.

"Would you like coffee?"

"No."

"Some fruit?"

"No," again.

"Water?"

He just looked at me, flipped open his tools, and turned to the huge pile of paper I set out.

I licked my dry lips, feeling I had started up the steps to the gallows. "Yes, well, then, why don't I leave you to it," I said as calmly as I could.

"Don't go far," he said. "I may have questions."

I'll just be hiding upstairs. I needed prayer time alone. Please-God-don't-send-me-to-prison prayers. And about two hours later, I heard Mr. IRS call my name. I went down. He said, "I can't account for $35.26."

"That's a penalty for a late payment. There's a receipt for it." I dug it out. I actually located it, even with shaking fingers.

And that was it! My math skills were better than I thought. Everything balanced and could be allowed for. I thought I'd faint. He stood up and began digging around for his coat.

I walked him out. On the way to the door, he stopped in front of a painting. "Nice," he said.

My keen awareness that I needed money caused me to blurt out, "Would you like to buy it?"

"Oh, no." He looked shocked. "I could never afford it."

We said our goodbyes. Back in the family room I took in deep healing lungsful of air. I had thought I could never manage an audit for three years of non-filing—and I passed.

JUDGMENT DAY

"**N**o landlord in his right mind would welcome a single woman with five children. Not in Chicago or anywhere else," my divorce lawyer said as we worked on the settlement. My husband and his lawyer looked at me as he went on, "She has to keep the house." Keeping the house was vital; it would give our children a familiar shelter in a time when their parents were breaking up the family.

It was still the mid-1970s and my husband's lawyer was alarmed by the paltry amount of child support, even though he had set it up. "This money will go through that family like salt through a dog! I *wish* you two would reconcile!" he said to Dan and me, with an angry look. "And there will be no alimony. Only child support. After all, if she marries again, we don't want Dan supporting another man's pleasure!"

Broad smiles around the table, except on my face.

My stomach lurched. Is that what they thought marriage was? Pleasure? I shot my lawyer a warning look; he stopped smiling and looked down. My spouse and his lawyer appeared to find this remark wonderfully witty.

Could the three of them hear my heart pounding at that? I kept my shaking hands in my lap. And reconcile? I felt attacked and furious. All my years of work and pain to get to this point, and this dim bulb wanted to throw them away. Like many people, he was annoyed at me for saying what appeared to be a perfect marriage was a mirage. And I was entirely to blame for wanting to escape it.

We worked out a settlement that seemed agreeable to the men at the table. I had privately told Mr. G that I would take nothing, anything to get away. He had said, "Now, now, let me do my thing. I'll handle this."

Dan did renege twice on what we had agreed, but in the end, Mr. G went ahead with a settlement the other lawyer and he could agree on. Dan blocked three court dates at the last minute. Mr. G said, "We have to go ahead if he doesn't show up this fourth time."

When the lawyers gave this hand-off to me—the twelve-room house outside Chicago, the five children—I had another problem as well. Because it was I who wanted this divorce, my in-laws and my spouse told everyone that it was because I had "serious mental problems."

Mother-in-law had advised Dan to put me in an asylum and to get me shock treatments to "fix" me, somewhat like an auto tune-up. After shock treatments, they could expect me back in service. Clearly, my not wanting to stay married to her son meant I was insane.

At the time, it seemed odd that the lawyers would give me all that responsibility when I was crazy. And why did Dan want to keep his marriage to a "seriously mentally ill woman"? The children told me their dad's mother often said, "It must be terrible for you children to be in that house with that mother of yours!"

Yes, would anybody but a lunatic volunteer to raise five children alone? Who would want four boys and a girl as the older ones entered puberty, those Golden Years of Adolescence? Perhaps my sainted mother-in-law was right: spending time in a nice, quiet, mental hospital might be like a vacation—clean sheets someone else washed, meals others cooked, curtains I didn't have to iron—compared to our home where the walls throbbed with rock music. And the music itself—Rolling Stones' "Can't Get No Satisfaction," Pink Floyd's "We Don't Want No Education" and The Who's "Who Are You?"—pretty much covered the main themes of what my teens grappled with.

Compared to my dad's melancholy records in our home— "Heartache," "Your Cheatin' Heart," "If I Didn't Care," and "You Don't

Love Me Any More"—my kids' rock music was far more energizing, up-beat and listenable.

And I could have all that hard rock right there in my own living room, almost 24/7. Who wouldn't trade that for a psych ward?

Then, too, Dan's mother had noticed my sketches from an art class. I worked from "life," as they say, using nude models in class. She decided my drawings of naked women meant I was a lesbian, so she shared this insight throughout the extended family and our Catholic parish. That mental ward began to look even more attractive—I could sit around talking about ME to shrinks and groups of crazy people instead of listening to my husband talk about himself, and to my children complain about their lousy teachers, their friends, their lack of friends, their icky lunches and why they couldn't do their chores.

In the 1970s most people believed women belonged in the home and in marriage, and mothers stayed home. Away from school, children played together outside or they ran back and forth to each other's homes—because their moms were there. There was a strong animus against women in the workplace. The *Chicago Tribune* in 1973 published a letter from a woman who wrote "working women are destroying the American family." Further, rather than welcoming that second paycheck, husbands were jealous. What if male co-workers found these working wives appealing and seduced them?

How did a nice Catholic girl like me get into this situation? I had grown up in a small mill town on the Hudson River. My father, mother, and all our relatives were Catholics. And so, the emotional and mental landscape of my childhood and adolescence formed inside the strong-box of Catholic belief. I had no idea I had options, that there were other ways to think and believe.

Sunday Mass attendance was required; we risked going to hell for skipping it. Boring sermons interspersed with vivid descriptions of hell made me feel sick. The sermonizer would outline visions of eyeballs boiling in their sockets as the fires of hell consumed us sinners. Yet we would never escape. Just as Prometheus got his liver pecked out only to have it grow back, the never-ending fires of hell would rage on for all eternity, especially for the sins of our senses.

Annual weeklong retreats for teens at local churches included evening sermons on all Ten Commandments. But the ones "Thou shalt not commit adultery" and "Thou shalt not covet thy neighbor's wife" were the most popular. They gave the retreat master a chance to dwell on the "unspeakable and filthy pleasures" these entailed.

Retreat nights on these commandments drew teens from all parishes for standing room only. I heard boys in the vestibule warning each other not to miss Thursdays when the "good stuff" came up. For the other Commandments, most boys just weren't there.

Fear of hell entered us with our mothers' milk. Long before we had any experience of sin, we were imbued with a terror we didn't understand, a handy tool for parents and teachers to keep us children in line. Adults and especially our Dominican Sister teachers said, "You're on your way to hell!" as they scolded over even small infractions. Only an unusually spirited child could withstand this prediction, and I was not one. I never heard anyone say, "There is no hell!"

At our parish school, these nuns dwelt with relish on how we would be stabbed with pitchforks and fire would forever burn our skin, all inflicted by Lucifer—the Bad Angel who defied God and was cast into hell.

In church we were told to rise above our own sorrows as we looked at the statues of Christ on the Cross, blood dripping from the nails that held him. Our suffering was nothing compared to His. If we were in pain, we were told to "offer it up" for souls suffering in Purgatory, a sort of Green Room for the dead whose souls were not quite ready for heaven.

This Church I believed in was also capable of great beauty—as when it filled our ears with magnificent music, where stained glass windows filtered sunlight through multicolored panes and incense perfumed the atmosphere. Choral voices would rise in harmony, and the spectacle might include a visiting bishop slowly pacing the center aisle in gorgeous, gilt-trimmed vestments, jeweled Cross on his chest. Monsignors in purple walked behind him, a cardinal in crimson.

In the past when I went inside any Catholic Church, I sensed God's presence and felt comfort and protection. I had believed when I spoke to God in prayer, He heard me. The Church had been my early refuge from parental abuse, a safe home. To leave my Church broke my heart—far more than leaving Dan. Divorce meant excommunication, the Church's form of shunning.

And it was our house itself that provided the turning point for me to forge ahead and leave my spouse at any price. Unknown to me, Dan had not made the interest payments on a large second loan against the house. And he had sold the stock that was the collateral, without telling anyone. Once the bank discovered the loan was not secured, they called it for immediate payment. The notice came one lunch time when Dan was traveling as usual. The enclosed note had to be signed by my husband and me to forestall the house being seized.

When I read this real estate loan notice—to be "paid in full within ten days" —I realized that the house was in my husband's name and *mine. We* owned the property. Jointly. This came at me like a thunderbolt: So I *did* have a financial leg to stand on after all. Previously when he threw in my face that I had no money, no resources, I crumpled. Yet here was concrete proof that I had power: I could refuse to sign this.

I kept this to myself for the time being, but feeling panic-stricken, I did call the divorce lawyer. He said, "All right, we have ten days."

He was surprisingly calm, and I wondered how many calamities like this he had met over the years. He helped me negotiate to keep the house.

And a few weeks later, I was on my way to court to testify that I wanted to end my marriage. And lose my soul. My lawyer had asked me to meet him at his Chicago office and walk over to court with him. As we waited for the elevator that morning, he said, "I hope you know how much it means to me to be able to do this."

"Do what?"

"To walk across Daley Plaza together. I have two clients in the hospital this morning. One with two bullets in his back and another with four."

I was in a daze and didn't realize how relieved he was that I was intact. He had told me "not to date or do anything that might antagonize" my spouse. My lawyer had never mentioned his concern that I might be in danger. But my shrink and two friends had told me they thought homicide was a possibility in the weeks leading up to the court date.

As we entered the Civic Center and looked for our courtroom, I told him I was really nervous.

"Now there's nothing to be scared about," he said. "It's all very cut and dried. I have a list of questions I'll ask you. All you have to do is say 'Yes' to each."

The courtroom was thronged that December day with well over a hundred people, no empty seats. All had their winter coats on and sat looking forward, silent and grim. I scanned the rows hoping to see a kind face. And there in the very back wearing dark glasses on this dark day, I saw Dorothy from our art class. My heart gave a thump; she had promised to come, and she did. I felt tears start spilling and brushed them away.

As my lawyer and I walked the long aisle to the bench, he said out of the side of his mouth, "Uh, oh. We've got a tough judge. Margaret O'Malley."

My heart sank. She did look tough, and that Irish name meant she must be, or used to be, a Catholic. So what was she doing in divorce court? Catholics were forbidden to divorce, could no longer receive Communion and at death, would go straight to hell. A few minutes earlier, I had heard this judge refuse a decree to the woman ahead of me, telling her, "You go home and work harder on your marriage. You've been married only eleven months, not enough time." Tough judge, indeed.

As I settled on the edge of the witness chair, the judge asked the lawyers, "Where is Mr. D?"

My husband's lawyer said smoothly, "Mr. D is traveling. On business."

My husband had refused to come to court, over and over. He'd said, "This is bad for my image." This was the fourth court date he had brushed aside.

She looked at both lawyers, said abruptly, "Well, he should be here," then said, "Proceed."

My lawyer glanced at a piece of paper and began questioning me. He started by asking the date of my wedding and suddenly St. Mary's church flashed before me. My heart thudded; I saw colors from the stained-glass windows, azure, crimson, gold, flooding in with the fragrance of lilies and carnations, and I heard the organ playing "Mother, at Your Feet Is Kneeling," as I lay my bouquet on the Blessed Mother's altar.

I forgot to breathe.

My lawyer looked at me over the top of his glasses, a warning sign. I pulled in a full breath and answered him. He went on, "Had your husband been away for long periods of time? Leaving you alone with five children?"

"Yes." I could barely talk. I gripped the partition in front of me so hard it made my hands ache.

"Did your husband refuse to have you see a psychiatrist? Did he refuse to pay for a psychiatrist for you?"

"Yes."

"When you were finally able to get Mr. D to go to a psychiatrist, you went for a year—is that correct? For marriage counseling? And at the end of that time, the psychiatrist determined it was futile?"

Judge O'Malley–not looking at me–broke in: "The name of the psychiatrist?"

The questions continued. "Your husband hit you from time to time inflicting bruises?"

(I don't remember, I don't remember! But the doctor used to point to bruises on my arms or legs and say, "Where did those come from?")

I just said, "Yes."

"You gave him no provocation for this?"

I choked. "Yes."

"Several times he broke things, including punching a hole with his fist in the bedroom wall?"

"Yes."

"Did he creep his hands around your neck and choke you at times when you argued?"

"Yes."

"Were there bruises on your neck?"

"Yes."

"Frequently criticized your judgment in the handling of the children?"

"Yes."

"Leaving you alone with them for extended periods of time?"

I felt miserable with each new probe but continued to say "Yes."

"You developed symptoms of dizziness, difficulty in breathing, extreme exhaustion, difficulty sleeping, and weight loss for no physical reason?"

"Yes."

"Your doctor attributed this to the deterioration of the marriage?"

"Yes."

The judge interrupted. "The doctor's name?"

After I answered, my lawyer continued, "Your husband moved out about a year ago or more with no provocation on your part? You gave him no reason to leave?"

I wasn't sure about this, but he was nodding vigorously at me. "Yes." It was harder to talk.

"Prior to his moving out, you had begun divorce proceedings on the grounds of mental cruelty?"

And so on. These questions soft-pedaled his bullying and abuse, his breaking my nose, choking me until I blacked out and so on. My lawyer told me beforehand that he and the other lawyer had negotiated what they would present. There were some issues, for instance, that I had wanted to kill myself to get away from Dan that they agreed not to bring up.

My husband's lawyer butted in from time to time to ask, for instance, "You do understand that this settlement can never be changed or improved?"

The tough judge sat there expressionless, glancing from one to the other. She didn't once look at me. I felt myself perspiring into my Mollie Parnis designer dress. It was the only one I could still wear after the weight I'd lost leading up to today.

Suddenly, Judge O'Malley slid the left sleeve of her robe up over her elbow, leaned forward with her hand out to the lawyers and said, "Give me that decree. I'll sign it right now. Then I want to see the two of you in my chambers. Now."

As she stood the bailiff intoned the words for a brief recess, the lawyers followed her out, and I was left sitting there in the witness box in a daze. What had happened? Everyone seemed to be staring at me. I felt impaled. I didn't know if I should stand, step out, or sit still. Or run away. What was going on?

I sat. No one spoke to me. Time crept by on hands and knees.

At last the bailiff called, "All rise!"

The judge returned to her bench, and my lawyer walked toward me with very pink cheeks. He was smiling, a jarring note in this courtroom. He told me I could step down; he must have seen how shaky I was and gave me a hand.

Then the bailiff called the next case.

It wasn't until we got to the courtroom lobby that he explained. His smile still lit his face as he said, "She complimented us! The judge! She said we were both to be congratulated. That's what she called us to her chambers for." Looking like a pleased child, he savored this accolade as he shook my cold hand in both his warm ones.

My husband's lawyer barged in between us to shake my hand and wish me good luck. He didn't look so happy. But I couldn't pay attention to him; I wanted him gone.

My lawyer said, "I'm anxious to get this completed, so I'm cutting my fee in half. Your husband still has to pay that half, but this way it will be over and done with sooner."

I kissed him right there in front of his colleague, and he blushed. Then he hugged me and kept touching and squeezing my hand. "Have a nice time over the holidays!" he said. Christmas was the next week, but I couldn't think about it now.

From the corner of my eye, I could see my art-class friend, still in sunglasses, waiting by the door, hesitant to interrupt our glee. I was in shock, but a pleasant shock: it was over. I had met the devil and worked with him. Hell and be damned! We won. I won. The bully lost. Whatever would come next, right then I felt like I could handle it.

Dorothy and I went to enjoy a celebration lunch on LaSalle Street close to Civic Center. Being near City Hall, we were soon surrounded by mostly loud, hard-drinking politicians, aldermen.

I looked around us; we were the only women there.

That First Christmas After

The divorce decree was signed on December 16, 1976. Nine days later was our first Christmas as a "broken family" to use the term then in vogue. Dan had moved out, but I invited him for Christmas day; the children asked me to. I lived in dread of having him stop by, never knowing what mood he might be in. These moods were directed at me and not the children.

Money-wise, I had gotten down to only supplies for pancakes and Kool-Aid. But knowing how important rituals were for children, I wanted to make this first Christmas as good as I possibly could.

When the kids asked if we could still have a real tree, I said yes, a big one like we always had. Fortunately, the week before the holiday, I was able to sell a painting named by my seven-year-old Martin as "Little Boy Looking for God." It depicts a small boy in a church walking to the altar–so I had enough cash for a tree and for "fixings" for dinner. I put the tree up and the kids and I worked on finding candles, tidying, peeling potatoes, pie-making, table setting and the myriad tasks that go into having company—in this case, their dad.

He got to our house a little after noon. We exchanged gifts. He gave me a gold-color medallion inscribed "You are free to be your true self here and now. Jonathan Livingston Seagull."

He must have felt giving me permission was appropriate. I tried not to laugh or feel offended. I knew I was free and didn't need a bird to tell me so. However, I did not point this out because this day was for avoiding saying anything that would set him off. (Jonathan was not my kind of philosopher, although I thought parodies such as Marvin Stanley Pigeon in *The New Yorker* were fun.)

Martin gave Dan a card he had made with a tiny drawing of Santa, reindeer, a tree with gifts and a fireplace. Mart was ten. He wrote:

"I'm so sorry that you had to go
I know that I will surely miss you so
Wishing you a very merry Christmas and a happy new year."

I hadn't seen it beforehand, and I choked up when he showed it to us.

For our festive dinner, I made the usual roast turkey, bread stuffing, mashed potatoes, quarts of gravy, white corn, salad and pies. We lighted candles and Dan had brought wine. Looking around the table at all the faces, he said, "This is a wonderful dinner. Thank you for having me."

Beth said, "You're welcome to come anytime, Dad." She was fourteen, and I felt uncomfortable about how grown-up she sounded, like her dad was a complete stranger. But I realized she meant the effort was up to him to arrange for it.

As we passed the platters back and forth, Dan said to me, "Did your brother send me a gift?"

"Not that I know of. Why don't you ask him directly?" I said.

"I don't want to do that," he said.

"Did you send him one?" I asked.

"No," he said. Odd that he expected my brother to give him a present if he sent him none. And I had thought of my siblings as *my* family, but over the past year Dan had flown to visit each of them more than once without telling me beforehand. This hurt. I had been close to my sister and brothers as we grew up. I loved them.

They told me, "Dan called and asked if he could stop by for a few days." I hoped they might tell him "No" out of loyalty to me. But they didn't. They lived in New York and Oregon, far from Chicago. From what they later said, he liked to sit around drinking with them in the evenings; their talk included discussing how mentally ill I was. (Years later when I told people I worked with about this perception of my "illness," it brought on hearty laughter. My boss told me he considered me the "office therapist." Men and women often called on me for advice.}

"Dan seems to be looking for agreement," my sister said. I suspected they were afraid to contradict or offend him. His being six feet four and heavy gave him an intimidating presence. Though I realized long ago that they stopped being part of my support system, it hurt that he drew them to himself for support. I would have liked them to refuse to have him visit. On the other hand, it never occurred to me to look for any kind of agreement from Dan's people.

The only Christmas gift my in-laws sent the children was a subscription to a Catholic magazine, *The Ligourian*, published by the Redemptorist Priests of St. Alphonsus Ligouri. Articles on "The Value of Suffering, Bible Quiz. Understanding the Psalms," etc., filled its pages. (The kids put it in the trash whenever it arrived.)

After our holiday dinner as the kids cleared the table, Dan went out to the living room and fell asleep on the couch. Greg said affectionately, "Look at Dad. How can he sleep like that?"

"Yes, with all the noise and him with leg up in the air," Matt said.

After he left, the kids told me about a champagne party Dan just given. Martin and Justin had tended bar. (I didn't know about this before, because I would have objected, since it was illegal for minors to tend bar.) The boys told me about old friends who were there and that Dan's secretary got drunk. Mart said, "I took her out to the elevator because I was afraid she couldn't find the button to press."

I felt bad hearing about a champagne party at his new apartment. He complained so often when he had to send me child support money, how it involved "great sacrifice" on his part. Giving it to me, despite it being part of the settlement, usually came with a lecture about how he couldn't afford it.

"I just can't give it to you this month," he would say. That week he had just paid a lot of money for new furniture for his apartment, and Greg's tuition was unpaid. The times when I didn't get the child support money, he said, "You deserve punishment, for what you did to me. And I will punish you." He said this before the divorce and after.

My great sin was that I had made him look bad by telling the world I couldn't live with him. At the moment, I couldn't pay Greg's tuition at Fenwick, the Catholic high school. I had put the other kids in public schools, but Greg's father had graduated from Fenwick.

The principal called to rebuke me for my arrears: "Now, Mrs. D., we *all* have financial problems, but you *owe* us this money," the priest started in. "A lot of families have trouble making these payments, but *they* make the sacrifice." He ladled on Guilt as only a Catholic priest could do. And yes, I felt deeply guilty. To the bone.

I was dying to tell him that my child support money hadn't come that month. But I had promised my children I wouldn't tell anyone about the divorce. And I wondered if I had, would this priest throw Greg out of the school to prevent his contaminating others? Probably. For my son's sake, I maintained silence. It was humiliating. Never did I regret my choice to divorce, even in the darkest moments. It was worth it.

My former friends thought divorce was contagious. This attitude went beyond shunning me; many stopped inviting me to any social gathering. As a single woman, I was socially unacceptable, a pariah. I remember standing in a circle of couples at an Aspen weekend–one I had arranged–and one man invited everyone standing there to come visit their vacation home in Vail. "Except you, of course, Anne."

He was rude to exclude me but he pointedly did. He had told me that he saw "no reason for divorce." As he put it, "My wife and I have had OUR problems. But WE always worked things out." Then he looked at me in a way that made me feel I was an Untouchable from India. I had to "Keep Smiling" and not voice the rage I felt.

And I still had to go forward with routines like dealing with the mandatory behind-the-wheel parent hours that took time and rapidly advanced my aging. I figured once each of them had a driver's license, they would think they knew all they'd ever need to, and my admonitions would fall on deaf ears. Therefore, I even made them turn the radio off while we practiced. I used to think to myself, "I want to have no regrets."

Drivers' Ed instructors insisted we parents log time riding "shotgun" while the neophyte drivers became "comfortable" behind the wheel, in my case, our Volkswagen microbus. I would brace my feet against the dashboard and we took off.

Since we lived a block from a chain of graveyards, with headstones in German, I thought the area could provide a helpful reminder that infractions of driving laws held serious consequences. The speed limit there was usually five miles per hour—perfect for my nerves. Granite and marble headstones made sturdy buffers, should any child go off course. Once Waldheim Cemetery was mastered, we moved on as most other parents do to empty parking lots, local roads, rush-hour traffic, and finally the expressway.

For that, on my first time with one son as we entered the On ramp, the car would not pick up speed. Suddenly he said, "Oh, my god, I've still got the parking brake on!" and released it. An eighteen-wheeler came up behind us at speed, swerved up on the grass to our right and kept on. I took many deep breaths and we continued on down the highway.

Just before my student drivers got out from under my supervision, we would drive to Lower Wacker Drive, usually at night. I thought the homeless and vagrants with their ragged blankets, cartons, and oil drum fires provided a cautionary reminder. When I did this with son Greg, he said, "We're really down here to look for relatives, right?"

"Very funny. Just keep your eyes on the road, would you, please? And lock the doors."

KIDS AND THEIR FRIENDS

My children's friends were often at the house, and occasionally wandered into the kitchen to see what I was working on for dinner. They would stand, inhaling, keenly interested in food and food subjects as they patted the refrigerator affectionately. They continued to be around after the divorce the same as before.

Sometimes I would turn the oven on low and have an onion in there. "Something smells wonderful!" one boy or another would say as they passed through. I did make sure to leave out cookies, pretzels, and fruit.

A friend who liked to hang around our house throughout high school was Chet. He and Matthew met one summer at the local swimming pool. Matthew had inherited my penchant for attracting strays, and so when Matt came home for supper, Chet often tagged along. Having another kid at the table occasionally was not a problem as long as I had extra bread, noodles and potatoes. But when Chet-for-supper threatened to become a habit, I would tell him, "We are going to eat now, so it's time you went home, Chet."

"Oh, that's OK. I can wait. I'll just sit in the living room," he would say. And I had to tell him we needed to be "just our family tonight. We have some family things we have to talk about."

When he did eat with us, he liked to talk about his injuries from diving off the high tower.

"See, sometimes I land on the concrete instead of the water," he said while my kids would nod and continue eating their chicken stew. Then he would add that "I sometimes ride on the tops of cars, you know, 'surfing.'"

I looked up warningly at my children, who knew this was a forbidden activity. But he said, "My other injuries come from informing for the local police. Me and some other guys like to keep our ears to the ground."

I could hear someone say quietly, "So does that mean you're a narc?"

Chet ignored this, saying, "We hear a lot of stuff about drugs and can pass it on to the cops."

"Really?" I said. "Jus, please pass me the salt?" Not having foreseen this turn to the conversation, I didn't at first know how to stop it.

Taking more mashed potatoes, Chet said, "Gee, I haven't had hot food cooked on the top of the stove in so long. . . . And I have a commander," he kept talking. "Or at least I had one until he got shot to death three weeks ago. Four bullets."

The other kids looked at me, looked at each other, said nothing, used their eyebrow semaphore to signal "Wow" to each other, then went back to eating.

Chet's grin lit up his whole body as he said, "I want to be a cop. I'm fifteen now and my morals are all set. For the rest of my life. So I'm going to study sociology and all that stuff." He was still talking. "And then go to the Police Academy. To be a good cop.

"My life has been threatened," he went on, "and I love it."

I felt bad for him. I had wondered where his mom was. He never mentioned her, but once in a while, his father came over on a bicycle to get him. I had noticed lately Chet looking at Beth with longing. Maybe he wondered if she was a good cook. She had told me she wasn't interested in him. Summer was almost over and I was glad. The pool would soon close, and that meant Chet would go back to his school, far from ours.

As I sat thinking about that, Justin blurted out, "Chet, you smell really bad!" Bodily hygiene was not among Chet's virtues, though his daily swim helped, but I hadn't noticed until he was inside the house.

The other kids murmured agreement with Justin.

"Well! Thanks a lot!" Chet said. He didn't seem embarrassed. But he did stop coming by soon after school began, to my relief.

One boy who was at the house often was Mart's high school friend Don. He liked to sit on the threshold of the door between the kitchen and dining room. We had to step around or over him. "Don, are you sure you wouldn't be more comfortable in the living room? We have lots of big chairs and you can spread out," one of us would say.

"Here's fine."

Then, just before Mart and Don graduated high school, Don's parents moved to Washington, D.C. Don was supposed to move with them, but he wanted to be near his friends. He asked if he could live at our house for the summer. At first it seemed do-able, but when he said, "I don't want to have to stay here every night. If I feel like staying somewhere else, I want to do that, and not have to report in to you."

That was a game-changer. Don was 17, and I said, "Don, you're still a minor. If there's a problem, I'm responsible. If the cops come looking, I'm on the hook for knowing where you are. I can't agree." (I later learned he also liked to drop acid.)

He was furious and so was my son. It was one thing for my own children to come and go, but Don was not mine. Would his parents give me money for his food? No, he said.

I had barely enough money for food for us. I heard later that his parents had taken offense when he didn't want to go with them and his little brother, but preferred to live with me.

In my defense, I said, "This is not Mother McKneally's Home for Wayward Boys."

It took a few months but they forgave me and later when they were both in college, Don occasionally sent a postcard, with the return address "Prairie Baby" that asked, "Mom, is it OK for me to come home this weekend? Love, Don."

The handwriting was so like my son Justin's, that as I read it, I thought it was from Justin, but Justin never asked permission to come home. He just showed up but of course, he was blood kin.

Beth had a good friend, Colleen, whose parents were the classic Irish types who believed sparing the rod spoiled the child. One Saturday night, she and Beth came home late, and Beth asked, "OK if Colleen stays over tonight?"

"Yes, of course," I said and got ready for bed. Much later, Beth woke me. Colleen's parents were furious that she was staying here and were coming to get her. Matt was still up and answered the door in his briefs. Matt was more than a head taller than the girl's father, and muscular in the way only a gymnast who worked out every day can be. He said later, "I wanted these people to know they were intruding, so I answered the door in my underwear."

The parents stood on the doorstep until I came down to let them in to the entrance hall. The father said, "Where's Colleen? Upstairs? I'll go up and get her." He started toward the stairs and had one foot on the second step.

"You will not go upstairs in my house!" I said loudly.

He stopped. "Well, then, I think I'd like to have the police here." He had a pronounced Irish brogue. He turned and came back down to stand in the hall next to his wife, who had said nothing. She seemed cowed.

"Good idea. I'll call them," I said.

I went into my office and called our police station. "We have a situation here. A father has come over to make his daughter go home with them, and I'd like an officer to come over. She doesn't want to go with him."

The officer said, "I'll send a patrol car over. It will be just a few minutes."

Shortly, I looked out to see two uniformed officers approaching the front steps clanking with their equipment–night sticks, handcuffs, weapons. I let them in and said, "This is Mr. Flaherty and his daughter is upstairs. She doesn't want to go home with him."

"How old is this girl?" one officer said.

"She's seventeen," I said.

"Would you please get her?" he said.

Beth brought her friend down into the front hall; Colleen's face was red and wet with tears. She sniffled. Beth said to me, "She's afraid she'll get beaten."

The officers had walked over to talk quietly by themselves. Mr. Flaherty said, "Don't we get to tell our side of the story?"

"As far as I'm concerned, you don't have a side." The officer turned back to his colleague and continued chatting about a recent arrest north of here. Matt and Beth stood there, eyes wide, alert and quiet. Colleen sobbed quietly nearby The smell of beer was palpable, and Matt raised his eyebrows as he caught my eye. I nodded.

Her mother said, "She's going to be a drunk just like her father."

An Irish witch's curse.

The officer in charge took me aside and said quietly, "I'm sorry, ma'am, but we have to let her go with her parents. She's underage, and it's the law, I'm sorry to say."

With a triumphant smile, Mr. Flaherty and his wife took their daughter to their car. They walked on either side of her, gripping her arms.

The officers said again, "We're sorry, but there's nothing we can do. The law is the law."

But they did do something: the next day I had a call from a teacher at the high school. She was Colleen's homeroom teacher, and said, "Colleen has told me several times that her father beats her. I never believed her, but the police contacted DCFS and .they called me. I wanted you to know that I will follow up on this."

Beth had told me that Colleen was beaten with a tennis racket held to the side, so that the frame delivered painful blows. Beth had seen the bruises.

She also told me that the teacher who called me had gone into Colleen's class and called her into the hall. She put her arms around her and said, "I am so sorry I didn't believe you before when you told me about your dad. What can I do to help?"

Beth didn't like this girl's father; he often scolded her. She said, "You always told me I had to respect adults who earn respect, but this man—I have no respect for. I don't like him for what he does to Colleen."

Son Greg's friend throughout high school, college, and beyond was Kelty—Mike Kelty. They were buddies for pool-hopping, pickup basketball games, and other activities I was not aware of at the time. If he were in the house or outside playing Frisbee, and it was dinnertime, as part of the family "Before Dinner" routine if Mart or Justin were setting the table, they might say, "Is Kelts staying over?"

"Just set him a place. I'll ask him," I'd say.

Years afterward, Greg would tell us at dinner about the times when he and "Kelts" used to get beer when they were underage.

"We waited outside the liquor store and asked a guy going in to buy beer for us. One time a cop pulled up beside us and Kelty took off. The cop grabbed me and put me in his squad. He said, 'What did this guy look like? The one who said he'd buy beer for you?'

"I wasn't anxious to rat on the guy so I looked around and saw a lot of guys in plaid lumberjack shirts. I said, 'I think he was wearing a plaid shirt.' Then I looked up and across the street I could see Kelty in the window of Arby's eating a beef sandwich and laughing his head off, pointing at me. Even he had on a plaid shirt. I told the cop I didn't see the guy anywhere and after a while he let me go."

Kelty was around in good times and bad. It was comfortable to have him there, not quite the same as Chet.

And when it was time for me to move out of the big house, he and his brother helped us move. It took a huge, overloaded truck. The two of them and my boys piled it high.

We had a bamboo peacock chair that had been in the house since I married. It squeaked when we sat in it and dropped little bits of itself on the floor over the years. It was more than time to let it go. Greg said, "Let me handle this." He took the big, clumsy chair out into the grass, and with great enthusiasm and an axe chopped it into small pieces as I watched.

We ceremoniously burned it in the fireplace.

Having the kids' friends around was not so much of a problem, but having Dan stop by unexpectedly was. The settlement had specifically indicated he was to give me advance notice whenever he would stop by to pick up the children. But he often came over without letting me know.

When he did drop by, he made derogatory comments. For instance, he would pop in and notice Matthew cleaning out the fireplace and dumping ashes into a big garbage can. In a bitter tone, my former husband said, "Oh, I see you are keeping a garbage can in the fireplace room."

There was no point in my saying, "No. It's just while we empty out the ashes." He didn't listen. And it was hard enough to get the kids to do their jobs without his negative comments.

I was tempted to say, "We are getting a garbage can for every room. And wait till you see upstairs!"

He passed on into the dining room, saying, "I see you have broken more panes of glass in the door. Well, this old house sure is falling apart!" The broken panes had just happened. I did get them fixed, but his pessimism had been a downer throughout our marriage.

From time to time, the children stayed with him for a weekend or for ten days in the summer. After one visit, Beth told me, "It's boring mostly. Dad doesn't know my friends, or what I'm studying in school. I think he feels bad about us. But I don't like going out to restaurants. Maybe once a month, but not four times a week."

It made me feel good to know she liked eating at home, or at least, I thought that's what she was saying. She went on, "And when we need groceries at Dad's, I'm the one who has to make the list and do the shopping. Also, Martin and Justin tell Dad what's wrong at home. They fight all the time when we're there.

"Dad makes someone, usually me, sit between them in the car because they hit each other. Then when we get back to his place, they make up for it by hitting each other more."

I could hardly stand them after they had been with Dan. They fought far more after a visit. Sadly, I had to face that there were things I couldn't control, and this was one.

Sarah, the school therapist who had met with the children and me, had said the children needed to be with their father so they could see what he was really like. With great misgivings, I agreed to let them stay with him on some weekends. But I resented and could not control that Dan opened his liquor cabinet to the children, all of them, so they could drink freely. As my son Matthew said, "The other kids all drink while they are with Dad." Matthew didn't drink at all, so he just withdrew.

One time two years after the divorce, my former husband invited me to Thanksgiving dinner at his house. He said, "so we could all be together."

I accepted—unwisely. As it turned out, I was to roast the turkey and bring it with me. I did, partly to make sure I had a good dinner. What I got in return was an ear-and-eye-ful of everyone's behavior as they drank and traded sarcasms at the table.

I noticed all of them made fun of their father every time he didn't get the point of their joking: "That was an airplane joke, Dad. Over your head!" Mocking laughter followed. All five of our children were there and several of their friends.

I sat next to Beth's college boyfriend who said quietly to me, "Are you shocked? At the disrespect? This is how it is all the time."

Although I was not ridiculed, I felt really uncomfortable, and really like screaming. They weren't like that with me. If it had been my home, I would have told them, "Hey! Cut it out. Right now!"

I regretted agreeing to be there. It wasn't a happy getting together, oil spilling out on troubled waters.

It was savagery.

I made my goodbyes as soon as I could, but waited until I turned the key in the ignition to let the tears start. I had kept it together till then. But I was alone now and could let my tears of relief and sorrow fall: Relief that I had escaped this marriage and his culture. Sorrow that my children were part of this still.

My work was far from done.

Am I Lonesome Tonight?

"You really ought to start dating again while you still have some looks left." After my divorce, advice like this came at me like gunfire. The worst offenders were my own family — my brother, for instance, who added, "These years won't go on forever. Is there someone at work you could go out with?"

Then my mother called to say, "What about someone from church? (I was the only divorced Catholic in our parish in the late '70s.) You should date. You need a husband, someone to protect you."

"Mother, I . . ."

She went on, "You know perfectly well that without a father those boys of yours will turn into drug addicts, alcoholics, and homosexuals. They can't be normal!"

Using a different approach, my sister took each of my children aside and asked, "Why doesn't your mother date? What's the matter with her?"

My children were baffled by comments like these. The five of them saw no reason for me to date, and they didn't understand why anyone would ask *them* about my dating, as they pointed out more than once at dinnertime.

My non-Catholic family doctor: "Are you dating yet? Why not? (He usually asked this during a breast check.) I think you ought to be fitted for a diaphragm just in case."

On my car radio Gracie Slick sang to me, "Don't you want somebody to love? You'd better find somebody to love!"

I felt I had violated an unwritten code that everyone should be in quest of a partner. Clearly I was out of step. I never wanted to marry again, let alone get involved with someone, after escaping an abusive marriage. Lately I had begun to feel lighter and even more, happy. Grateful for being free from abuse. Productive in my teaching. Connected to my children.

But to people who thought they knew me, I didn't know what I was missing.

Self-doubt took over. Was Mother right when she said, "You *can't* do it, raising those children by yourself. You need a husband, and *they* need a father." Every time Mother called — she lived on the East Coast and I, near Chicago — she brought it up. I reminded her they had a father, and he still paid child support, most of the time; he just didn't live with us. Her phone calls usually started, "Dear, have you found anyone?" No how-are-you.

If I followed her advice, I'd need a plan. And where would I find a suitable candidate? The most likeable men I knew were already married. And having children in the house complicated the plan — teenagers lying around the living room guffawing at each other's jokes could crimp any budding relationship. So if I even had a date, I had better meet him away from the house and this ready-made family.

And that house! To a real estate agent, it was a "handyman's delight." Fifteen rooms with a full (and often flooded) basement, large rooms. Sometimes it felt like Miss Havisham's mansion in *Great Expectations* when every fall, mice came in. (Not mice living in my old wedding cake.) These were field mice who came through chinks in the foundation every year with the first frost. They colonized in the soft earth under the porch where they set up camp like French revolutionaries, establishing supply lines from our kitchen, and training each other in survival skills. I had almost gotten used to having them invade each fall. And recently I noticed someone had taped on the baseboard in the kitchen a tiny WANTED poster with a drawing of a mouse.

It wasn't just me who thought the mice were almost family. One night I was sitting in the family room with Justin, fourteen, who was studying history. I had student papers to correct. Mart, twelve, came in; he couldn't seem to get through any door without banging against both sides with books, legs, head, elbows. He said, "That Sampson creep! I swear he's humor-impaired. In science today he said, 'Boys and girls, Uranus has a diameter of over a million miles.' And *I* said, 'That's funny. I'm pretty sure mine's only an inch.' And he sent me to the principal! Whaddya suppose is the matter with that guy?"

Justin glared at him and he sat down, settling in to read *National Lampoon.* And for a while all we heard was the icebox turning on and off, and a stifled snort from Mart. Then Justin looked up from his text and said, "Listen! They're back." A rustle came from under the fridge. We looked at each other. Then came the snap! of a sprung trap.

Mart got up and went to the kitchen. He called, "Mom, look! He's so cute! This little mousie is wearing a beret and carrying his French book. He's probably on his way to school. And we've killed him!" I heard him take the trap to the back yard and clang the lid on the garbage can. He came back in muttering, "We never get to keep pets," and settled down again.

And now the only sound was Mart slapping his thighs and sliding his feet down the wall, "Hey! Listen to this! There's this article about the Early Warning Signs of Sex. (Helpless laughter) And how to prevent it. SEX! And the way to prevent sex is with a diagram. The diagram shows the path from sex to early death!" Howling, he dug the back of his head into the arm of the couch.

Justin said calmly without looking up, "Would you just shut up? I've a test first period. If you have to laugh, go in the living room."
After my mother called again, usual message, I decided to try a singles group advertised in the local paper. These groups — Discovery, Aware, Spares — offered mixers where they discussed topics like "How to Fall

in Love with the Right Person" and "Are You a Veteran of Love and War or a Casualty?" A Single-Mingle group was having a talk on Female Sexuality.

As I checked in, I got a name tag that was sure to remove layers of nap from my sweater. It said "Hi, I'm Anne" in tiny letters so any man facing me would have to lean into my bosom to read it. Rewriting "A N N E" on it so anyone could read it from across the room, I walked inside.

A woman in a black tent dress began talking; she told us she was a sex therapist at a Northwestern University clinic, and that she ran weight-loss sessions. She shifted from ham to ham as she talked and looked over our heads as she drifted from female sexuality to touching and being touched. "So important — for all of us! If we don't get skin contact daily, our spinal cords will shrivel and dry out!"

At this, the men and women near me looked scared and gray-faced. And terribly single and vulnerable. She also shared stories about her own sex life. "You know, the first time I brought a man home, my two children called Grandma on the phone as soon as my bedroom door closed! And Grandma was so upset that she had Grandpa call me — in my bedroom!" The speaker looked at her fingernails, waited a beat, then said, "And by the way, the man was black.

"But this made me re-think my parenting. I mean, if I could bring home a lover, there's really no reason my children shouldn't. Well, my thirteen-year-old son thought that was wonderful," she said. He started exercising his new privilege at once. But her daughter said she "wanted to wait for a while, which was a healthy choice for a ten-year-old."

Saying, "Now we will all practice Touching, and I'll lead," she instructed everyone to lie on the floor. As people moved chairs, I retrieved my raincoat and quietly left.

The next morning as I made coffee, I found a note taped to the ice-box. On a scrap of paper in tiny writing was:

NOTICE!

Camembert, our brother-in-arms, is dead!
I promise to avenge him!
(signed) J. Roquefort, *Capitaine*,
Loyal Order of the Mouse.

I thought how different the children of last night's speaker seemed from my kids, who wrote these notes and hadn't asked to "exercise sexual privileges." Sure, they were messy and grouchy and tried to weasel out of their chores like all teens, but they had also learned to cook their own breakfasts and make lunches. I still made dinner so we could eat together.

Later that week I went for a checkup with my doctor. As I undressed, he called loudly from two rooms away, "Say, Annie, did you ever get to use that diaphragm I got for you?"

Wrapped in my hospital-issue paper gown, I went to the door, "*Would* you mind! When I am ready, and *not* before, I will get involved in some kind of ..."

He was contrite as he came back into the room: "I'm sorry. I really want you to have some fun. I don't mean to imply you aren't normal, not at all. Lots of people don't have sex and lead happy lives. The saints, for instance ....."

"Would you just do my checkup and let me out of here?"

"Annie, I know you are dedicated right now to raising those children, and you're doing a great job, but someday — sooner than you think — they're going to grow up and out of your life." He patted my shoulder kindly, "You have to start thinking about what — or who — will take their place."

My one divorced friend, Lenore, agreed with my mother and doctor that I should be out meeting men, so she invited me to the Embassy Ballroom. "It's on the West Side of Chicago. Nice place to meet people. The guys are mostly widowers. Music you can dance to."

"Wait a minute," I said. Lenore already lived with a guy and her own two kids. "Why would *you* want to go?"

"One, Sylvio works nights. He won't know. And two, his divorce isn't final. That wife of his still has her hooks into him. This will give me a little insurance. Come on, let's go; we'll have fun!"

And so, a few nights later, we headed for the Embassy. As she drove, Lenore said, "Whatever you do, don't have any alcohol! No drinks. There's no telling what can happen if you drink."

I agreed.

"Okay, whatever happens tonight, we leave together, promise?" she said.

I promised.

The Embassy, a converted movie theatre, had its seats removed to form a dance floor; heavy maroon velvet drapes hung along the walls. An all-male orchestra in tuxedos played fox-trots and an occasional waltz, usually the "Tennessee." Everyone in the ballroom seemed older — or maybe they just looked old. Many women wore floor-length dresses; the men, three-piece suits.

I asked for a glass of water on the rocks with a twist of lemon. The bartender, a chubby young woman in a tuxedo, made a face but fixed the drink. Lenore waved to me, as she headed for the dance floor with a tall, serious-looking man. She mouthed, "Remember! No drinks!" and disappeared into the crowd of dancers.

An older man with ears like batwings appeared at my elbow, wrapping his hand around it. He pointed to my ice-water-with-a-twist and said, "Drink that. I'll get you another. Then we dance."

A business-like agenda. I drank up at one gulp. He looked pleased, but was disappointed that I didn't want another. We began dancing to "Are You Lonesome Tonight?" as he told me he worked in the garment district. His suit looked hand-tailored. He asked what I did for a living, then interrupted to ask my dress size. He held me tighter. I pulled back.

Speaking around his breath mint, he said, "What's the matter?"

Everyone circling us wore those doomed looks I saw on subway passengers in the winter. Lenore and a man with long white hair shuffled
past. He looked like he'd just gotten some bad news. They weren't talking.

A polka started, and my partner held firmly to my waist as he said.
"We'll stand on the side for this one." He seemed breathless; we watched
the dancers move to the relentless rhythm, like performing a penance. I
uncoupled us, excused myself, and went to the ladies' room.

As I entered, a woman combing her long, blonde hair looked up
at me and the attendant, then said, "If he bought me dinner, does that
mean I have to sleep with him?"

"How old is he?" said the attendant.

"I don't know. Fifty-five or something."

"Then the answer is 'yes.'" The attendant wiped out a few sinks, rat-
tling her tips dish as she flicked by. "Ya know, we getta nice classa people
in here. No rough stuff, men gotta wear ties. Mostly nice guys."

"When you say 'In here,' you mean out there in the ballroom, don't
you?" My eyes met the attendant's eyes in the mirror. She paused, then
said, "Yeah. Of *course*, I mean out there."

As I did a complete valve-and-ring job on my makeup, the attendant commented, "Rouge. Lots more rouge. Those lights out there, they
make a person like you look dead." She sat on the sinktop, lit a cigarette,
and said. "Ya know, I just buried my sister."

Other women came in, touched up their hairdos, refreshed their
makeup, complained about watered drinks, left. As I added more and
more color to my face, the attendant said, "Ya know, I used to do cosmet-
ics for the remains at a burial home. But the quiet got to me." Squinting
at my face in the mirror, the attendant said, "And those older people,
awful lotta work getting them ready for viewing."

So I rouged my chin and forehead as well.

"Better," the attendant said. Suddenly, she jumped off the sink saying, "Geezis, what happened to you?"

Looking happy and excited, Lenore had burst through the doorway
with wisps of hair stuck to her forehead, her blouse torn, and mascara

streaking down one cheek. "I've just had the fright. Of my life!" She sure didn't look frightened.

"Okay. Guy from here, right?" The attendant settled back, lit another cigarette, nodded at me. "I knew it."

Lenore patted her hair into place as she met my eyes in the mirror. "This guy. Could *not* speak English. We were dancing. All of a sudden we get near the door, he picks me up and starts outside with me. I'm yelling, 'Stop! Wait a minute! What're you doing?' I'm hitting his back with my fists. And everybody around me ignored us. Like I'm just another drunk, right? 'Put me down!' I'm shouting."

"Lenore, my God . . ."

"I'm not finished. We get *all the way* outside, it's raining, and finally, finally this guy from security looks up and decides to come out. He pulls on me, the guy pulls, and then I get away.

"But here's the beauty part. The guy told security he only wanted to take me home with him." She glowed.

"The Sheik of Fullerton Avenue," said the attendant, tucking Lenore's blouse back in. "Honey, never go no place with a guy who don't speak no English. It's un-American. Where's this button? I'll sew it on."

I opened the door cautiously; the corridor looked clear. Back at the bar, I asked for an olive in my ice water this time. Someone came up behind me to ask in my ear if I'd like to dance. I turned to face a tall, nice-looking man in dark gray. A silver tragic mask held his string tie together. "A friend made it for me," he said. It looked like a death's head, a grinning silver skull. As we joined in dance, he managed to press his every possible body surface against me. As I struggled to breathe, I thought, "Is this the fun my brother wants me to have?" and my partner pulled me closer, murmuring, "I want to take you home with me."

Arching my back away from him, I said, "Dancing is dry work in this ballroom, isn't it? Let's stop for a drink." I saw Lenore down at the end of the bar talking intently with a man. His ears stood out from his head like open doors on a cab.

After Lenore called loudly, "I'll have another Martini," I heard her invite him for Thanksgiving dinner, "because nobody should be alone on Thanksgiving!" Although with two children and a live-in boyfriend, she was unlikely to be alone; still, the holiday was a week from now.

And what happened to our "no drinks" pact? Exasperated, I walked into the corridor to see that it was still raining hard. The security guard came up behind me to say, "You must be awfully fussy not to have found a fella by this time!"

"Not yet!" I edged away from him back towards the ballroom. "Still looking!"

"I get off in half an hour," he said. "What do you say we . . . "

I headed back to the bar to hear the bandleader announcing the last dance.

As the lights came up, I realized that Lenore was smashed. She fought off the attendant hunting through her pockets for the car keys. "No, no, I drive better when I'm drunk!" Lenore shouted. The attendant and I wrestled Lenore into her car. Yelling, "I had at least seven Martinis! Seven! And I never drink!" Lenore curled up on the back seat.

I felt bad as I drove us home in the rain. I had looked forward to our talking over the guys we'd met. Somehow I managed to get Lenore awake and inside her house. No one was up. I heard her singing her way up the stairs, " . . . the night they were playing/ That bee-you-tiful Ten-nisgame Waltz."

When I got home, the doors had been chained and bolted from inside. The lights were out. I rummaged for pebbles and sticks. Standing in the rain, I threw them at the darkened bedroom windows.

A window lit up, and a frowzy head appeared against the light: "Oh, Mom! Did I lock you out?" Then I heard feet inside running down the stairs.

"I'm sorry, Mom; I forgot you weren't in yet. Did you have fun?" Mart said as he let me in.

"Well, mostly I met . . . some really lonely people," I said, hanging up my raincoat.

"Sounds kinda boring," Mart said. He ambled back to bed.

Turning on the kitchen light, I saw a note on the icebox —

ATTENTION!

Imperialist dogs! You bait traps with cheap generic
peanut butter when our babies need cheese!
This is an outrage! It shall not go unpunished!
   P. Gruyere, *Brigadier*, Loyal Order of the Mouse.

A tiny splotch of ink was next to the signature. I checked the traps; still set, but now the bait had been removed. Baiting and setting traps was a nightly task the kids rotated. Tonight I reset them, then wrote on his note in tiny letters:

M. Gruyere, Brigadier:
Defy at your peril! Traditional order will be defended.
Madame la Guillotine still waits!
     — Sovereign Majesty

Then I went to bed.

A few weeks later, I went to the auto shop to get my car. I had gone there on my bike, and as I tried stuffing it into the car's trunk, I looked up to see a mechanic smiling at me. He came closer and said, "I wouldn't want you to think I'm a male chauvinist pig, but I saw you wrestling with that bike. Would you like a hand? I'm Johnny."

"Actually . . . Yes," I said. "I'd . . . like that." And together we loaded the bike in the back of my car. He turned then and stood there, calmly smiling, his hand on the door handle. He had a great smile. It made me really nervous. I licked my lips, wondering if he could tell how nervous I felt. I thought I was giving myself away, and this was like the way dogs can smell fear.

"You know, I'll get off work in just a little bit. Would . . . would you like to have a cup of coffee?" He smiled again. "With me, I mean."

While he seemed really sure of himself, I was a wreck. Why? Did I want to get away from him? He had asked if I had time for coffee. Did I? I felt disoriented and needed a moment. He continued to stand there. Okay, coffee wouldn't be a date exactly. My dad used to say, "When in doubt, always say No." And I wanted to sort this coming-out-of-left-field invitation out. So I asked for a rain-check until the next night when we could have coffee and dessert.

As I drove home, I felt my spirits rise. Was it having my own car back? And I could listen to my music now on my radio, rock or even opera if I felt like it? Or was it that a good-looking man found me attractive? Could be. And then "Are You Lonesome Tonight?" came on. I didn't feel lonesome now, but it did feel nice to know that someone was interested in me — asking more than "What's for dinner?"

Then I remembered: I couldn't have him come to the house with my teenagers underfoot — not to mention Roquefort and his relatives.

Still, he seemed nice, he was really good-looking AND he knew how to fix things. Cars at least. But would he want to go out with me if he knew about my kids . . . and the mice? Could he fix those? Better call him and ask if we could meet at a restaurant. Just the two of us.

That evening, I sat in a rocking chair going over bills in the family room. Greg, my oldest, came in, turned more lights on, reached up to touch the ceiling with the tips of his fingers, and said, "About when?"

"About when what? And what happened to 'Hi, mom?'"

"About when do you think we'll have dinner?" He lay down on the couch, open-toed sneakers braced against the end.

"I don't know. I haven't thought about dinner yet." I had thought about Johnny, though; I was wondering if now was the time to tell Greg I'd be going out for coffee the next night. On a sort of date.

"What's in the pile? What'd you have in mind foodwise?"

"These are bills, and why do you always ask what we're having for dinner?"

"Oh, I don't know. I just like to think about it." He took inventory of his dirty, broken fingernails with a distant and surprised expression, then said, "OK, if we're not eating for at least an hour, I'm gonna make myself a couple of burgers and some fries. I'm starving."

He rummaged around in the kitchen, patting the refrigerator affectionately as he talked to himself, orchestrating the warming of rolls, banging the frying pan on the stove top, heating fries, molding hamburgers, chopping onions, "where's that ketchup?" while singing "We . . . Don't . . . Need . . . No . . . Education!"

I called out, "Say, Pink Floyd, make me one?"

The next evening I did meet Johnny at a restaurant. Toward the bottom of his first cup of coffee, he mentioned that he was divorced. "I even have a little girl — but she lives with her mother." He looked sad, then said, "who punishes her by making her do *housework!* "

I thought of my children; they each had regular kitchen chores and might even be doing the dishes — with lots of fighting in between — as I sat there with Johnny. He had his hands curled in front of him, and now he examined his fingernails, frowning. "You know, no matter how hard I scrub, I can't get all the dirt off." He turned his hands over and spread his fingers out. I could see some blackness under the neatly trimmed nails.

He shook his head, looked up at me and said, "Another thing, just so you know. My name's Gianni, short for Giovanni. My dad grew up in Calabria, then came over to the U.S. But enough about me. I'd like to get to know you a little better," he said. "Do *you* have children?"

Whoops. I looked around for the waiter.

He asked again. I set my cup down carefully. "Some." Time to come clean. "I have five. Four boys, one girl."

"Do you let their dad see them?"

"Yes, and he seems more interested in them now than when we lived together." Should I mention they stay with their dad once in while? Meaning some nights I'm by myself. Better hold that thought.

I looked down at my apple pie, warm and fragrant — delicious. And I hadn't baked it. And how long was it since I sat in a restaurant with just one other adult? As I ate, I had my left hand next to my plate, and Gianni reached across to gently touch the tips of my fingers.

"And what about *you*, Anne?" He looked into my eyes; how really blue his were. And how large and dark his pupils. "How long has it been?"

"How . . . long?" I said. He couldn't mean . . . no, of course not.

"How long since anyone made you feel . . . protected or cared for? It sounds like you are the caretaker. And I'm sure you're good at it. But who takes care of you?"

Tears stung my eyes. After what I had known, kind words were painful. Harshness, I could handle. I took a deep breath, then looked up blinking.

"Tears, Anne?" He smiled tenderly.

That brought more tears, and he held out a white handkerchief. "It's been hard, hasn't it?" he said as I wiped my eyes.

I glanced at my watch, not sure what to say. "I'll . . .I have to get back," I croaked. "The kids . . . need help with their homework."

"I'd like to drive behind you to your house, just to make sure you get in okay."

And so we did that and, as I got out of my car, the moonlight on the snow was breathtaking. A clear night, sharply cold with just a silver ribbon of cloud. Gianni put his hand gently on my shoulder, then he looked around at the sidewalks. My children had made a path only a shovel's width from the garage to the house. The neighbors had cleared off their walks right to the parkways. We stood by my back door where hedges, heavy with fresh snow, leaned over the walk.

Gianni squeezed my hand gently and said, "Would you like me to talk with your boys about shoveling these walks? I think they'd listen to me better 'cause I'm a man. I don't mean that as a criticism. But there's nothing like a man's influence." Had he been talking to my mother?

Looking at the walk, the moonlight, the peace around me, I felt something settle inside. Someone else telling my boys to shovel the walk wouldn't get them to do it. That would just push them away. Whatever it took to get the job done, or not done, was up to me. Gianni didn't belong in the middle.

I took a deep breath and said, "Thanks, I appreciate that, Gianni. But this is between them and me. I'm not done with working on them."

I choked on that, and Gianni squeezed my shoulder. Then he said, "I just thought I could help. But it's up to you. When can we get together again? We could see a movie or have supper or even go dancing. Next Saturday?"

And when Saturday night came, three of my boys came into the hall to meet him. Greg took Gianni's hand and said seriously, "What time do you think you can have her home by?"

"Yes, just exactly what are your intentions?" Justin asked. My sons stood there laughing, arms across each other's shoulders. The three of them were already taller than Gianni.

Greg held the door open and said in a falsetto, "Now listen here, I don't want you two watching any submarine races off Navy Pier. You don't know what it is to stay up late, worrying about someone out in a car till all hours . . . ."

We went down the outside steps laughing together.

Sexology

When I first had children, I told myself that I could handle questions about where babies come from, but I was sure it wouldn't come up for a long while. And part of me wondered: why can't my kids just learn about sex from the street like everyone else? Then one morning as I doled out oatmeal, my four-year-old looked up into my face and said, "How does the daddy get the baby inside the mommy?"

Her question stopped me in mid-ladle. My mind flashed to my mother, seeming nervous or angry, handing ten-year-old me two leaflets. "I want you to read these," she said. "When you are finished, put them back in this drawer. Your brother will read them next year."

The titles, "A Girl Becomes a Woman," and "A Boy Becomes a Man," meant nothing. "Girl," from the Department of Agriculture, had cross-section diagrams of a woman's abdomen, outfitted with the usual: womb, vagina, baby upside-down inside. With multi-syllabic words like menstruation, insemination, gestation, it was written like a scholarly article on genetic variants in plants. Had I been interested in sex—I was not yet—I would have decided against having any.

So that breakfast time, I just answered my little girl's question. I said, "He does it when he loves her." I kept serving.

She said, "Oh," and went on with her cereal.

The other children continued their "Stop looking at me!"

"I was not!"

"Knock it off, you guys," I said. No one asked for more about babies. From the next room, I heard my husband saying loudly to himself, "Whew! I'm sure glad it wasn't me she asked."

Since this topic had come up, I figured it would again. And it sure did. When they did ask, it was always random. After that first one, I fielded occasional questions when asked. It seemed to take a while to sink in. They were curious about everything, like "Why don't we fall up into the sky?" But long explanations just bored them. Having descended from hedge-row teachers, I naturally liked explaining till people "got" it, but about sex I held back from going further unless asked. We had a blackboard in the kitchen for noting needed groceries, and I sometimes used it to draw answers to questions about whatever had come up—gravity, babies, lightning, etc.

Movies and TV shows make a big deal out of the "Moment" when kids ask their suddenly perspiring parent where they came from, and that parent feels a need to tell it the "right way" so they don't scar the child. I thought setting up a formal talk might alert a kid to suspect something strange was about to happen.

My husband had told me that when his father gave him the "birds and the bees" talk, they were in a car, and Dan said, "I still remember every tree, bush, and leaf we passed while Dad just kept talking and talking. I couldn't wait to get out of the car."

I hoped to avoid that reaction by doling out facts in bits and pieces as the need came up. A doctor friend told me he took his children to watch elks mate, so they would know the basics of intercourse. When I visualized it, I knew I didn't want to watch that myself, and I thought my kids might be the same.

Senior year in college (in the '50s) we were told to assemble in a lecture hall for a routine talk by the doctor who took care of students whose medical problems could not be handled by the campus Infirmary.

This doctor entered the lecture hall without speaking and stood behind the big lectern. He picked up a piece of chalk and drew a long line across the four blackboards behind him. We sat there, open-mouthed. At the far end, he turned and made another line a foot below it and joined them at one end. Then he said, "This is ah, um, the male penis."

It was? Spread out across those blackboards, it must have been about twenty feet long. Most of the girls had never seen an erection, and this had to be the member of a mammoth. I began to giggle. I tried to hide behind the girl in front of me, and I heard a few stifled snorts behind me.

The whole time Dr. M talked, he kept his back to us. It was just as well that anyone who already stated her intention to enter the convent had been excused.

"Are there any questions?" Doctor said. I remember a couple of suck-up types asked about the Catholic injunction to have "as many children as God sends," and Dr. M defended the party line. He comforted the concerned by saying, "You don't have to have them all at once."

The Pill was being developed in the later 1950s and not yet available. None of us would hear about it here since contraception was a mortal sin Any Catholics who wanted to prevent conception could use the Rhythm Method. He talked a bit about Rhythm, but indicated "that was for later."

Many in my class went on to have seven and ten children; I had five and stopped. Ten seemed a lot more than I could handle, yet my husband had his heart set on having that many as did a lot of his friends. And yes, we argued about that.

I wanted to avoid passing on attitudes like what I was also exposed to in high school. In my senior year our convent school in Newburgh, New York, hired a young female gym teacher fresh out of New York University, to replace a seasoned veteran of the Catholic school system. We students really liked this new teacher—a smart-alecky, loud-voiced, jock type with a New York accent.

During a health class our new teacher talked to us seniors about sexual hygiene and mentioned masturbation. Health class was a New York state requirement, with obligatory topics from the board of health. Our teacher was following the curriculum.

However, some girls near me looked shocked; most of us knew that the Catholic Church condemned masturbating, a mortal sin. Miss M tried to lighten the atmosphere now feeling tense, by joking that "If you don't know this word, you are either lying or you don't know what the word means."

Later that day, two seniors went to Sister Principal, but we didn't know it. The following day, all seniors were summoned to an assembly. Five Sisters were there, and Sister Principal hefted herself onto the stage to talk to us. We didn't know it was about our health class at first, but I had a foreboding. Miss M sat over on the right side of the auditorium; she was crying and snuffling loudly.

Sister asked what exactly Miss M had told us about masturbating and called on *me* to answer. "Specifically, Anne."

I stood and mumbled something about, "She, ah um, err, told us it was stimulating yourself…sexually…"

Why, oh why, did she pick on me?

Sister Principal was quite pink in the face as she said, "What I don't understand is, why didn't you girls ask one of us?"

"Us" were celibate Sisters of Saint Dominic who had taken the Vow of Chastity. How in God's name would any of us even think of talking to them about sex? Let alone anything else personal. This was a boarding school and the boarders' letters–incoming and outgoing, even those in French, German, or Spanish–were always read by a faculty member who spoke that language. Outgoing mail was then sealed and put in the post. If any incoming letter seemed steamy or contained difficult family news, the girl was sent for to discuss it. Some letters were not given to their recipients.

There were no lay members on the faculty except for the gym teacher. Any day-hop—a student who lived in town as I did–caught smuggling a boarder's letter to an outside mailbox was expelled at a general assembly. This was not legend; I saw it happen.

As Sister Principal talked, we girls squirmed. Miss M sat across the auditorium sobbing as four other Sisters stood in the aisles looking furious. Sister Principal was the Grand Inquisitor, and we girls were all cowed. She went on to lambaste us for having listened to such "terrible talk." There was no discussion,

The upshot was that Miss M was fired on the spot; she was not to finish out the year. No more health class, Sex Ed, or sitting around in the gym bullshitting about whatever, often school restrictions. The boarders especially needed her sympathetic ear, and she let kids smoke there.

She told us earlier she had to get out of Manhattan to recover from an unhappy love affair. She hoped to escape to this bucolic retreat for a year. What she got instead was humiliation. To me the worst of it was that she was not wrong–and we never even got to discuss venereal disease.

So I had lots of experience about the wrong way to talk about sex, but not much help in finding a good way. As I fumbled through this situation, not everyone appreciated my approach. A case in point: One day Justin was on St. Luke's school playground with his fourth grade friends, just the boys, and their talk turned as it usually does at that age to how men and women made babies. The boys each had a theory and Justin told me he said, "No, no, you guys got it all wrong! Here's what happens." He was describing intercourse with his ten-year-old enthusiasm when he told us, "I suddenly felt a hard pinch on my ear."

He said the other boys' eyes bugged out. Sister Mary Beatrice had been listening and now took action. As Justin explained it to us at dinner that night, "She frog-marches me back inside and gets her face up close to mine, still holding my ear, and she says, 'How dare you talk like that?'

"So I told her those guys had it wrong, and my mother told me how babies get inside the...."

"And Sister says, '*Nice* people don't talk about things like that. Ever.' She made me stay inside for the rest of recess!"

Although we all scoffed at Sister's remarks, I was deeply angry. I didn't like having my children in Catholic school as it was. This was the grammar school my husband had attended. As soon as I divorced, I moved four of them to public schools.

At about this time, a friend met me for coffee to talk about problems with her thirteen-year-old son. She said, "This is a difficult age. We are fighting a lot. I know you have a lot of boys, so I figure you must know something. This kid, I bought him a vibrator and showed him how to use it."

Our eyes met in the mirror. I saw mine bulge as I gasped, "Why? Couldn't you let him figure this out for himself?"

I shouldn't have said it. She flared. I saw red spots on her cheeks as she spat out, "I'm sure if I had more education, I'd know better how to handle this." She got up, turned on her heel and stomped off.

At dinner–meat loaf and mashed potatoes–that night, I mentioned this mother's solution. My kids collapsed with laughter. Beth had a mouthful of potato that she guffawed out on to the tablecloth, "The poor kid!" she said as soon as she could talk.

"Why would that mother do that?" Justin said.

Matthew said, "Ee–yooh. That's disgusting! Please say you made that up." He pushed back from the table to look at each of us.

"That woman is a pervert." This from Martin, seven.

Greg, a junior at a Catholic high school taught by Dominican priests, said, "We were told that that's a sin, self-abuse." He looked around the table, said, "And that we shouldn't do it." But he was smiling.

Years later, Martin called me when he was a college sophomore to verify this story. His roommate had refused to believe that someone's mother would do that. I heard laughing in the background. "It's true," I said. "Want me to tell him?"

I had a copy of *The Joy of Sex* in the bookshelves, and every once in a while, I noticed it set down in a different place. As Beth put it, "Oh, Mom, somebody's always looking at it."

I also had my nudes in charcoal (male and female) on the walls of my art room upstairs. *Joy* was a bit more advanced with its graphic pen-and-ink drawings of naked couples. My room had eight casement windows, lots of wall space, and I used to tape my most recent drawings on the bare spaces. When Greg's high school friends were outside shooting baskets, they would look up, see my drawings, and I could hear them roar laughing.

And later when Justin was in public high school, he was on the Student Council. They were asked to vote on whether art classes should have nude models for their life drawings. Justin told them, "Vote yes, it's excellent practice for drawing."

A good number of parents heard about that, got involved, and made sure that any models appeared fully clothed, even to shoes.

Dan's parents had started a group years ago called Cana Marriage Preparation to give premarital talks to Catholic couples before their nuptials. The members of the group presented a positive outlook on marriage and family life. Mother-in-Law often told me that people looked up to her and Dan's father as a "model couple"–in contrast to my own "terrible" parents, as she often referred to them. As bad as my parents were, they never told people they were an example for others to copy.

Member couples were also trained to provide talks at Catholic high schools—to give positive talks about married life, children and so on. Dan and I had been part of this system early in our marriage.

I also gave talks about childbirth at these schools. I often ran childbirth films at home to use in these classes. I checked and mended any worn places—no point in having the movie break down with the baby only half hatched.

My children sometimes stopped by to watch. I didn't have any movies about how the baby got in there, though. My audio-visual aids included films on family-centered childbirth and whatever lap baby I had at the time. In those schools at that time a small baby was a great novelty. Lots of the kids, boys as well as girls, asked to hold my baby. I always said, "No, he (or she) is quiet now. But being held by a stranger upsets this baby."

When I went to a boys' Catholic high school, St. Mel's in Garfield Park on the near West Side, I took my fri0end Marnie with me. It was 1967 and I had been enthusiastic about having the two of us give a talk about family life. But when we entered the lobby, a man in uniform was walking back and forth with a drawn pistol at his side. Not in a holster, just loose and at the ready.

She and I locked eyeballs; I said through my teeth, "Are you sure you want to go through with this?"

And bless her heart, she said, "I will if you will." Nodding to Security, we went inside this male enclave. I had my small baby, and she had hers. Her dear little black girl was an instant hit.

I felt touched often to see that high school boys like these were so interested in our babies. They asked questions like, "Do you *really* love your children? Really?"

Another boy raised his hand and asked Marnie, "Do you punish your kids? How?"

"I have four other children," she said, "and I have a long wooden spoon. When the kids see that come out, they know it means: *Someone* is going to get it!"

The boys chuckled appreciatively. I vouched for how well-behaved her kids were; her family had come to our house one night during the rioting after Martin Luther King was killed. They were really good kids. I was proud to have her with me that day, a mom doing her best to be a good mom. At this Catholic school, I thought it was good for these boys to meet someone who belonged to the Radio Church of God, as she told them, not just another Catholic mom like me.

At another school, a girl handed in a slip of paper with this, "Is it enough that your husband doesn't beat you? Or is there more to marriage?" Tears came to my eyes; she came up to me after and looked so pretty with her long blonde hair and blue eyes–and so wistful. My worst times with Dan hadn't happened yet, so I encouraged her. "It doesn't have to be like that. A good man won't beat you."

One talk I gave at a suburban high school to boys at the request of the gym teachers. A boy who sat in front with a tape recorder asked, "This isn't exactly on the subject, but can I ask about kids getting along with their dads? My dad and I fight all the time. Can you give me any pointers?"

I did my best with such a big audience, and fortunately, a coach came over to me and said, "That kid who asked is blind, and I had no idea he wasn't getting along with his dad. I'll follow up on this. I'm so glad it came up."

When I gave a talk at a Christian Brothers boys' high school in Chicago, one veteran priest said, "I agreed to have this talk, but I have to tell you. These boys really aren't ready to listen to talk about Marriage. I *know* them, and they are really involved in their basketball and football, and what their teammates are doing. Working out and competing is their life now. Girls are a small part of the picture and thinking about marriage is way off in the future." I did give the talk; I hoped it might plant a seed or two..

I think back to those talks; how different it is today, with some mothers encouraging "boy-girl sleepovers" for high school kids. Not all adolescents are ready to jump into bed. I know the ripening arrives at different times for individual kids as they go through puberty. While it's true that kids mature earlier these days, pushing them before they're ready is cruel.

And speaking of how important sports teams were for teenage boys, when Greg, my oldest, made the Varsity basketball team, he told us that his coach had hired a barber to cut the Varsity team's hair short, after they made the team. Greg usually went to a local barber, so I said, "Do you want to go to the barber here and get your hair cut the way you like it?"

And Greg said, "Ah, no, mom. See, this is free and besides all the guys on the team do it together. This way everybody knows you made the Varsity. The haircuts are in the gym and after the haircut, you walk around it. There are a lot of kids on the bleachers and they clap and cheer and catcall. It's a ceremony."

His team was one of the best in the state, so walking the halls with short hair was significant; getting "balded" was a sacred ritual. Girls were pretty far down the list of interests compared to this recognition.

When Beth was a junior in high school, she wanted to ask one of Matthew's gymnastics teammates to the Sadie Hawkins Dance. Every year the high school provided this opportunity for the girls to invite boys to this informal dance; it was popular. Bill was a handsome well-built athlete who attracted a lot of girls. Coached by her brothers she nervously made the call from my home office with the door shut.

I didn't hear anything for a while, but I saw the office door was open. No Beth inside. I went up to her bedroom. She was under the covers with the pillow over her head. The boys were behind me. When I went to her, and touched the pillow, she pulled it away. Her face was red. "I'm so embarrassed!" she said. "I asked him, and he said, 'No!'"

The boys, Matthew and Justin, the gymnasts, were angry for her. Matthew said, "A lot of gymnasts aren't into dating yet."

Justin said, "I haven't seen Bill talking to any girls," and other comforting comments, even "Maybe he doesn't know how to dance."

"Yeah, and he doesn't want to look stupid."

Her friends knew she wanted to ask him. He was just another boy involved in his sport and not ready for any boy-girl involvement. Or maybe, I privately thought, he liked just being with the guys on the team. Last time I checked he still hadn't married.

One morning I went to call Martin for breakfast. He was four and had the covers over his head. When I pulled them back to see his face, he popped up with a big smile and said, "Hiya, Sexy!" then collapsed laughing. I smiled; no point in making a big deal of it.

To me it was like when very small children use four-letter words. Yelling at them and punishing ensures they will do it again. I remember being four and I used a bad word, which I do not recall. All I remember is that a cleaning lady at my mother's request had cut a small circle of brown laundry soap, held my nose until I opened my mouth and put the soap pill on my tongue. Then she held my mouth shut. I remember the evening well, being out in the grass, not liking the soap taste, and wondering what I had done.

And no, Martin didn't call me by that name again.

One night at dinner, Matthew said, "I want to say something. Beth has a Biology teacher, Mr. R, who does something . . . interesting. My friends who had him say he tells the students when the discussion gets to Sexual Reproduction, that he makes the students get up in class and tell the exact date and details of their first experience of a Wet Dream, noticing the sheets are wet."

"What?" Justin and Martin said together.

"What about girls?" I said.

Matthew said, "In the case of girls, an erotic dream."

I sat back, shocked. I thought, Beth and her classmates are freshmen. Matthew was a sophomore then. He went on, "My friends who had this teacher told me that Mr. R would lower their total grade average by a full point if they refused to tell, or they said they never had this experience."

I felt my face getting hot. I said, "He has no right to this information. It must be humiliating."

Greg looked up and said, "What he's doing is wrong. That man has no right."

The two younger kids just sat there with big eyes.

I said, "The Bill of Rights was written to protect people from this kind of invasion. Mr. R is violating the first and fourth Amendments. And free speech means the right NOT to talk if you don't want to."

"What's the Fourth?" Justin said.

"Unreasonable Search and Seizure," I said. "That covers personal stuff. The kind of thing I mean when I tell you that I hope you have your own private secrets. I have secrets of my own private life, and no one has any right to pry into them.

"What I'm saying is, if you don't want to tell, you don't have to."

Thirteen-year-old Beth said, "Well then, if he asks me, I'll just say I think it is wrong for him to ask us things like that, and that he is violating the Bill of Rights."

She sounded so matter-of-fact. And she knew I would back her up. I'd get into it if I had to, but I thought it would be best coming at the teacher on the student level. Telling principals never got real traction in my experience. But if a kid spoke up in class, others could join in. She told us one night a few days later that Mr. R was going to take the Biology class on a field trip. She said, "I told him I didn't want to go. He wanted to know why. I said, 'I just don't want to.' He even followed me out of class to ask again."

I never heard any more about this after that, but it felt good to know she was armed and already showed the courage to stand up to him. .

In those times, the 1970s, there was a belief that people had to "share" about their sexual feelings, even when a person has a sense that tells him or her, "No, don't do this." In my therapy group, I asked why the others were willing to talk about their sexual experiences, and Dr. H said, "The idea behind that is, if you can talk about sex, you can talk about anything."

I felt my hair standing up on the back of my neck. So talking about sex was a kind of door-opener. I said, "Anything? OK. Would you folks like to tell us your annual incomes?"

No one said anything; they squirmed and looked at the floor. Not even the therapists commented.

When Justin was sixteen, I was sharply aware of an uptick in phone calls from girls for him, and of their appearing at the door unannounced. He was more into student activities than his older brothers and I was concerned that I might have left out something about protecting himself. So one night at dinner after the others had left the table, he and I were still sitting there. I said, "Honey, I wanted to talk with you about sex."

He flashed a big smile, put his arm across my shoulders like a favorite uncle, and said, "Sure, Mom. What would you like to know?"

FAREWELL TO OUR HOUSE

I step outside and turn my key in the lock for the last time. I have come to the end of a long road as solo homeowner of this house. I had groped my way–at times in darkness–inventing as I went.

As my children changed and grew, I changed and grew along with them. While I started with low self-esteem. I worked through challenges as they rose, and I grew stronger with each one. I had emerged from a childhood of abuse, only becoming aware of how bad it was as I nurtured my own children. Later my marriage became abusive, and I developed tools to resolve that, too.

Throughout the times of struggle. I discovered solace in watercolor painting, comfort in friends I made through art, strength in my joy with my children. I had never expected to be happy, and yet I was. Joy and happiness surprised me, and I felt I was doing important work in raising children who would mature into sound adults, and not spend their teen years in mental clinics as my younger brother did.

It is time for another family to grow and thrive here. Other children will live in our house–it's a good place for kids to grow up. I have already met the new owners, a family of grandparents, parents, and small children. They will live here, look out through my windows, sit at my fireplace. In weeks to come I will drive past and see little children running through the grass and laughing as mine once did. I will see a porch swing settling between the apple trees and hear children calling to each other as I pass.

And for me, it's time to make my way into a new life. This one has accomplished what I set out to do: raise healthy children, and that job is complete. Time for new challenges and to absorb all I've learned and use it in new ways.

My walk-through has been to say goodbye. As I shut the back door for the last time, my house sends back an echo from deep inside, empty and hollow. Tears rise in my eyes. I still have the key in my fist. I could go back. But now my house is only bare walls and floors, no longer a home.

No, I think, this house and I have done our job–done it well, the job Dan and I gave it. The mortgage that kept me awake is paid, my stiff climb is over, that phase of my life is complete, and I can turn to new challenges.

Our children are up and off and out into their own lives and homes.

Author Biography

A native of upstate New York, A.X. McKneally taught at the University of Illinois at Chicago. She also worked in newspapers and public relations before embarking on a career in corporate America. She has five children. *Family Dinners – A Memoir of Hard Times, Hope, and Laughter* is her first book.